# The Tennis Junkie's Guide (To Serious Humor)

Happy B-day
Love
Mom & Dad
8.31.08

# The Tennis Junkie's Guide (To Serious Humor)

*Dave Whitehead*

Writers Club Press
New York Lincoln Shanghai

# The Tennis Junkie's Guide (To Serious Humor)

Writers Club Press
an imprint of iUniverse, Inc.

For information address:
iUniverse, Inc.
2021 Pine Lake Road, Suite 100
Lincoln, NE 68512
www.iuniverse.com

ISBN: 0-595-25828-X (pbk)
ISBN: 0-595-65364-2 (cloth)

Printed in the United States of America

# Contents

## Part III    The People of Tennis

# *Preface*

Have you ever noticed that tennis is almost always written about as if it were some kind of natural disaster? Serious tennis writers are constantly warning us about the pitfalls common in tennis: how to avoid them, or in most cases, how to get out of them. Countless tennis-writing professionals are, right this minute, pounding furiously on their keyboards, valiantly trying to translate their brilliant tennis knowledge into words that will help their readers play better, practice better, and even choose partners better. Typical musings from this group are, "How To Play Good Tennis On Bad Courts," "What To Do Until Your Serve Goes In," and "Three Easy Steps To Running Around Your Backhand."

Occasionally, a writer will pen a "lighter side" tennis piece such as "The Lighter Side of Tennis Elbow." "Lighter side" articles are always welcomed, at least by me. However, since these types of articles are about as frequent as a hacker with a sharp fashion sense, I can only conclude that no one else has developed the requisite appreciation for this sophisticated type of humor. I attribute my own vast understanding of this humor to having continuously coped with numerous and recurring match defeats. As a matter of fact, my many losses have propelled me far beyond the "lighter side." Indeed, I now wallow where no tennis writer has gone before—in blatant humor. Therefore, in the face of no known market for, or even prospective revenues in, tennis humor, I have gone ahead and courageously written about tennis' humorous angle. That's just the type of guy I am.

Yes, in this very book, for the first time, is tennis humor as you have never seen it—flagrant. That's right; you can't miss it! Well, maybe some of your more simple primates can. But, if you want the truth, the truth is: Tennis IS a naturally occurring problem, similar to dandruff. End of discussion.

Since there is no profit in the truth (reference your state's lack of penal codes under "tabloids"), most tennis writers treat learning tennis as any other honorable endeavor, like learning a foreign language or constructing your own backyard compost bin.

Tennis instructors and parents all put a spin on this "honorable" viewpoint. Witness Forest Hills' mother's philosophical explanation of the mysteries of tennis to young Forest:

> *Tennis is like a new can of balls; you never know when you open it if they're going to be day-ud.*

No one knows precisely what she meant, but we tennisologists consider it very wise.

# *Acknowledgements*

Many people made contributions to this book in unique ways. Some were more direct than others, but all were essential and all are immensely appreciated.

First, I want to thank the many, many nameless players and hackers that I have encountered over the years who have made vital contributions in their own inimitable ways and without whom this book would never have been conceived.

I want to thank the helpful people at iUniverse.com for their countless contributions. I'd also like to thank Mellanie Bauslaugh (Abstract Design), whose cover design inspiration gave this book its curb appeal, and Chandra (scribendi.com) Clarke for her important editing contributions. I thank them all for their efforts on this book's behalf.

I want to give special thanks to Bev Buckley, a former women's tour player and current superb tennis coach at Rollins College, for finding time during her busy season to give this book a technical review. I want to express thanks to Mike Kreiss, Dennis Oppeltz, John Smallfield, Dr. Denny Huston, Guy Fritz, and Dr. Ted Teacher for their distinctive inspirations.

I want to especially thank a couple of people who never lost faith in what I had to say. When it looked like all might fall into silence, their encouragement gave me the strength of voice to press on. For their unflagging support, I want to express my sincere appreciation to Rick (mountainghost.com) Johnson and to my daughter, Kellie. Without their unrelenting enthusiasm for my creative side, I would never have completed this tennis classic.

Most of all, I want to thank my wife, Molly, for her assistance and support throughout the course of this endeavor. From conception to completion, she was a valued friend and resource on whom I could always rely.

# PART I
## Tennis Parts

o o o o o o o o o o o o o o o o o o o o o o o o o o o o o o o o
*"'Tis better to run around a backhand than to curse it."*

*—Confusion*

# 1

## *This is Your Brain on Backhands*

WARNING: The Surgeon General has determined that backhands act as a hallucinogen on your brain and should be stroked only as directed.

Picture this:

A serious male, deep in his thirties, standing in your kitchen. Straightening up as if you have just walked in, this serious guy looks almost annoyed. "All right," he barks, "one more time."

He walks briskly to the stove and lifts a black skillet off a gas flame. He shows you the skillet. "This is backhands," he explains. He holds up a raw egg. "This is your brain." He breaks the egg into the skillet. CRACK! SNAPPLE! POP! "This is your brain on backhands," he states flatly. CRACK! SNAPPLE! POP! "Any questions?" he demands, as if we had better not.

A long time ago, before nylon, some geezer tennis player with a diary once noted that it was easier for a camel to fit through the eye of a needle than to hit an outstanding backhand. Well, that isn't true! Damn close though. The pros aside, hitting an "outstanding backhand" is more of an oxymoron, such as "overhead slam." (Well, it's an oxymoron in my game.) Realistically, on a scale from losing your car keys (easy) to public speaking (difficult), hitting an effective backhand is as easy as slicing bread with a wrench.

You see, backhands were bestowed by the Creator unto man (*man* in the philosophical sense) as an impossible dream. According to The Plan, impossible dreams provide us the impetus to improve ourselves through continuous and strenuous efforts directed toward futile ends. (*Algebra, the Northwest Passage, radial tires*, and *Gore-Tex* were merely incremental warm-ups.) Yes, backhands were designed to completely provoke and frustrate us so that we might learn patience and wisdom. But, like so much else (i.e., artificial insemination), man mucked up the plan. Man invented two-hand backhands.

For the moment, let's focus on REAL backhands, the one and only one-hand kind. The kind *I* hit!

By virtue of The Plan, learning a backhand is an enormous under-taking. First, one has to recognize a backhand when one sees it coming. This recognition skill is often more difficult than it sounds. Why? The reason is many players with one-handed backhands, and all hackers, EXPECT to hit forehands. When I say, "expect to hit forehands," I mean they pray for forehands to the point that they devoutly ignore all backhands, even in Ping-Pong. They ignore them in the hope that by denying their very existence in the universe, any shot directed toward their backhand side will supernaturally be sucked into some other-dimensional, space-time continuum. Then, after a brief time, the ball will miraculously reappear above the baseline and land "out." That or these geeks will try to hit backhands as forehands.

Forehands can produce a hypnotic grip on some players; especially when their backhands are as appealing as soap-on-a-rope. These players always stand waiting expectantly for the next shot, (1) on the backhand side of their court, with (2) a forehand grip and, (3) already turned halfway facing a forehand. If they are wrong and discover they have failed to sacrifice a sufficient number of tennis balls to the god of back-hands, their eyes bulge out in fear when they realize they must execute their emergency backup plan called *The Run-Around.*

The run-around happens when a doofus elects to run around his or her backhand to hit the ball as a forehand. Why go to such exhausting lengths? To hit the ball back, of course. They know their backhands are so unreliable they could just as well be stroking the ball back with a salad fork. Anyway, the run-around requires that a player turn to prepare for a forehand and then sprint backward to their backhand sideline. Ideally, they can then use their superior forehand stroke to hit the ball back. Alas, this player usually ends up getting to the ball just in time to abruptly swing his chicken-wing forearm at it, miss it, and have the ball bounce up into his crotch.

Secondly, you have to decide what you're going to do with your non-racket hand while your good arm is committing a backhand. (Remember, I am not talking about the pernicious two-hand backhand.)

Modern tennisologists recognize that there is more than one school of thought concerning the "other hand." One school of thought is the *Sum Of The Moving Parts Backhand Theory*. This theory stems from the principle that the fewer body parts you involve in stroking, the fewer things there are to go wrong. Proponents of this theory tuck their shriveled non-racket hand into a pocket. In a pocket, their palsied opposite hand is safely out of the way until they need it, like during a service toss, opening a can of balls, or writing a check to their tennis therapist. These players are geeks.

Another school of thought is the *Harmonic Convergence Backhand Theory*. Proponents of this theory grasp the throats of their rackets with their free hands. Using both arms harmoniously in backswing, they then use both arms again to initiate forward momentum. Once their backhands are powered up, they release the throats of their rackets like a cruise missile from a B-2 bomber.

This theory is named after those planetary Harmonic Convergences. A Harmonic Convergence occurs when all the planets line up like a cornrow. This phenomenon mysteriously initiates a period of global goodness and understanding hitherto unknown because the planets had previously been aligned like your backhand stroke: in CHAOS! Evidently, once every Ice Age or so, the planets align causing a passing outbreak of peace and the end of trickle down economics, and which coincidentally, is about as long as it takes to master this backhand method.

Of course, the last theory is the *Two-Hand Backhand Theory*. This method of hitting backhands clearly amounts to cheating. Real backhands are difficult by definition. The very term *backhand* is derived from the ancient Greek *back*, meaning 'to strike' or 'make violent contact with,' and *hand*, meaning 'air.' In fact, I hereby dub the two-hand backhand as the *quasi-forehand*. This type of backhand is akin to holding a steeplechase race and letting one competitor run around the obstacles. I will save analysis of this backhand type for my closing opinion.

Third, and finally, one must hit the ball with the racket. Okay, you have taken $1800 worth of tennis lessons so that means your pro has taught you: (a) how to recognize a backhand, (b) how to prepare to hit a backhand. And, (c) how to hit a ball that has been slowly guided right to your racket strings with professional precision.

You are now ready to learn how to strike a ball that is flying toward you from across the net. That's also the bad news, because you must now impersonate an anti-missile defense system to intercept the streaking tennis ball before it strikes the back fence as an embarrassing winner. As an ex-tennis hacker, you can understand why the Department of Defense spends billions of dollars on computer programs each year trying to figure out how to accomplish, essentially, the same thing.

Here's the process: The ball comes bouncing toward you. You prepare as you always do, you reach down to make sure your protective cup is in place. You amble over to the ball with your racket back and ready. You then begin your swing anywhere from just after the nick of time, to one half second after the nick of time.

"No problem," you think. "Like my user-friendly forehand, I will merely alter my swing. The ball will zip past my forward hip. I will adjust my wrist forward...WHAT THE?!" You suddenly realize that your backhand does not include a built-in Plan B like your forehand! You can hit a serviceable forehand off your back hip, ala Plan B. Backhands, however, require that you either hit the ball in front of your body or look like you've somehow inserted your racket into an electrical wall socket.

I don't want to totally mislead you. Like the occasional gold medal-winning US Olympic hockey team, good backhands can happen. Ken Rosewall, for instance, owned a good backhand. You may have heard of him. In one-hand backhand circles, he is known as a "Dude." Then again, being 5'7", the backhand gods obviously made him pay for his unique skill with his height. Some other players to have mastered the one-handed backhand are Stephan Edberg, Pete Sampras, Martina Navratilova, and Steffi Graf. Each had a one-hand backhand and yet was ranked #1 in the world. After that, the list gets shorter than a boot camp haircut.

The irreducible fact still remains that it is wholly unnatural to have a superior one-hand backhand. So, personally, I'm keeping my cup.

## *Two-Hand Backhands:*

Okay, I have put two-hand backhands off to their rightful place–last. I will now discuss the wimping of tennis, that's right, the fiendish two-hand backhand. Normally, the less said about this mongrelized and cowardly method the better. However, I have to get this off my chest.

Today, alas, there are nearly as many people with two-hand backhands as there are tennis players. Whatever happened to good ol' one-hand backhands? I remember a time, by cracky, when everyone had one-hand backhands. They were as numerous as forehands, and so exclusively abused that some club's entire memberships formed support groups like *Backhands Anonymous* and *Up Your Backhand*.

These days, the only successfully competing one-hand backhands are the pros' or by an occasional sunscreen-deprived old fart who cackle "by cracky" as their standard interjection. Nowadays, all players with one-hand backhands are young misguided players with long arms who waste no time attacking the net. There, they loom menacingly until they are passed by weaselly little geeks with two-hand backhands. Sadly, it now takes a freakish, sideshow type of one-hand backhand to make a living playing with one.

Have you also noticed that since two-hand backhands have infested tennis, the sport has lost much of its innate grace and beauty? Now tell me, whose backhand would YOU rather watch, the legendary Gabriela Sabatini's or some two-hander's? Gabriela's, of course! Real men could sense the musky animal magnetism of Gabriela's ripe, well-developed, one-handed backhand. In fact, if you had taken the time to exam Gabriela as closely as I did, you would have come to the same inescapable conclusion: Gabriela is a, er, had a long, sensuously elegant, one-hand backhand that commonly drew "oooo's" and "aaaahs" from aroused spectators. Conversely, two-hand backhands are short, brutish, and usually accompanied by boorish grunts.

(I want to spotlight one extraordinary form of two-hand backhand. It is a form that is so elegantly built and well-proportioned as to be worthy of admiration. That backhand belongs to Anna Kournikova. Anna's backhand is marvelously constructed from the ground up. She gracefully glides to her backhand with her smooth long legs. She transfers hot, pulsating energy into balls by rotating her exquisitely honed hips. Finally, her exceptional upper body development is an asset that never leaves her stroke flat. As a guy, on behalf of guys everywhere, Anna, we salute your backhand.)

Ahem, how has this two-hand tragedy happened, you ask? Simply, one day some whiny, sniveling wimp came along wanting to learn to play tennis. Possessing just enough physical strength to push the buttons on a pocket calculator, this hormoneless geek found some bleeding-heart teaching pro, who, in instinctive sympathy, advised, "If you hit your backhand with two hands, you might be able to hit the ball back."

Did that greedy pro or little dweeb care about tennis' grand one-hand tradition? No! Instead, the nerdy dweeb selfishly wanted to play better tennis. So, the little geek started using the devious, two-hand backhand. Of course, as usually happens, he mastered the stroke in about twenty minutes and the following year won The US Clay Courts!

Do you know how long it takes to learn a one-hand backhand? Real backhands take years of sweaty, determined effort, and that's just to learn how to change grips. It's not fair! I demand a recount!

Is it any wonder that two-hand backhands proliferate across this great nation's tennis courts like Amway distributors? And, these blasphemous backhands are cutting through the once venerated one-hand backhands like a weed-whacker. They are hit harder, and yet are controlled. They are hit at impossible angles, and still land in the court. They have also made my game completely and hopelessly *obsolete*!

A contributing factor to this mutation of tennis is the ever-increasing amount of prize money. Tennis' traditional values are being corrupted, by cracky! In our current social environment of nuclear family meltdowns, diminishing tax deductions, and gum disease, today's players will stop at nothing to win. They will do anything from using two hands, to acupuncture, to even ingesting repulsive health food, such as *live* bacteria cultures in the form of yogurt! Gad!

Yes, I have witnessed the sport evolve into a Schwartzenegger-esque style of terminator tennis. Every time I hit the ball to a two-hand backhand, I hear it coolly assuring me telepathically, and with a German accent, *Ah'll be baack.*

Today, when I hit to my opponent's backhand, I hear his thundering return, BLAM! Reeling backward, I attempt to fend off its crushing power. I slice my backhand back, desperately trying to hit the ball to his "weak" backhand. BLAM! He steps up and cracks another incoming, bazooka-style, two-hand backhand. Pinned against the fence, I chip it back, at the same time asking myself, *Where the hell's his damn backhand?!* KA-BLAM! "Nice shot," I mutter obligingly as the ball whistles off the sideline and puts a hole in the windscreen. Meanwhile, I am thinking, "I hope you fall on your trophy and impale yourself on the figurine's tossing arm!"

(Although, today's trophies are different inasmuch as they are plastic and would break if you fell on one. Back when I was young we had real trophies, by cracky! Those trophies were fashioned of real metal and genuine compressed sawdust. Of course, if we consider that many of today's trophies are pieces of paper with dozens of zeros printed across them, and represent enough cash to buy a congressional sub-committee, perhaps pining for the good ol' trophies may be a bit like fondly reminiscing over jock itch.)

Actually, I am not really bitter. I mean when it comes right down to it, who needs trophies, or even victories, to be a good person? I know it sounds like sour grapes, but it's not. Really. If I am lying may my keyboard turn into unflavored yogurt right this minu

# 2

## *Forepla—Hands! Forehands!*

Forehands are like chocolate. We all adore them. Okay, for the record, there is a certain percentage of demented people on the planet that do not care for chocolate, and an even lower percentage that shun forehands. But who can take such tasteless numbskulls seriously? Chocolate, for instance, is so unusually good that many fundamentalist religious sects are considering re-classifying it from a dessert to a vice.

Of course, vices only exist in the philosophical sense. They are something debated regularly on radio talk shows and in Internet chat rooms. A vice can realistically be described as something that is much too fun for your own good.

Vices are all relative, too. What are vices to some people are not vices to others. Take drinking and prostitution. Of course, if you did, you would hear a violent uproar from these large and vociferous populations. Closer to home, I consider it my wife's vice that she wins all the arguments.

If you are a beginning player, your reputation will depend on your ability to distinguish your forehand from your backhand in public. Luckily, you can easily differentiate a forehand from a backhand by doing a little homework and using my handy, two-step method of stroke recognition:

## *Dave's Handy Two Step Stroke Recognition Procedure:*

1. Find a tennis court; any court will do. (However, if glowing like a neon geek concerns you, I would recommend the courts at the local junior high school. Only festering hacks in running shoes and accompanied by their dogs that pee on the net poles would ever play on those courts. Junior high school tennis courts have resisted all forms of repairs originating from natural disasters like rain, sand, weeds, and even drifting landfill debris. These courts are so neglected and unsanitary that even the homeless avoid them.)

2. Have someone you can trust to keep a secret bounce a ball to you, first on one side of your body, and then the other.
   The side of your body that you hit the ball on is your forehand.

   If you somehow hit the ball from both sides, then the side on which you hit the ball the farthest was your forehand. It also means you have the talent, after thousands of dollars of tennis lessons, to become a rung-in-good-standing on the local tennis club's ladder.

   If you failed to make any contact at all from either side, get another friend who knows how to toss a tennis ball better. If even that fails, I understand stamp-collecting can be rewarding.

   Since you're reading this book, chances are you're a tennis junkie and already own a reliable forehand. Also, I'm willing to bet you live for your forehands. That is, with the possible exception of you players with quasi-forehands; they are NOT pure backhands at all. That would be the one-hand backhand. It takes an indecent amount of talent to perform a one-hand backhand. In fact, the lousier your backhand is, the purer the player you are. It also means, the more you rely on your forehand.

# *SRI*

To better illustrate your forehand reliance, clever tennisologists have devised a formula that lets us determine our *Stroke Ratio Index* or SRI. The SRI was developed by our friends, the tennisologists, as a way to quantify the degree to which you rely on one stroke or the other. Teaching pros use it to sound analytical.

First, under the guidance of your pro, assign your forehand and backhand a strength index from between the numbers 10 (the perfect stroke) and 0 (eggplant). Let's take me, for example. I will assign my forehand a value of 7.5, and my backhand a value of 6.9. (Hey, it's my book and I will assign myself whatever score I want.) Using the formula: forehand over backhand (f/b) x 100, my ratio calculates out to 110.8. Calculate your own SRI and plug it into the following table:

## *Dave's Stroke Ratio Index Table:*

| SRI: | Degree of Reliance Reference: |
|---|---|
| SRI > 200: | The wind created by your forehand stroke could put out most kitchen fires. Your backhand reminds others of a frozen turkey wing. |
| 100 < SRI < 200: | You are normal. You have a workable balance between your strokes. You don't have to run around your backhand, probably because you are too lazy. But your opponents pound your backhand until it crumbles like cornbread. |
| SRI < 100: | Your backhand has a cult following and geeks make fun of your forehand. According to the world's leading tennisologists, this score is purely theoretical. |

Now, there are good forehands, awesome forehands, and then there are awesome-*looking* forehands. To the average tennis player, any forehand makes the sport worth playing. As a matter of fact, if it were not for forehands, most players would be bowlers.

In short, forehands are fun. However, players can take their fun so seriously that they run around their backhands to use their fabulous forehands. This particular sort of fun-seeking can become an addictive vice, overcome only by a 12-step program devised by your pro. However, if you are successful at running around your backhand and can drive your forehand shots forcefully back-across the court and down-the-line, you are immensely formidable and are called a *forehound*.

As mentioned, some forehands are incredibly awesome. They pin you to the back fence like a centerfold on a wall and leave you feeling just about as dressed.

Awesome-looking forehands make you cringe *before* the ball is struck. Therefore, this type of forehand leaves you ill-prepared to continue the point. I knew a guy named Mike Kreiss. He was a very, very good player. He had an excellent, highly effective forehand. Its effectiveness was due chiefly to the fact that it was awesome-looking. I mean, when he wound up to murder his forehand, he growled like an engine-revving dragster at the starting line. His muscles would ripple in anticipation of smashing the ball's guts on his strings like a fly. His face would contort in grim determination. His eyes would blaze down on the ball in malicious fury. His windup ritual looked more malevolent than *escargot!* Seeing this terrible display, I would retreat to the back fence and cower into my duck-and-cover ready position. (This ready position was based on the duck-and-cover drill we learned in grade school; it taught us to hide from nuclear bomb explosions by crawling under our desks.) Anyway, he would drive his forehand hard and deep to my wincing backhand, just like any respectable player. Of course, I had no chance of getting to it because it took me too long to get up off my knees.

Occasionally, nature plays a trick on us tennis players and creates a mutant. That is, sometimes a player's forehand gene is recessive and his or her backhand gene is dominant. Of course, I am talking one-handed backhands here. Two-handed backhands are always dominant. I know of another player, Dennis Oppeltz, with the backhand-dominant gene. Dennis' backhand was more reliable than tax increases. It was amusing to watch him play those players unfamiliar with his game. They would habitually feed his Rottweiler backhand, and he, in turn, would maul them with it. Too bad his forehand was the Chernobyl of forehands. At any time or place, his forehand might melt down into a flashflood of unforced errors that could sweep away entire matches.

I'm sure you can rely on your forehand too. That is, you can rely on it to be virtually ignored while your opponent zeroes in on your hapless backhand. I'm beginning to suspect that Darwin must have developed his "survival of the fittest" reasoning after playing a few tennis tournaments.

In conclusion, although there are some minor variations between forehands, you can always count on it to be the most common of your opponent's arsenal of weapons, then his moby serve, his wall-like volley, and his spiking your sports drink with Ex-Lax. You know, the usual suspects.

# 3

## *Serves: It's Your Fault!*

A player friend of mine (John Smallfield) once observed, indeed, he made it axiomatic by printing on a bumper sticker, "'Tis better to serve than receive." For a great many of us, 'tis also more difficult.

Serves are like nuclear reactors, public transportation, even pork and beans. They can be your best friend or your worst nightmare. It's a matter of perspective. My meaning is that if you serve effectively (over 100 MPH), serves are a profoundly moving experience! Otherwise, they are more like some self-inflicted, spilled hot drink wound.

On television, servers regularly pummel luckless returners with their atomic service bombs. It's so common, everybody expects all players everywhere to hold their serves. It is considered "normal." Consequently, losing your serve is seen as equivalent to poking yourself in the eye with your thumb, and worthy of an automatic nomination for the Nobel Geek Prize.

During its lifecycle, a tennis player's serve will run the gamut of effectiveness. The service lifecycle consists of a beginning, middle, and an end.

In the beginning, a young novice's serve is a lamentable *putz*. (Tennisologists have labeled this blooping type of serve, the "putz." It is named for Sigmund Putz who invented the foot fault.) With years of practice, the putz slowly grows into a dominating weapon. With decades of practice, those cannon-like serves shrink back down to a worn old putz again. Now, that's normal.

## Service Motions

Serves are hit in all sorts of fascinating ways. Some are blazingly fast. Some are glacially tame. Some serves are intensely gyrating. Some are flat (without spin). Some go in the service court. Most serves go in the net. And, all of these service types can usually be observed during the course of a single game.

Additionally, all serving motions are unique. The FBI could identify players by their service motions alone.

Some serves are smooth as cream and some are geekier than Big Bird dancing a *rumba*. Some servers go through a long, ritualistic windup before patting the ball like it was a baby's behind. Some servers compactly hold their racket back over their shoulder, toss the ball, and then smash the air out of the ball. One unbelievable server I actually witnessed, started his service motion at the back fence, then walked steadily toward the baseline while flapping his arms like a rush-hour traffic cop overdosed on glazed doughnuts. When he reached the baseline he would windmill the ball over with a rigid arm. (I only saw him that once. He was quickly felled by the teaching pro's tranquilizer dart and laid across the hood of his car with a warning message pinned to his shirt.)

Many players hit their serves from inside the court. Serving from inside the court is an annoying symptom of that classic tennis insecurity–*Neil Armstrong Syndrome* (details coming). However you hit the ball, it will almost assuredly go directly to one of the places you pray it won't. Those places are in the net, out, or to your opponent's expensively trained and ferocious forehand.

## Learning To Serve

Why are serves so difficult to learn to hit when it is the one shot you get to set up all by yourself? If you are like most players, your serve causes you to ask yourself every day: "What the hell is going on here?!"

Let's look at some common service difficulties. First, the serve requires pinpoint control of not only your dominant arm, but also the one you hide in your pocket at formal get-togethers because you only trust it to scratch an itch. Yes, the "other" arm can readily transform your serve into a rendering of that classic comedy skit: *Who's On Serve?* Here's how; while your good arm is waving your racket behind your back and around your head like the flag-man at the Daytona 500, your hapless excuse for human symmetry must deliver the ball to the strike zone just as your racket comes streaking through it. These complementary actions take exact timing. And this timing requires years of practice to blend harmoniously together—but that's only because it requires the coordination of a brain surgeon to learn, and about the same expenditure in lesson money.

Second, let's assume you have invested the normal several years and thousands of dollars, and you now possess the skill to move both your arms at the same time to a common goal: the serve. Now, all you want to do is make the ball land in the service court. And you may. Then some fungus-for-brains yells, "FOOT FAULT!"

"Foot fault" is what cowardly whiners cry when they become upset at repeatedly being aced. It means 'cheater.' Those sniveling weenies quietly allow you some aces during your first couple of service games. After that, unless you show immediate signs of a total loss of muscle control, like double faulting four times in a row, they will march to the tournament desk to request a foot fault judge.

Calling for a foot fault judge is tantamount to yelling, *you fungus pustule! I hate you and the car that brought you!* Face it. When is the last time anybody called for a foot fault judge when (1) they only mildly disliked their opponents, or (2) they were AHEAD? Almost never! I say "almost" because those people do exist. They are the overcompensating morons who, as children, used to pull the wings off helpless insects, and today drive slowly in the fast lane.

Of course, they are right. The disputable fact is your serve is probably teeming with the heinous *Neil Armstrong Syndrome* (NAS). Tennisologists inform us that Neil Armstrong Syndrome is either a geek's way of maintaining balance while serving, a misstep, or a player's way of cheating. Whatever the reason, they define it as *one small step for the server, one gross violation of the rules of tennis.*

Happily, a normal foot-faulting problem can be remedied. All it takes is the same sort of determination and money that it took to learn your serve in the first place. Just go to your pro and hand him a blank check. You will see results in no time. That is, you will see your account balance drop like swimsuits at a nude beach.

Correcting your serve will require hours of patient reconstruction. Accordingly, tennisologists compare the ease of altering your service motion to changing a flat tire during a blizzard—in your underwear. But, that's what pros are there to do—fix faults. They will fix every fault you can commit, except asphalt. Asphalt requires a proctologist.

## *Normal Serves*

If you are a normal player, you imitate the pros by crushing your first serves with a generated two tons per square inch of service force, regardless of your inability to control it. In this way, you publicly demonstrate your superior service skills by slamming the ball directly into the back fence. Temporarily humbled, you then putz your second serve over the net in a pitiful effort to bloop the ball into play. Subsequently, your opponent's service return zips past you faster than a New York taxi in the rain. You continue in this vein until you lose your serve. Why? Because you're normal.

Fortunately for us, our opponents are as "normal" as we are and lose their serves at roughly the same rate. This combined loss of serves entitles us to proudly assert at club social functions that we were *on serve*[1] until the tiebreaker (when, because of nerves, you putz-returned even your opponent's putz serves).

---

1.    To win or lose games at the same rate as your opponent.

Of course, in a pinch, you can always revert to the devious under-hand serve. I say "devious" because it catches your serious opponents off guard. They think you are *giving* them the ball! Ha, ha. They catch the ball with a quizzical expression, and you dutifully claim the point. It works like a charm. It also works exactly one time. After that, your opponent is on to your under-handed ways and will lie in wait for any opportunity (including changeovers) to send a ball rocketing directly into your crotch.

You can see why serves represent a lifelong commitment to learning: learning to putz, learning a second serve, and learning to come up with varying excuses about why your serve has been "off" since you were 12 years old.

# 4

## *Carpe Pointum, a.k.a. The Volley*

Along with the serve, volleys are the stock and trade of real tennis players. The volley is a shot that is snatched straight out of the air. No speed reducing bounces here. Volleyers must handle and redirect unadulterated power, just like a president's mistress.

Volleys are for the brave and adventurous tennis player. They are for the player with the courage to change his or her world. They are for players forged with a courageous spirit that inspires them to attack first and ask strategic questions later. They are for those players with the reflexes to protect his or her vital organs from steroid-bloated, tennis-playing brutes with muscles on their fingernails and turbo-charged groundstrokes. In short, volleys are for *real* tennis players. (It's not that baseliners can't be real players, it's just that volleyers *must* be real players.)

The scary thing about volleys is that, like trains and bad report cards, you can see them coming. Volleys are typically heralded by a rather strong and potent serve. A frequent scenario is this: a player, usually large and sporting facial hair, starts the point by hammering a serve into a blur. Subsequently, the returner lunges weakly and is barely able to float the ball over the net before his racket is wrenched from his grip by the biting power of the serve. The server, anticipating this puny return, and seeing the helpless ball drifting high in the breeze, glides confidently forward into the court. He/she attacks it, driving the ball into a corner for a dazzling winner, a la Minnesota Fats.

The aforementioned point scenario has been labeled *The Wimbledon Scenario*. It was named after Horace B. Wimbledon who inadvertently invented the attack game by continually returning even mediocre serves in a novel manner—high, short, and softly. It became notorious as the "float like butterfly, sting like a dandelion" stratagem.

*The French Scenario* is the opposite of The Wimbledon Scenario. The French Scenario happens when both players stand at the baseline powerfully clubbing their strokes back and forth until one of them develops cramps in a major muscle group.

Another signal of the impending volley is the *approach shot*[1]. This type of shot occurs when both players are in the backcourt slamming graphite ion-emitting forehands back and forth. Then, quite involuntarily, one player produces a shot that bounces about service line depth. The other player, sensing an opportunity, drives a stabbing approach shot deep and down the line. Then, he or she quickly closes to the net to await the easy volley. (In this case, that "she" is downright rare. At any given time, the women's tour includes maybe one aggressive volleyer. For this reason alone, that lone stalwart female should be ranked an honorary #1.)

Most women do not serve and volley. Recent studies by some of the world's leading tennisologists have concluded that this is principally due to substantial amounts of the hormone, *Keepemstroken*. This hormone sends an overpowering signal to the brain to pound endless groundstrokes. The more Keepemstroken your body produces, the more time you spend running around the backcourt. Serve and volleyers hate the effects of this hormone on opponents. After losing an extended *moonball*[2] rally with a baseline specialist, a frustrated volleyer will often shake her fist and let slip, "You wimp! Play like a man!"

---

1.    A shot players use to end tiresome rallies.
2.    A lob hit for no apparent reason.

All volleys are not created equal. (I'm sure our forefathers would have mentioned this fact in the bylaws had they not tabled it in committee because they were busy writing important historical documents like the *Declaration of Independence*, the *Constitution*, and various *Jim Crow* laws.) A small minority of volleys are awesome put-aways like the ones the professional serve-and-volleyers hit, roughly after every "in" first serve. The majority of club volleys are, on average, decent shots that also land in: *in* the net, *in* the fence, and off the frame and *in* your eye.

Another, even smaller, minority of volleys are those frame shots that land in the court; the kind geeks hit when they play you. These are the most effective volleys of all. A volley off the racket frame will almost certainly win the point. You might try it yourself on your next match point. But, if you are playing doubles, warn your partner first. Otherwise, should something go wrong, he or she may feel compelled to frame shot your ear.

## *Volley Worries*

You need a conspicuous amount of courage to be a good volleyer. That's because there are a number of things you need to worry about while volleying.

One worry for the volleyer, at least while playing doubles, is your partner's serve. Specifically, that your partner will serve the ball softly and short while you are standing at the net trying to look inconspicuous. This type of serve leaves your skin vulnerable to instantaneous welting. This danger exists because returners will often jump at the chance to play a little intimidation game with the net person by drilling a bloodcurdling power stroke right at his or her aorta. (**Dave's hint**: If you cannot find (and keep) a steady doubles partner, see your pro about some service lessons.)

Also, it can happen that, although your partner has a good serve, it can stray. More accurately, it can stray 110 MPH right into your backside. This is always painful. It is sort of like hitting yourself on the shin with your racket, but different because YOU ARE NOT THE IDIOT! So, it is advisable to stay on speaking terms with your doubles partner.

The biggest worry for the volleyer is the net. Not so much hitting the ball into a net that hangs there like an ominous spider web ensnaring flying tennis balls. No. Rather, because it can be extremely dangerous to your more indispensable body parts. I am talking about the dreaded *net-cord* shot. A net-cord shot is ordinarily a titanium-powered forehand or quasi-forehand that has been slammed directly at you, but then slightly rerouted by casual contact with the net. Instead of being rerouted around your body, the ball tends to leap up over your racket and into a favorite nostril. These shots put the fear of double faulting their match point away into most volleyers.

Still, there exists a more dangerous and terrifying situation. A situation that, the very thought of, causes even the most intrepid serve and volleyer to tremble in horror. It makes me cringe just typing this: the net with *holes*! The truly diabolical thing about a net with holes is the false sense of security you feel when you know the ball is not coming over the net. Just when you have relaxed your vigil, POW, right in the *groin*! I don't know about women, but men will drive to the next county to avoid playing on a court with holes in the net.

Speaking of nets, maybe the most disturbing net type is the chain link type. Besides producing an annoying, tinny *chlang* when a ball smacks it, this type of net also launches the world's tallest net-cord shots. Normal net-cord winners are blown up into suicide lobs. Really. I have seen incredibly blazing passing shots miraculously transformed into lazy, short lobs. Still, we men will play on courts with this kind of net because studies have shown that they are highly resistant to unauthorized holes.

The very last skill a volleyer must learn is when NOT to volley. Experienced volleyers will let you fire away with booming salvos like the USS Iowa. Then they'll calmly turn aside and watch the ball remove paint two inches outside the line. On the other hand, it is completely common to see good, technical volleyers leap high into the air to return a shot that had been cleared for take-off over the back fence and into a nearby storm drain.

It should be obvious by now that if you volley or plan to volley, you need to be assertive and brave. So, drop your vegetarian diet. And, ALWAYS check the net for holes!

# 5

## *Service Returns are Easy (If You Have Your Receipt)*

A sun-tanned man in a dark trench coat and sunglasses approaches the Sgt. Pepper soft drink machine at the Inner City Recreation Center. Disregarding the nine-fingered, switchblade knife juggler, he calmly plunks a few coins in the slot and presses a button. A cold tea drink rolls out and lands with a *thunk*.

Annoyed, but not dismayed, the man curses silently to himself, inserts his last coins, and this time carefully presses the proper button. Out plops a small tape recorder. His eyes cautiously scan the area. Satisfied, he presses "PLAY."

> *Good morning, Mr. Phlops. Your mission, should you choose to accept it, is to return serve, not just any serve, but the powerful first serve. As usual, if your skills are discovered deficient, your pro will disavow any knowledge of you or your service return. Good luck. This tape will self-destruct in seventeen seconds.*

The man sets the tape recorder down on the bench. Three gang members waving sawed-off Uzis quickly scoop it up and run to a waiting car. The car blows up in a small mushroom cloud; the man grins. Then his countenance hardens. The look of hard determination reveals his grim decision. He will return serve.

Service returns are difficult shots. They often involve trying to hit a tennis ball traveling upwards of 120 mph. Now, consider trying to hit them without life insurance. Whew! It's a good thing we don't play with golf balls like some sports I won't mention.

What about your service return? What do your opponents call it? Do they say it is a brick wall? Or, like mine, a dessert topping? Chances are, when you are playing an addle-brained clod, it is an impenetrable armored wall. On the other hand, if you are playing the person you suspect is having an affair with your spouse, it turns to Cool Whip. If you are a relatively typical player, it's both, and usually within the same game. Why? Because you are not hitting a typical shot. You are returning a serve. Service returns are very routine, atypical shots.

Returning serves is frequently an exercise in jury-rigging a stroke that will return the ball over the net. When you are returning a strong serve, you can't do it with an organized shot like you can the other tennis strokes. You don't have the time to hit the ball with your normal full backswing and measured footwork, or to follow through with your arm wrapped around your neck like a nervous anaconda. Such returns only work off those rare serves that only clear the net because the wind is behind them. Instead, you must lunge and swipe at the blurred ball like a drunk at a passing Coors truck. The unexpected truth is: as long as you get the ball back it doesn't matter how you look doing it, which is good, because you're certain to look pretty foolish.

Everyone knows that the hardest, toughest serves are the ones YOUR opponent unleashes. In contrast, for example, if you were to walk past a hundred friends during their matches, not only would you be very tired, but you would also observe that 90 percent of their opponents' serves are putzes.

My opponents, and probably yours, are different. Always. (My wife says it's what I get for taking the Sports section into the bathroom.) Example: you and your opponent are warming up, rallying smartly back and forth, and you're feeling rather comparable. Then you warm up your serves. You begin easy as you try to break through that feeling that makes us think our arms have been shrink-wrapped across our chests. Then your bemused opponent opens up his arsenal of various, murderous and ravaging serves that leave you wondering if you weren't his final post-steroid overdose, rehab match before rejoining the pro circuit in Europe.

There is a certain look a server takes on when he or she hits the ball well and on purpose. It is the look of a deeply ingrained confidence, and it's indelibly written all over your opponent's serve. As you both continue warming up your serves, you try to keep up with your opponent's bullets by demonstrating that your service power is similar to his (the ones bending your rackets into coat hooks), except your serves tend to ricochet around inside nearby bleachers. Meanwhile, his serves hit all the service lines, whistle by your ear, and wedge themselves in the fence, leaving your racket flapping in the air like a kite caught on an antenna.

When the match is underway and your opponent is still bouncing serves off the line and into your chest, you are honor bound to give him his first few service games. Then he is honor bound to be a sport and let you return a few serves with your racket. If instead he smirks and continues to drill casual aces, it is okay for you to start claiming apparent liners for yourself. I say "apparent" since he crushes the ball so hard, can you really be sure the ball was *not* out? No. As a matter of opinion, not even NASA could track anything traveling that speed. It's the same reasoning they use with firing squads. One of those rifles contains a blank. You can't be sure yours wasn't the one. So, don't feel bad. Life's too short, especially if you are the part of the firing squad without a rifle.

In response to your change in line calls, your opponents may take matters into their own hands. Rather than calling for an umpire, they may begin serving the ball so far inside the lines that even career politicians would be forced to call them "in." If your opponent begins serving balls inside the lines, fall back on Plan B: request a foot fault judge. Who cares if the guy really foot faults? Again, you can't really be sure your opponent isn't doing it. Heck, he or she is standing on the other side of the court.

Most players with functioning sweat glands find a foot fault judge wreaks havoc on their serves. Even if they have written and notarized proof that they have never foot-faulted before, they still can't be absolutely positive. Right? I mean, who watches their feet when they serve? Okay, maybe a gang member with a newly stolen pair of $150 "Airhead" basketball shoes. But gangsters mostly stick to recreational activities other than tennis (i.e., self-tattooing, drug-trafficking, and drive-by bullet sculpture). Anyway, in the most successful havoc cases, your opponent's first serve will begin to not only miss by entire court lengths, but their second serves become more like backcourt, overhead drop shots.

Then again, there are those players that can ONLY serve. These players are annoying because while warming up their strokes, they spray balls all over the court like aerosol air fresheners. This spraying forces you to walk around the fences to gather up the balls, thus giving you plenty of time to plan your next three-day vacation, which, of course, you do. Then, from out of the sun, your opponent serves up two aces and two serves that you quickly convert into *forced errors*[1]. All of a sudden, you are down a game and you haven't even packed yet.

If my opponent's strokes routinely ended up with the ball wedged in the throat of his racket, it only meant that he balanced his game with a sonic boomer first serve. Loud cracks of thunder would issue from his serves as the ball flashed past the corner of my eye like a yellow ghost. Then, if I could manage to push a return back, he would trip over his own racket in a futile attempt to move his body toward the lazily bouncing ball. Again, balance. This dork reaction would reveal his true identity as *The Incredible Geekman*, offender of all that's coordinated. I hate being *on serve* with those types.

---

1.    Errors with built-in excuses.

So keep working on your service return. You'll know when it has blossomed into respectability, because when your pro watches you play, he won't wear a bag over his head.

# 6

## *High On Lobs*

A lob is generally defined as a shot hit softly and high, and usually beyond a frustrated net-person's reach.

**Dave's Note:** A lob hit to a person standing in the backcourt is called a *moonball*. This shot is cleverly named for the fact that since your opponent will let the ball bounce, it gives you enough time to "moon" him.

### *Lobs, The Background*

Lobs were devised by smart-ass little players with pocket protectors in their shorts. These geeks realized that they were frequently being forced into weak court positions that required drastic defensive maneuvers. (Translation: the ball had bounced too far inside the line to call it "out" and not be head-butted into a coma.) So, they concocted the lob to incense their crudely one-dimensional opponents. Once lobs were let out of the can they spread like two-handed backhands. Today, viciously nerdy lobbers lob until their exasperated opponents hammer their rackets into circles the diameter of net poles. These passive-aggressive lobbers then continue lobbing until their opponents run out of rackets.

As a result of this geek-by-association, lobs get no respect. People with effective backhands regard lobs as wimpy shots. Likewise, lobbers are considered to be petty cowards incapable of executing real strokes, or geeks with only enough strength and imagination to launch the ball up safely into the air like a flare. Real players eventually designed indoor courts to constrain hardened lobbers.

Today, lobs are pretty much like chaperoning–a lost art. Young players today don't realize it, but a lob can be a very useful shot, especially against those gorillas that hate them most–volleyers. As volleyers rush snorting to the net like a Hollywood cokehead, a well-placed lob sends them into a frenzied retreat while muttering nebulous but audible threats of mischief, like pouring Gatorade into their opponents' tennis bags.

The net-person ordinarily expends a great deal of physical effort securing the potent net position. This effort usually manifests itself in the form of overpowering serves or explosive groundstrokes, and then sprinting up to the net. These net-persons, subsequently, tend to become visibly irritated when they are forced to give up their net position because of a stinking, no-effort lob. After all, they must start all over again at the baseline, wait for another short return to assail, and then re-storm the net to volley their opponent's shot away for winner. A good plan, unless the dork lobs again, which of course they always do.

When the lobber is also a Hall of Fame dork, the energy supply of attacking tennis players is sapped more quickly because of the added embarrassment of losing to someone who looks like a pre-pubescent charter member of an after-school science club. These dorks use a strategy of alternating strokes and lobs. This strategy takes advantage of the tendency of real players to repeatedly attack and retreat until they eventually become delirious with thirst and imagine they see a stream of cool water flowing on the far side of the court. Crazed, they then charge forward again and fall across the net.

If you are wondering why you lose to those skinny-legged, pencil-armed geeks who lob over your head until you get cramps in your neck from looking up more often than visitors to the Sistine Chapel, the answer is: your overhead sucks. Sucky overheads are symptomatic of players who over-compensate for their lack of control with exaggerated spikes of power. These players are always young males who consistently demonstrate the pinpoint precision of a D+ student.

## *The Boys*

For young males, tennis is a modern form of the ancient warrior's code, dubbed by sports anthropologists as *The Code of Macho*. These adolescent boys view lobbing as a concession of superiority in a test of strength. If a boy were to break down and lob, when there was even only a theoretical chance of hitting any other shot within ten feet of the baseline, they would suffer a humiliating public loss of face or, at least, an acne eruption more conspicuous than Mt. St. Helens.

The whole point of The Code of Macho is that boys can hit any shot as long as it approaches the speed of an Indy car. As a hypothetical example, if one boy were to crack an overhead to his opponent's forehand, his opponent is not only expected to hit his forehand back as a passing shot, but he is code-bound to try to crush it back even harder than the overhead. In fact, all points progress this way under The Code of Macho. Boys play points wherein each succeeding shot is hit harder than the previous one. This pattern continues until one of the players is unable to control the ball and drives it over a fence. Though a boy may lose 6-0, 6-0, if he plays by The Code of Macho he is considered a respectable opponent. Conversely, if a boy collapses into manifest sanity and issues a deliberate lob, he is considered a wimp, unable to withstand the rigors of real tennis, even if he wins. The rest of the code-keepers subsequently ridicule and ostracize that boy for a period of time not less than the next tournament. Only the next tournament allows the code-breaker an opportunity to redeem himself by blasting all strokes into any of the following code-approved areas of the court:

1. in

2. out

3. the net

4. into the fence

5. over the fence

Boys are allowed a few extenuating circumstances when breaking The Code of Macho. Boys are allowed to lob without tainting their otherwise macho reputations if: (1) they are the best player in their age group in the city; (2) they are hitting the ball from outside the fence; (3) they have a tattoo on a prominent body part; or, (4) they have a criminal record.

## *The Girls*

In the past, especially in the youngest divisions of girls' tennis, the lob had evolved not only into a standard defensive shot, but an offensive shot, and in severe cases of pre-adolescentitis, a serve as well. As you might guess, points could last quite a while for these girls. In fact, two 12-year-old girls set the record for a single point. They played a point that lasted one hour and included 1029 shots. Counting the serve, 1004 of those shots were lobs.

This old lob mentality is why "macho" has traditionally been ignored in girls' tennis. After all, few girls wanted to work out with heavy metal objects. They preferred the smooth curvy look, and just didn't care if they hit the ball hard enough to drive staples. Today, with the emergence of enough prize money to start a private university and personalized weight machines, where you can sit down while you pump iron, all players are working out and getting much stronger. Girls are even showing signs of taking up The Code of Macho, except there is still no stigma associated with lobbing.

So use lobs judiciously; but don't be surprised to hear a gang of boy players call you "wimp" or "geek." Then again, just go downtown to someplace like "Burt's Tattoo Depot" and have a tattoo of a fierce-looking, cobra-headed, tennis racket injected into your forearm with needles the size of turkey basters. It's a simple way to "free the lob."

# 7

## *Are Overheads Over Your Head?*

Overheads are a sensation. These types of shots are powerful explosions of guided velocity that have well-deserved reputations as dramatic point-enders. They're point-enders, that is, if you're watching tennis on television.

Every pro on television has a dynamite overhead or else they'd be bartenders. I have even seen pros crack overheads out of the air, three feet inside the baseline! The pros on TV laugh in the face of lobs. "Bwahaha," they guffaw as they crush overheads into the corners with the same disdain they display when the clown ahead of them at the airport car-rental counter rents a *Hyundai*.

As the average tennis player watches tennis on television, s/he sees confident professionals routinely smash overheads away for impressive winners. These viewers can't help but notice how explosive overheads draw cheers of admiration from the excited and appreciative crowd. This overt adulation can sometimes cause a tennis player's baser instincts to surface. These players frequently decide that they, too, would look good winning points in similar climactic fashion. So, they begin rabidly crushing every ball, shoulder high and above, like a lumberjack on a double espresso.

All players want to hit those shots that they have the most confidence in. That confidence allows them to execute elaborate and gaudy, heavy-duty swings. Forehands, for instance, are being smacked with great gusto and are forcing errors daily because they are the easiest

41

shots to boom back for most tennis players not yet suffering from moonball-induced brain damage. Unfortunately for many players, the overhead is not one of those shots.

The overhead is a peculiarity. It is the only point-ending shot that is as effortless to learn to hit effectively and consistently, as it is to convince the IRS to let you claim your dog as a dependent. This difficulty stems from the fact that overheads are a close relative of the serve. Very close. I mean, *incestuously* close.

Overheads fall into one of six categories:

1.  *The Killer Overhead.* This is the kind of overhead exhibited by professional players with boxcars of product endorsements. It is also the phrase most of us use to describe our overheads to strangers.

2.  *The Common Overhead.* This particular kind of overhead is hit with modest speed, often down the middle of the court, thereby allowing any geek with blisters to lob it back into play.

3.  *The Blazing Overhead.* This overhead is hit dead on the sweet spot of a racket traveling at the speed of the average ballistic missile—to the wrong places. Blazing overheads are always sent rocketing:

    a.  into the back fence

    b.  over the back fence

    c.  into the net

    d.  into the ground in front of the net

4.  *The Putz Overhead.* This overhead is a shot that is patted back up into the air and over the net with about as much meaningful depth as The Hokey Pokey. Terrified baseliners use it when confronted by lobs at the net. It is also the leading cause of injuries for tennis geeks.

5. *The Blazing Putz Overhead.* This overhead is a Blazing Overhead, except that you wildly miss the sweet spot. The usual results of this type of overhead are:

   a. A miss-hit off the frame that ends up working as a drop shot that bounces just over the net and spins back onto the other side.

   b. A miss-hit off the frame that flies off sideways and makes lobbers laugh.

6. *The Header Overhead.* The overheader misses the ball entirely and it bounces straight off his head.

Overheads are extremely effective against lobs. Against other types of shots they are less useful. Just the same, to do battle with loboholic dorks you must learn to hit overheads.

Unfortunately, overheads are more difficult to master than lobs. Tennisologists' studies have determined that it requires roughly 10,000,000,000 brain cells, working in harmony, to execute a single common overhead. Lobs require 106. (As a reference: chewing a stick of gum requires 121.) Now, geeks have billions of brain cells engaged exclusively in conceptual thought such as fractal geometry and string theory development. That leaves them with about 150 brain cells dedicated to muscle management and how to make themselves look "sexy." These limited mental resources explain why lobs are as second nature to geeks and dweebs as dandruff.

The problem is many tennis players don't know brains cells from bran flakes. As a result, they don't take their overheads seriously enough. They see those palsied little lobs lofted up in the air by some palsied little geek, and think, *Chalk up another point for Mr. Slambanger.* Of course, after scorching their first five blazing overheads into the back fence, they see the subsequent hundreds of palsied little lobs and think, "Oh *bleep.* Come on. Get this overhead in. Easy. Eeassy. *BLEEP!*" Soon, our hero is *putzing* overheads all over the court like a seagull with the runs. Finally, the only approach to the net he/she makes is to shake hands in defeat while the match results are broadcast over the public address system and citizen band radio.

Overheads and serves, as mentioned, are severely similar. In fact, they are as different as domestic and imported beers. Serves require you to wind up like the Maharishi Yogi meditating in the *pretzel* position. Then, as the ball floats on a cushion of air, it pauses for you to cream it at somebody.

Overheads are perilously different. Overheads require that YOU wait. As soon as the geek you are playing launches a lob, you strike the pose of placing your racket head on your back with your "good" hand and point up at your target with your "other" hand. You then wait in that position as the geek's lob flies upward. You wait as it zooms past low-flying aircraft. You wait as it pulls alongside a balloon sent up by the National Weather Service. You wait as it reaches its apex and starts back down. Then you wait as it comes hurtling at your head like a deadly, yellow, pterodactyl turd. By the time your wait is over and the ball has fallen to within striking distance, and assuming all the blood has not drained from your hands, you then have the opportunity to hit a ball that has attained the same velocity as a super-collider electron.

Good players let these high-flying lobs bounce—ONCE! (An important distinction.) Letting hyper-high lobs bounce produces a second, far lower lob that falls at a more manageable speed. Of course, players must often return these lobs before running into the back fence like a mosquito into a can of Raid. Now, if the lob bounces over the fence, that player must then quickly run out the gate to return the shot from the middle of a seniors' water aerobics class.

So, if you want to inoculate your game against those neurotic lob-ophiles you need to develop your anti-lob device: the overhead. Seek professional help.

Just think of how you will awe your friends and rivals. Think of the satisfaction that you will enjoy when peers upgrade your overhead skill to "decent." Just think of it. Did you think? Okay, now think of a way to duck out of playing those lob-mongering geeks until your overhead pops up on your game's radar screen. Reference Chapter 47, Excuseology.

# 8

## *Shot Droppings*

After scooping up hundreds of drop shots on the second bounce, I have concluded that drop shots are either very good or really, really bad. Namely, when my opponent's hit them, they are very good. When I hit them, they are frighteningly awful. Oh, I have hit my share of great ones, mind you, just rarely on purpose.

### *Drop Shotting*

Used prudently, drop shots are a (practically) no-lose shot, even if you don't win the point. I mean, even if your opponent surges to the net like some sort of racket-wielding rabid dog and contemptuously bashes the ball out of the reach of your comic interpretation of a backhand, it's okay. You will have sent a message to your opponent that you will drop the ball short whenever you feel in the mood to mock him or her. That knowledge will make your opponents so nervous that they develop sudden ulcers, keel over, and forfeit. Or, they will start giggling uncontrollably and thereby lose valuable concentration brain cells. Either way, your outlook is good.

If you are like I am, you mostly attempt drop shots when you have forced your opponent to the back fence to retrieve one of your better lobs, and where he/she has trapped his or her foot under the/thee chain link fence and is unable to get free. Or, he/she has returned the ball, but has fallen down and is rolling in agony while clutching a major leg joint. Tennisologist studies have determined that as your opponent is busily using his or her racket as a crowbar to pry the fence off his or her foot, or is flailing back and forth on the ground holding a leg in the air, you will be able to successfully drop the ball over the net 67 percent of the time.

In those rare moments when I attempt a drop shot, and my opponent is uninjured and unfettered by the fence, I tend to send them a little too high and a little too deep. Okay, I typically limp off the court with red ball marks raised on various parts of my body. Curious spectators will sincerely ask, "Why did you lob short so often?" (I found the best reply to be, "Go to hell!")

What makes drop shots so great is that they are so unexpected. You approach the shot as if you were going to hit it as usual—out. Your opponent backs off the baseline with his or her index finger already poised in the "out" position. Then you drop shot the sucker!

In theory, your opponent is so stunned at your unexpected display of dim strategy that he or she staggers for a second, then races to the ball and lunges for it as if it was the last bottle of beer in the cooler. If your opponent gets the ball back, chances are excellent that he or she will simply run into the net, thus awarding you the point. Or, you will be right there to smash it between his or her legs in a bold stroke of pure intimidation.

(Doesn't it bother you when we writers write awkward sentences in an attempt to placate various politically correct groups? An obvious example:

> *Then, he or she, armed with his or her racket, waits for his or her college professor to come bouncing by like a high forehand to thwack him or her upside his or her head, because he or she gave him or her a 'D-.'*

If we were to de-gender all of our pronouns, as some advocate, we would clearly require other words to replace them. In other words, "woMAN," "perSON," "huMAN," etc., would be unsuitable. Perhaps, for the children, we should take the *hu* from human, and the *per* from person, and combine them into the gender-neutral term *huper*. It would mean 'Homo Sapiens without glands.' Fortunately for us, there is no such thing. Unfortunately for us, lawyers and political interest groups wouldn't care. These groups would find new and innovative legal ways to use this term against us normal people. So, forget I brought it up.)

For many players a drop shot comes even more unexpectedly to the hitter. That's because, at the club level, a drop shot is commonly due to a miss-hit. These miss-hits are typically full-swing, graphite-powered shots, intended to be forceful put-aways deep into corners, but which *boink* off the frame instead of the strings. The result is a lazy drop shot that floats over the net and then dives for the ground like it was home plate. These types of shots are frequently flat-out winners.

Now, these types of winners infuriate your opponents. They'll stand there, hands on their hips, glaring at you. This glare means, *only an unethical twit, with toenail fungus, would stoop to accept such illegitimate gain.* But don't even offer to play two. Those people use the same glare when you win the spin for serve. They're just jealous they didn't miss-hit the ball first.

At all levels of play, the best drop shot has consistently proven to be the net cord assisted drop shot. This shot is essentially the same as the miss-hit, except the ball shoots screaming off the racket with a distinguishable vapor trail. Then, just as it looks as if it will cross the net cleanly, it smacks the tape with such a CRACK that career military and law enforcement personnel instinctively take cover. The ball stops dead like an F-14 Tomcat landing on a carrier deck and then drops sedately over the net for a winner like an escaped convict in a wool optic yellow jumpsuit.

Of course, the net cord drop shot is a very difficult shot to hit deliberately, even with practice. So I strongly advise you to not waste time practicing it. If you are currently practicing this shot, cease immediately! If you will not stop, for heaven's sake be discreet, and do not let the children witness such wanton self-indulgence.

## Being Drop-Shotted

Now, if YOU are on the receiving end of multiple drop shots, your opponent is telling you 1 of 4 things: (1) You need to lose weight. (2) You move with all the agility of a city bus. (3) You are a poor tennis player, a fine yo-yo, but a pitiful tennis player. Finally, (4) you are too damn good and "I am going to tank this match as quickly as possible so I can buy a stress-relieving six-pack."

It is important to ascertain the proper meaning associated with your opponent's drop shots. Therefore, ask yourself the following questions. Could your opponent's drop shotting mean reason #1? Sure, your spouse and doctor have been nagging you to shed a few pounds, but they have been for years. Besides, you always figured that you looked pretty good for your age. However, if they have, AND your opponent drop shots you more than once on purpose, you have incontrovertible evidence that you ought to lose those extra 50-60 lbs.

Could the reason your opponent's drop shot you be reason #2? Do you move around as if tractor-driving vandals have plowed the court? Sadistic opponents with copious, fast-response muscle groups like to watch the gravitationally-challenged plod around the court until they lose track of the score via unconsciousness. If your opponents are amused by your best efforts, consider it proof of #2.

You will discover that most of your confusion will occur when choosing between reasons #3 and #4. Therefore, I have supplied a handy scientific technique to help you distinguish between the two. Here is how you use this handy scientific technique:

## Dave's Handy Scientific Drop-Shot Decipherer:

Wait until the match is over; then check the score. If you lost, it was #3. If you won, it was #4.

# 9

# *Half Volley: The Shot Feared 'Round the World*

Half volleys are unavoidable shots that you should always avoid. I could probably stop there, but that's never stopped me before.

The term "half volley" has been borrowed from the ancient Phoenician *half* meaning 'incomplete,' and early English *volley* meaning 'shots.' (In certain British Commonwealth countries it also means 'rally.') So, *half volley* is therefore a bi-rooted term meaning, literally, 'incomplete shots.' It is a historical term referring to bullets landing in front of targets.

I will now describe what a half volley is for you hackers. A half volley is a *frustrating piece of*—wait we don't want to corrupt our young readers. Tennisologists' current definition of "half volley" is *a shot hit between two and 13.7 inches off the ground as the ball rises.* In other words, the ball is struck just after it ricochets off the court right in front of you as if the court was Teflon-coated. Returning a shot less than two inches above the court requires more luck than Russian Roulette. After a ball has risen more than 13.7 inches, it is considered less a half volley and more of a shot that is hit *on the rise.* "On the rise" is another tennis term meaning: *To hit the ball back after it stops being a half volley, and before your opponent can fully recover his court sense.* In still other words, your chance of executing a decent shot rises directly with the ball. Get it? Depending on your level of play, hitting on the rise enables you to either (1) better finish off a point, or (2) look like a hockey goalie blocking moldy yellow pucks.

Before we further delve into the mysteries of the half volley, let's establish what they are not. Half volleys are not intelligent, funny, rich, or Episcopalian. Half volleys are not even volleys. Nor are they half of anything, not even half effective. More precisely, half volleys are almost wholly *ineffective*. They are largely futile shots because they are so difficult for us to execute without exorbitant amounts of luck. Period. Unless you net-cord the ball over the net, it is almost impossible to not set up your opponent. But I'm getting ahead of myself.

Now, should your half volley defy all tennis logic and drop in, it is first required by natural tennis law to float serenely up into the air like a small fuzzy hot air balloon. This sleepy sight instills in your opponents roughly the same amount of dread and concern that Einstein had for long division. In fact, the chances are excellent that you will be irked by your opponent's outright guffaw before he or she pulverizes the ball back into (1) your side of the court, or (2) some notably sensitive and private part of your anatomy.

Of course, if you are willing to practice half volleys daily for a few decades, you may be able to make the ball hit the tape in such a way that it drops over the net and onto the court like an anonymous hit-and-run gift of zucchini on your porch. Yes, and pie-eating contests are sophisticated cultural events.

So, half volleys require a great deal of skill to execute, and that's just to be able to put yourself in extreme physical danger.

## *Singles Half Volleys:*

In singles, a half volley is regularly experienced after a serve and its subsequent return, or after an "approach shot." An "approach shot" is 'a shot you hit on your way to the net.' It is named for the fact that the point is quickly approaching its conclusion. The approach shot is a favorite shot of you attacking-type players who use it to set up your half volleys, and which ordinarily prevents you from having to execute those annoyingly technical volleys at all. In any event, half volleys usually occur on the way to the net.

So, why do players brave these menacing half volleys to go to the net? Simple: advertising. The net is promoted as the power position on the court by formidable tennis institutions, like your club pro. Teaching and media-prominent pros, who handle half volleys like Shakespeare handled English, constantly dangle the net in your face like a cheesecake.

*Reality Check #1*: Most would-be net players only get part way to the net before their opponent's return comes diving back at the ground in front of their shoelaces. At this point, they meekly pop the ball up with kibble-like half volleys.

Sometimes, half volleys occur while you are standing idly in the backcourt, watching the match, as your opponent drills a shot just inside your baseline. In this instance, you can do one of two things: (1) hit a difficult, full-swing half volley from the baseline, or (2) do what we regular players do, call it "out."

## Doubles Half Volleys:

In doubles, most half volleys are likely to be delivered as service returns or, heck, just about any time that a player is inspired to volley. This doubles reality is why standing on the service line, waiting to volley is considered by experienced doubles players to be grounds for instant committal into the local Tennis Hall of Shame (THS). After all, you are just asking for half volleys, and that's if you are fortunate enough to escape SGT (Severe Genital Trauma). This, of course, presumes you are at least a net-playing wannabe. If you are the net-avoidance type, you are probably either an exercise obsessive-compulsive, baseline-hugging, singles player who gets manipulated into playing doubles by off-duty salespeople, or you are an "outed" sadistic lobateer who strays too far inside the baseline and receives a painful correction.

*Reality Check #2*: Half volleys are never tactical. They are always defensive and usually desperate. No player above an NTRP rating of-2 wants to hit this shot. Most players would rather play tennis without socks than try a half volley. Truth be told (and it sometimes leaks out in this book), most players would rather attempt ANY other type of shot, including the Kamikaze lob-volley (a suicidal shot whereby you are impaled by point-blank overheads that crash into your body like diving falcons in *snack* mode.)

In their endless quest for tennis truth and knowledge, our tireless team of tennisologists ventured forth onto our nation's courts, and after hours of intensive study concluded that half volleys are always hit in the following areas of the court, in order of most to least frequent:

1.   into the net

2.   under your racket

3.   into the courtside trash can

4.   over the net

Unfortunately, even if you skillfully lift the ball over the net and into the court, half volleys never draw the "ooohs" or even "aaaaahs" from a crowd that they deserve. This lack of adulation is due to the fact that successful half volleys are regularly returned as setups. In fact, these shots are never hit for winners, unless by serendipitous accident. (I used "serendipitous" because we tennis writers need to sound more author-like.) Just the same, crowds love forceful winning shots, and will wait in silent anticipation to see if the half-volleyer can dodge an instant appendectomy.

Speaking of crowds, have you seen the throngs of groupies herding around the top stars in any field of endeavor? Even the Federal Reserve Board Chairperson leaves a wake of groupies swooning. Well, tennis authors have groupies too. My groupie is Rap, my German Shepherd Dog. Actually, he is my groupie only when my wife isn't around. When she's around he attaches himself to her so closely that they get stuck walking through doorways. When my wife leaves the house the first thing Rap does is race around the rooms checking every window just in case my wife remembered she forgot something, but couldn't remember where the doors are. Finally, he will give up and lie down across the room, making sure to keep me in sight. In this way, he will be instantly alerted in the event that I spontaneously mutate into my wife.

So, half volleys require the skill of a world-class professional to not only hit effectively, but also to avoid having to hit altogether. Now, if we can just convince the general public of their level of difficulty, I'm sure we tennis players would get more groupies. Tell a friend.

# 10

## Lob-Volley: The Shot Nobody Teaches

o o o o o o o o o o o o o o o o o o o o o o o o o o o o o

*Overheads to the left of them.*
*Overheads to the right of them.*
*Into the Valley of Death strayed the Lob-Volleys.*

*—Al Tennisson, USPTA*

The lob-volley is a peculiar shot that, for some reason, has been granted the status of a standard shot by leading tennisologists. Okay, okay, it was in return for my promise of a rather sizable contribution to the retirement fund of the World Order Of Tennisologists (WOOT).

Lob-volleys are lobs that you hit without benefit of letting the ball bounce. Smart players know that bouncing is the intelligent manipulation of the Science of Friction. By letting the ball bounce, you let the court remove a generous portion of the ball's imposing speed, which gives you a better chance to control your shot. But, if you really want to be able to return forceful incoming shots, just stand ten feet behind the baseline. If you need yet more help managing ball power, stand with your back up against the fence. If you are still intimidated, develop a close meaningful relationship with a 10 gauge shotgun and watch tennis on television.

## *L/V Chip*

You only see lob-volleys on local courts and never on television because they are blocked by your television's L/V chip. Not long ago, USTA-bought FCC officials quietly mandated that television companies install this small electronic device in new television sets. The L/V chip detects incoming lob-volley transmissions and instantly overlays this message on your television screen:

**Please stand by. We are experiencing technical difficulties.**

Lob-volleys aren't taught by pros in full possession of their faculties. Sensible tennis pros won't even offer that the shot exists, unless you ask them directly. Nonetheless, it is a shot that pops up in matches, way too often.

## *The Theory*

The lob-volley theory, as it would be espoused on television by ex-tennis pro commentators who still execute flawless lob-volleys off searing overheads as routinely as cable television rates increase, is as follows. As you exchange volleys with your opponents they inexorably inch forward ('close in on the net' in tennis lingo), closer and closer, until you can make out their individual nasal hairs. Now, being the savvy doubles player that you are, you know that unless you can keep them away from the net and hitting the ball down at your shoes, your return shots are numbered. So, your highly trained reflexes (or perhaps brain lesions as we shall examine later) swiftly kick into action. You smartly punch the next volley that comes within racket distance deftly over the heads and out of reach of your surprised and humiliated opponents. In response to your strategy spasm, they quickly yell "yours" in unison, and then crash into each other while executing the crafty doubles *switch* maneuver. "Switch" is a doubles code word, shortened from: 'I want to play on your side of the court now.' The announcing player then takes off running in front of or behind his or her partner. In defense, their partner must then hustle over to the vacated side so as to present a set of moving targets. In a car, the switch maneuver is called a "Chinese Fire Drill." In tennis, this is considered an intelligent doubles action.

That's one theory of lob-volletivity. There is another theory however, and it says the first theory is INSANE! As usual, our curious and frequently mercenary tennisologists looked into the matter. In an under-funded shortcut study, these bottom line-conscious tennisologists speculated that the human brain might respond to over-crowding at the net with instant brain lesions. At least that's the conclusion the tennisologists plagiarized from the People for the Ethical Treatment of Rodents (PETR). The tennisologists somehow secured PETR's published report on the effects of over-crowding in laboratory mice that were confined to little cages with an itsy-bitsy net running across the center and surrounded by tiny windscreens.

According to the tennisologists, these lesions allegedly suppress an individual's natural irrational-thought filters, subsequently allowing unbelievably "mentally-challenged" tennis choices to slip through a player's brain synapses like illegal aliens across the border. Ultimately, affected players delude themselves into thinking they can execute ANY shot that their Veg-O-Matically diced brains can conceive.

(Incidentally, less biased studies proved over-crowding only gave the mice headaches and an uncontrollable urge to perform non-stop changeovers. Even so, it still seems to explain lob-volleys.)

Lob-volleys almost always occur in doubles, and only when both opponents are at the net with you. If you hit a lob-volley, your partner's position doesn't matter, except on the school prayer issue.

The reason you almost never see lob-volleys in singles is that, scientifically speaking, it would be INCREDIBLY STUPID! Even micro-brained, slaphappy hackers have figured that out! Okay, I got carried away. Hackers don't even know the shot has a name other than "pop-up." The only time you might want to hit a lob-volley in singles is if you are a highly-ranked professional, up to your armpits in deodorant endorsements, ahead a set and two breaks, AND your opponent has just tripped and fallen over the bench.

Eventually, our born-again capitalist tennisologists marched back to their labs with the aid of a generous grant from the Foundation for Victims of Short Lobs and Vasectomies (FVSLV). After many hours of intense note-taking in the study just mentioned, those tenacious pencil-wielding tennisologists broke down with finger cramps. But not before they uncovered the natural behaviors of the lob-volley shot! Here now, for the first time in print, are their findings.

Lob-volleys can be hit in one of two ways: (1) *accidentally*, and (2) *on purpose*. Of the two ways to hit this shot, "accidentally" is always the more beneficial. The reason is simple: you have a better chance of success.

Let's look at the actual numbers as prepared by our hard-working tennisologists. The average club player hits accidental lob-volleys for winners (over the heads of opponents and in the court) a whopping 19 percent of the time. Whereas, purposeful lob-volleys are hit for winners a calamitous 12 percent of the time! These numbers indicate that if you were to offer a lob-volley on purpose, you would be demonstrating the same amount of sheer court sense as a dung beetle.

So, as our tennisologist friends advise, don't do it! Just say no! They urge you to practice *safe* lobs. "Safe lobs" means that when you do lob, let the ball bounce first. So don't run out and put a condom over your grip.

If you're wondering if I've ever lob-volleyed, the answer is yes. But, that only reinforces my point. After all, how often do you hear my name mentioned in scholarly tennis conversation? Answer: never. Damn straight!

This brings us to the reason why pros don't explain how to hit this shot. It's not that they want to keep the knowledge to themselves for showing-off during exhibition matches, or even to spare you from looking like a clay-pigeon refugee from the skeet industry. No. Rather, they know you would probably go out and attempt this shot on your own, without proper supervision, and BE a world-class target. Pros know that any player who has not accumulated at least one Grand Prix point will most likely incur personal injury in attempting this shot. Which is no skin off their knees, except that those clay pigeons turn around and *sue* the pros. So they don't teach it, at least not without a written and notarized disclaimer. Without a disclaimer, pros would be at the mercy of lawyers. ("Mercy of lawyers," now there's an oxymoron.)

So, if any of you tennis players think you might want to give the lob-volley a try, run, don't walk, to the nearest phone. Call a sober friend. In a rapid, high-pitched voice, tell your friend that lawyers are stalking you. Then, beg that person to drive you to the nearest television factory to have an L/V chip implanted in your brain. Tell them Dave sent you.

# 11

## *Get a Grip!*

Grips. What kind of grip do you use? You probably answered leather, plastic foam, or some other derivative of duct tape. And that would be very impressive. However, I meant, how do you hold your racket?

I have noticed that there is practically no grip that someone, somewhere, is not abusing, even now as I wait for my spell-checker. Even so, there are the main grips, the main squeezes you might say. These grips have been given nifty and easily-remembered names. Although, for a secret purpose to be revealed later, these grips were named after airline companies: *Eastern, Western,* and *Continental.*

In the same vein, if you think you have invented a new grip and want to uphold this tradition, you might want to name it the "Delta," or perhaps for you two-handers, the "United." It might even prove lucrative (certainly more lucrative than naming it, say, the "Burlington Northern"). But those are just my suggestions.

Grips are very important when playing tennis because without one you would be playing handball. Trust me. You do not want to play handball, especially with a regulation handball. Regulation handballs are among the hardest things known to humans. I mean, they rank right up there in the Almanac of Hard Stuff. Some of the world's foremost hard things are:

1. diamonds

2. titanium

3. golf balls

4. world peace

5. cold fusion

6. Jeopardy

7. handballs

Some of you may be surprised that "handballs" is on this list. Obviously, you don't play handball. More the better.

Still, thank goodness the United States Handball Association (USHA), a foster cousin of the USTA, allows the manufacture of a milder pink handball. This ball, called the *pinkie* (by me anyway), is easier on the hands. It is the handball officially endorsed by the ASGW (American Society of Grimacers and Wincers), and real handball players universally despise it as wimp bait.

Real handball players are always male and always proudly in pain. You can tell who the real handball players are even when they are not running into the hard walls of oversized concrete boxes while engaged in inducing large, tumorous-looking swellings on their hands. Real handball players are the ones in muscle shirts trying to pick up women in bars using sign language. Often, they enroll in those offbeat extension colleges called "Self Individualization University," and take classes like *Indian Barefoot Fire Walking For Singles* and *Self-Flagellate Your Way To A Sexy New Look*.

Back to grips. The official rumors leaking out of the USTA about the geneses of the grips are: (1) the Eastern grips originated on the East Coast by snobbish Grip Nazis searching for the master grips. (2) The Continental is said to have its roots in Neo-Old World blacksmiths who always gripped their hammers in the same fashion. (3) The Western grip was developed by tennis camp dropouts in the Western USA.

## Eastern

Today, tennisologists mildly dispute the USTA's official rumors. Modern tennisologists believe that, originally, the only USTA-endorsed grips were first the Eastern, and then the Continental. They contend that the Eastern grips were handed down from generation to generation by well-bred players from Ivy League zip codes who snubbed baseball and joined exclusive clubs. Such players enjoyed shaking hands in gentlemanly fashion with fellow club members at every opportunity. These players extended this practice of shaking hands to their dogs and even their tennis rackets. Subsequently, they evolved the Eastern forehand grip gene. To this day, old-style pros teach this "shaking hands with the racket" forehand grip. It emphasizes that you place the "V" of your hand toward the relative "west" side of the grip. An Eastern backhand grip would entail presenting your hand to your racket for kissing like an Ivy League debutante.

These two Eastern grips require a disciplined grip change from forehand to backhand and back again. It takes many hundreds of hours of determined practice to develop a smooth transition between the two. Eastern grippers used to snicker amongst themselves at the sight of any uncouth grip type because it usually indicated ex-baseball players or unrefined blacksmiths.

## Continental

The Continental grip is used for both forehands and backhands. It was devised for less privileged players because learning only one grip required fewer costly tennis lessons. The grip sits halfway between an Eastern forehand and an Eastern backhand. Where exactly? Who cares? It's been extinct since the Nixon administration.

Unlike the Eastern grip, the Continental grip was first used by ill-mannered hacks from the other side of town who were too lazy to switch grips. These coarse hacks even succeeded in trading their classy European breakfast connotation in on some everyday airline (a bit suspicious). Then, just as the tennis establishment was becoming accustomed to this brazen grip, and even listing it in respected tennis journals, the Western grip burst on the scene like Viagra. Then came Rap music. Now, it's tongue piercing.

## Western

The Western grip, also unlike the Eastern, involves placing the "V" of your hand on the racket's relative "east" side. In fact, the Western grip is so far to the east side of your racket that there is NO Western backhand grip. None. Instead, players of the Western grip faith use the heretical, two-hand backhand. It doesn't matter how they hold the racket; two-hand backhands are always demonic.

The Western grip name incorporates many grips with varying degrees of westness. The Western grip can be divided into your basic *John Wayne Western*, your *Wild Wild Western*, and the extreme *(Sam) Peckinpah Western*. For each one, your hand slips farther around the back of the handle than the one before. The Peckinpah is performed by cupping your racket's handle from underneath.

Tennisologists suggest that the Western grip evolved on the hardcourts of Southern California to better negotiate the higher bounces that the harder court surfaces brought about. If this is true, what do you expect when you let your children play tennis without proper supervision and instruction? The parents of my generation did the same thing. And you know what happened? Two-hand backhands happened! YUCK! They should be outlawed. But can you imagine the backlash from the parents of little baseliners? I can see their bumper sticker now:

When Two-Hand Backhands Are Outlawed,
Only Outlaws Will Have Two-Hand Backhands

If you are the parent of a little two-hand backhand, you needn't worry. Today, anything goes. There are as many two-hand backhands infesting our courts as there are sport utility vehicles four-wheeling through parking lots. Today there are even two-hand forehands! It couldn't possibly get any worse. Although, I suppose two-handed serves would be worse. Two-handed beer mugs would be okay, though.

## Conspiracy Revealed

Okay. As promised, the big question on the minds of tennis players everywhere is this: What is all this geography doing in our tennis grips anyway? And, why do we tennis players predominantly fly these airlines (Eastern, Western, and Continental)? After some wild extrapolations from absolutely no evidence, I submit that a multi-airline company Political Action Committee (PAC) together with the National Geographic Society (NGS) has exerted undue influence on the United States Tennis Association (USTA). This PAC has, with money (\$) and/or all-expenses paid vacations to numerous tropical islands, bought the use of their airline names as grip names to shamelessly promote their companies.

There, I have revealed the reason for these grip names. If you fly any of these airlines or subscribe to National Geographic magazine, it is unquestionably because of the subliminal message in your grip name.

# 12

## *Clinical Depression: Clinic Dynamics*

Does anybody out there drill anymore? I mean besides Florida prodigies, dentists, and oil companies. How is it that adults don't drill? And, why don't women understand the chic charm of Saran Wrap blouses? Just asking.

Tennis drills are designed to isolate one shot or aspect of the game. Players use these drills to repetitively exercise different shots or aspects of their games in order to improve their muscle-memory, technical competence, and confidence levels.

Drilling different shots and bodybuilding involve similar concepts, except a bodybuilder's muscle-memory is HUGE. Bodybuilders are men and women who meet in smelly places lined with mirrors to lift heavy objects until their veins pop out and their sweat glands burst. By the way, these gyms are considered excellent places to meet members of the opposite sex. In a gym, you stand around lifting the equivalent of 89 rackets over your head until your muscles spasm into square knots. There are always a certain percentage of the opposite sex who finds such an exhibition completely alluring.

### *Clinic Balls*

In tennis drills organized by pros, the pro has a market basket of tennis balls for your hitting pleasure. These balls run the gamut of the tennis ball lifecycle. They include *Brand New* balls that the pro recently purchased at discount from the local Poverty-Mart. There are the *Good*

*Balls*; that is, the ones that retain 75 percent of their fuzzy lint and bounce more or less to industry standards. Also, there are the *Bald Bouncers* that are so flighty they achieve escape velocity via lob-volleys. The *Living Dead*: those balls that look good, but bounce more to watermelon standards. Finally, there are the often-useful *Bald Deaders*. Bald Deaders are old balls that only retain a 5 o'clock shadow of fuzz and plop instead of bounce. These balls are retained by the pro to pick up a geek's spirits.

Geeks, being geeks, sometimes get depressed after repeatedly being hit on the foot by tennis balls during a continuous hour of simple forehand drills. Therefore, the wise pro lets his geek students vent that frustration by hitting a tennis ball, as hard as they can, over the fence and into some native vegetation. In this way, geeks can regain a measure of self-confidence and self-esteem. However, as usually happens, the geek swings and misses. The pro then gives him two more chances to hit it over the fence. If that doesn't work, the geek is then given two chances to throw it over. Failing that, the pro allows the geek to cuss out the ball. So in the end, the geek gains a measure of cathartic revenge.

To develop a student's ability to hit a ball over the net, the pro repeatedly sets the student up with shots so easy that any third-grader with just enough physical coordination to safely play with rubber erasers could direct them away for winners. Of course, there goes any semblance to an actual match. Why? Because "winners" only exist at the professional level. At other levels they exist as "luck." Anyway, most beginning students are incapable of returning anything more difficult than lob-like drop shots.

In a real match, the going gets tougher. In a real match, balls are always coming at you faster than your ability to react. In a real match, all of your opponent's shots bounce in the court within six inches of the baseline. Of course, in a real match you get to call those shots "out."

## *Adult Clinics:*

In an adult clinic, you have upwards of 25 people in line practicing their strokes by waving their rackets in unison like a half-time Racket Swinging Precision Team. Then during a hitting drill, after they have each hit their ball quota, they get back in line where they have enough time to play a hand of Canasta before their next turn.

Pros know that bad things can happen when students stand around. Often, students will leave the court to gather the balls hit over the fence and never come back. Remember Custer's Last Stand? Those guys were just standing around in their little circle, and did they come back? No way. To avoid this dead time, pros go to great lengths to make sure that their students are not just standing around yawning like hopeless insomniacs. Even so, sometimes standing around is inevitable. That is why pros devised coed clinics. In all cases the pro diligently tries to keep everyone occupied with doing something to keep his or her mind from noticing that only one person can be actively drilling at a time. Some students are instructed to pick up the balls they have hit. Some are next in line and must be attentive to the drill in progress. Others can be found entwined in some "coeducation" on a nearby bench.

After drilling on one of the finer points of the game, like the "top-spin drop shot," comes the least fun of all, the ritual of picking up the balls. After hitting 500 balls to students lucky to pull out of their drive-ways without denting their cars, the pro is usually ready for a short break. Of course no one else is ready for any sort of break because they have been standing around for all but the four seconds it took to hit each of their six backhands over the side fence.

Still, picking up balls gives students a chance to engage in class bonding via this wholesome form of camaraderie. In coed adult classes, this usually involves students making passes at each other and/or the pro. In spite of this camaraderie, the balls are quickly herded together and placed back into the pro's basket. The adult classes always get the balls picked up quickly because they want to learn how to play tennis, even if it means picking up balls and playing a few hands of Canasta to do it.

## *Kids' Clinics*

Kids' clinics are a totally different animal. Unlike the good old days, by cracky, today's kids don't take clinics to actually learn tennis. Hell no. They are there to smash their 12 gauge forehands into the foreheads of fellow students whenever the pro turns his back. So you end up with anywhere from three to 25 kids (whose major goals in life are to eat french fries, watch MTV, and get away with an ever increasing number of social crimes and misdemeanors), standing on the court bored and actively not listening.

Today's kids don't listen to anything except TV, stereos, and delinquent peers. No matter what the pro says to instruct the little thought-resistant darlings, 9 out of 10 will not have heard it, because they were carefully studying someone walking his dog a half mile away. Even if we assume all 10 heard the pro, 9 out of 10 will not think that the pro has made a relevant point. In fact, kids genetically assume the pro is trying to destroy their already meager games by steering them AWAY from their own personally devised techniques borrowed from an NFL end-zone celebration. The tenth one is a confessed geek. Still, two of the nine will try it the pro's way exactly one time, because they are honor roll students. If the pro's way works, the pro is then entitled to try to change another flaw so obvious the Department of Defense wouldn't buy it. However, if the student's first attempt fails, they whine, "See, my way's better." The other seven don't bother to try it the pro's way even once. After all, they have been playing their way all of their tennis careers–about two days. And how long have they known the pro? Maybe twenty minutes. Besides, if the pro were really any good, he or she would have brought in someone "cool" for an exhibition match, like the reigning Miss Teen Bikini.

This brings me to the subject of the pro showing his stuff. Stuff-showing is totally unnecessary for adult students, because they pay the pro to teach them how to play tennis. The pro could be straight off the boat from Iceland, speak no English, know no tennis, walk on the court, take their money, and adult students will try to do everything mimed to them. Why? Because unlike kids, they pay the pro from their own wallets.

Conversely, pros must earn a kid's respect. Unless the pro has been on television, won a televised tournament they've heard of, or has the physical presence of a professional wrestler, kids assume the pro was hired right off the boat from Iceland with only enough tennis knowledge to teach them his or her name.

Therefore, a few ways to generate respect are (1) a flaming shot to the ear. Interestingly, this method is guaranteed to get their respect *and* make them hear better; (2) service aces; and of course, (3) trick shots. Trick shots include those hit between the legs or behind the back. Shots hit with severe spin that leave a kid believing in UFOs also work well.

## Ball Pickup

At this point, let's turn our attention to the herd of kids and the dynamics of a typical ball pickup session. At the end of a drill, the pro is confronted with 500 more or less evenly spaced balls lying: (1) all over the court, (2) all over the neighboring court(s), and (3) outside the court. The first thing the pro must do is dispatch someone to go outside the court to retrieve those balls hit over the fence.

Now, kids absolutely hate to leave the security of their own court. Outside their court, the designated ball-chaser must search through wild flora in often-disagreeable conditions, like *quickmud*. (Quickmud is a type of sticky mud that can suck ugly from a pig and yet immediately disengages from shoes the moment you step onto a tennis court.) Kids equate this kind of Out of Court Experience (OCE) with "work," and therefore something to be avoided.

Also, in the last decade or so there has been an increase in *Juvenile Loiterers* (JLs). Juvenile Loiterers are roving bands of grade-schoolers that pickup anything that is not bolted to something too heavy to throw. These bands are always "playing" unsupervised around public tennis courts. Whenever a ball flies over the fence, a JL will quickly scoop it up with larcenous intent and skip away with it, gloating. Then, a fellow JL gets jealous and decides it's his *legal right* to take a tennis ball, too. He'll march up to the fence and begin to pull a ball out from *under* it! He doesn't care if he is observed. He wants a ball and he wants it now! So the designated ball-chaser must go out to recover tennis balls from these amoral, thieving, juvenile delinquents in training.

Now, back on the court the real fun of a kids' clinic has begun: trying to hit your fellow student between the legs with a tennis ball. (You can see why the court is where the action is and why leaving it is not fun. In fact, kids consider leaving the court more than uncommon punishment. Kids consider it cruel and the pro to be reported to mom.)

You see, left to their own devices, a herd of kids will divide themselves up into gangs without regard to the distribution of loose balls. Why? Because kids are basically pack animals, and so they disperse into gangs to opposite ends of the court to fake retrieving the balls, but they are really establishing proximity to their targets. Then, instead of placing the balls on their rackets and carrying them back to the basket, one kid will launch a Mach 1 forehand drive to the basket on the opposite side of the court, where a few kids are debating the virtues of various contraceptive devices.

Why do kids blast balls? It's because kids are basically predators also. Yes, they are predators that feast on adult exasperation. Anyway, some kid is nearly hit. As if on cue, an epidemic of *Lemming Syndrome* breaks out. Lemming Syndrome forces children to imitate the actions of the most delinquent behavior they see. It is caused by an inherited virus that erupts in every juvenile under the legal drinking age when in the presence of illegal, immoral, or chaotic stimuli.

In a flash, a mushroom cloud of tennis balls eclipses the sun. A half hour later, once the kids are winded, the pro has regained order, and the damage assessed, it is not unusual for several students to have red welts, and at least one student to be writhing on the ground with an agonizing groin injury. It is also not unusual for the class to have ended. In any case, the balls are pretty much as evenly spaced as they were before.

You can see why kids think tennis clinics are way more fun than reading *Great Expectations*. Although their tennis skills increase in glacial increments, kids do learn a new sense of justice, namely: An eye for an eye, and a groin for a groin.

# PART II

## Tennis and Competition

o o o o o o o o o o o o o o o o o o o o o o o o o o o o o o o

*"I came. I saw. I got clobbered."*

—*Julius Loser*

# 13

## *Doubles and Being a Significant Other*

When four people play on the same court at the same time with the same ball, doubles happens. This form of tennis occurs most often when open courts are scarce, or when the players can't come up with the necessary money for a singles court rental, or they don't want to engage in any heavy breathing exercise with their pants on.

Tennisologists' studies have concluded that most men and women prefer to play doubles with their own kind: men with men, and women with women. You would think that mixed doubles would be the game of choice, especially among singles (spousally challenged) and married people whose spouses are out of town. But you would think wrong. Married partners break up faster than those makeshift couples the morning after booty call. Anyway, mixed doubles is not the dominant form of doubles enjoyed today.

### *Gender and Doubles:*

Since single-sex doubles has been identified as the most common form of doubles, a new breed of tennisologist called "behavioral tennisologists" is currently studying this single gender doubles phenomenon via grants from the Federal Government to some of this country's foremost institutions of minute detail. Their preliminary findings are out:

## Men's Doubles:

These behavioral tennisologists argue that doubles provides another excellent opportunity for men to engage in the ritual of male bonding. You know, that part of a man's life where he gathers with other males to talk about (do, if possible) gross and disgusting things that would never occur to a woman. For instance, what woman would celebrate a game-winning overhead by patting her partner's behind and issuing a belch loud enough to freeze a police SWAT team? Yet, we men bond in this way.

This type of male bonding is an ancient ritual that can be traced back thousands of years. Caves in France have been discovered that contain the earliest known evidence of what social behaviorists now identify as the *Male Belch Rite*. These ancient cave drawings clearly depict Neanderthal males standing around after a successful hunt, their mouths open wide, patting each other's behinds.

## Women's Doubles:

Unfortunately, few women experience the same thrill by participating in bondage. Too bad. When women play doubles, it's to thoroughly crush their scum slurping, slime oozing, wretched excuse for sluts/ opponents, and otherwise, fast friends. They suspend all rules and codes governing clean competition and fair play for the duration of the match. Afterwards, the two parties engage in small talk, like their husbands, and how they preach to their children that sports should be fun. After this light social interaction, they set up another match for the following week.

## Mixed Gender Doubles:

When mixed doubles *is* played, males are often wholly immersed in the very idea of bonding to the point of forgetting their children's birthday parties. Men will actually chase their partners around the court in a spirited effort to pat their partners' behinds. You can see why this type of doubles is often referred to as *four-play.*

The women of mixed doubles on the other hand, are primarily concerned with self-preservation. They intensely bob and weave around the court like a boxer. They try to present a moving target to their male opponent who (in testosterone overload), is trying to impress all women with his macho maleness by breaking the sound barrier with a tennis ball. These tendencies explain why nobody knows the score. (For more on mixed doubles see Chapter 15.)

## Social Doubles

Social doubles is mostly fun. Well, three-quarters fun, actually. Only three of the four players will be having a good time. The fourth player is, statistically speaking, a tennis social climber whose goal is to climb onto the club's 'A' Party Ladder. This player will be equating his or her opponents' like-ability somewhere between dental floss and the plague.

## Doubles Popularity

You might think that bonding and the wholesome competition it provides would be reasons enough for club players to prefer doubles to singles. Well, this turns out not to be the case! Random studies by skilled tennisologists of club players at the branch establishments of Sunset Days Home and Tennis Clubs in Orlando, FL, Scottsdale, AZ, and Sun City, CA have conclusively proven otherwise. The reasons the vast majority of tennis players play doubles are: (1) playing singles is so tiring, and (2) each player need only supply the balls once every four matches. As supporting evidence, these talented tennis scientists have documented evidence that the typical club player exhibits the lung capacity of a Chihuahua, the muscle tone of Jell-O, and the generosity of the IRS.

## Dave's 1st Doubles Tip

Since these studies show that many of you doubles players are sluggish, the following is my tip to the tired. **Dave's Generic Doubles tip**: If you find yourself out of breath during a doubles point, remember: when the going gets tough, the tough yell, "YOURS!" This one word instantly transfers responsibility for the ensuing shot from the most logical hitter—you—to your clueless partner. You can then take a breather while your partner dashes behind you to return the ball.

Yelling "YOURS!" is similar to yelling "DIBS!" as a kid. "Dibsing" was an unwritten rule of child property rights. The rule stated that the first kid to yell "dibs" in the direction of an obviously unattended object, no matter how remote, got immediate legal, territorial, and mineral rights over that object.

Similarly, "yoursing" is an unwritten rule of tennis. However, exercise the *Yours* maneuver prudently. In its worst cases, careless "yoursing" can lead to "competitive yoursing." In competitive yoursing, each player tries to sluff off his or her shot responsibility by being the first to yell "yours" during a point, and then sitting safely down on the courtside bench. Ultimately, the "yoursing" winner gets partner-complaining rights, and the loser suffers a mild recession in the local Doubles Reputation Market (DRM).

## Competitive Doubles

Competitive doubles requires a different set of skills than singles. Singles players are simply in a race to develop the better backhand. Doubles players, however, must develop a serve, service return, volley, and overhead. They should also develop a sense of how much court their partners can cover and then cover the rest themselves. Otherwise, a doubles player will quickly become a singles player by popular demand.

Doubles is a tough game to learn to play. Not only must you keep track of the ball, each member of the other team, yourself, the score, and your wallet, but you must also keep track of your partner—who is likely to be off playing doubles by him or herself. And, you must do these things all at the same time.

Tennisologists have devised more than one technique to overcome this continuous quandary of tracking a stealthy partner. But first, let me report that the USTA does not approve of the "Marco Polo" method whereby one partner yells "Marco!" and the other bellows "Polo!" in reply. Nor does the USTA approve of putting a bell around your partner's neck. However sensible for you, this practice does tend to annoy your partner and irritate your opponents who become increasingly hostile as their combined weights approach 400 lbs.

The USTA approved methods are (1) to watch your partner hit the ball (tennisologists called this the *Exorcist* method, because your head swivels around as you try to track the ricocheting ball), or (2) to react to your opponent's reaction to your partner's shot. This method is called the *Catatonic* method because you stare straight ahead as if in a drug-induced hypnotic state.

To keep things complicated, both of these methods have their disadvantages. The main disadvantage of the Exorcist method is that during a furious exchange of shots you are susceptible to whiplash. Also, opponents frequently tend to sneak around the court after they've hit their shots. Since you are not watching your opponents, you must then feel their movements with that valuable, yet elusive, *doubles sense.* "Doubles sense" is a set of survival skills that is acquired after several years of a partner's short lobs being converted into meteor-like overheads. (These types of overheads seek out the nearest exposed flesh like guided missiles and leave craterous depressions on them.) You might say "doubles sense" is comparable to a Jedi warrior's *Force* skills.

The main disadvantage of the Catatonic method is that because you are not watching your partner, you must use that doubles sense to follow what he or she is doing. Since you constantly get clues from where your opponents move and where they target their shots, your doubles sense will reveal that, statistically speaking, your partner is off playing somewhere safe and useless—as the Jedi equivalent of C3-PO.

Using your doubles sense as radar is a good thing. It helps you be a better partner. Still, if you can't reach the ball, it is by definition your partner's shot, and you should blame that person loudly and often at club social functions. As always, there is a trade-off. If you do complain, and during match play a ball is subsequently hit behind you, your partner may take the opportunity to return the ball via a swift detour through your kidney.

## The Rest of Dave's Helpful Doubles Tips

I have watched many club doubles matches and have observed that most players need advice in the area of playing doubles as a team, rather than playing separately together. Fortunately for you, I am a third rate pro[1] and here to help.

The following is a little pre-game checklist to help you prepare for your doubles matches. Let's begin with something that everyone except renegade Boy Scouts can do: prepare.

*1. Know your opponents' game.* The best way to know your opponents is to study them as they play another team. In so doing, you can obtain valuable insights into their match tendencies. All you need to do is gather the necessary data. It's easy. Hence…

## Dave's Easy Data Gathering Technique:

Arrange to watch your opponents play ahead of time. Obtain a thick notebook and write their names in large readable letters across the cover. Bring the notebook along with an adding machine and a pencil to your opponents' match (a calculator will do in a pinch). You and your partner should then sit down in a conspicuous location to watch.

---

1.    Really

Then, every time your future opponents miss a shot, scribble in your notebook while nodding your head knowingly. At the changeover, punch in random numbers on your adding machine and pull the handle with a loud mechanical *ka-ching*. Jump up and down in an obvious manner as you share your happy "discovery" with your partner. You may not actually learn anything about their match tendencies, but they will think you have cleverly uncovered some hidden flaw in their game that will allow you to trounce them without even taking off your sweats. They will stay up late that night worrying about what you figured out. They'll arrive for your match the next day tired and listless. Every time you win a point, they will shake their heads and think you somehow planned it that way, which you did. Ha, ha.

2. *Warm-up before the warm-up.* If you can't scope out your opponents before hand, the next best time to size them up is during the prematch warm-up. Therefore, the intelligent doubles team will warm themselves up early, before the formal match warm-up. That way, they can spend their time analyzing their naive opponents.

To size up your opponents, ask yourself certain questions. How do they handle slices? How do they handle topspin? How do they handle balls hit straight at their eyeballs? Are they bigger than you are? Could you call the lines "close" and get away with it? Or would they give you an on-court frontal lobotomy with their racket handle? A seasoned player will know these answers before the first point is played. Above all, make sure you ask them, "Are you ready yet?" every thirty seconds.

3. *The spin for serve.* The spin for serve is a frequently overlooked part of the match, yet it often sets the tone of the match from its very outset. The spin is influential because the team that wins the spin will usually choose to serve first. They then let their poster-child for high-potency steroids serve, pinning you cowering against the back fence while you hold up your racket as a protective shield.

To counteract this common serve tactic, decline to spin for serve until after the warm-up. Then, should you lose the spin, always choose to receive on the side where they warmed up. This annoys your opponents, because they must begin serving from the "wrong" side. They will think you are deliberately trying to get inside their sunscreen-fumed heads, which of course, you are.

These small steps will blow your opponents' cerebral thermostats. They will begin to aim their forehands and overheads at your lungs, instead of sticking to sound doubles fundamentals. Furthermore, these helpful hints will increase your tennis enjoyment without any practice at all. What could be better?

## *Optimizing Your Doubles Games*

There are a number of tactical ways to play doubles. Each style has its advantages and disadvantages. Each situation is both unique and commonplace. Any exceptional athlete could figure it out in a few years.

To optimize your doubles effectiveness, we first need to identify which style of doubles best suits your personality. Since personality type is a direct indicator of doubles style, let's examine this further. Are you a self-starting, self-serving, banzai bomber, or a cowering, weak-kneed, listless lobber? Do you try to outdo everybody in everything, like having the highest speed recorded on police radar to cultivating the largest overseas phone bill? Or are you the kind of person that cannot take sides in anything less than a full-scale thermo-nuclear confrontation? In other words, what is your intensity level? Fortunately, scientists have provided us with a couple of personal intensity categories: Types "A" and "B."

The first thing we must do to maximize your doubles game is ascertain what type of letter your personality is: A or B. To establish whether you are "Type A" or "Type B," I have provided the following handy personality test:

# *Dave's Handy Personality Test:*

1. **When the alarm goes off in the morning, you:**

   a.  Scramble out of bed, feed and walk the dog, change the oil in your car, and whistle *76 Trombones* as you get ready for work.

   b.  Roll out of bed, crawl into the bathroom, turn on the shower, and curl up in a corner humming *Old Man River*.

   c.  Never hear it. In fact, you have woken up more than once at your own autopsy.

2. **When you shop, you:**

   a.  Briskly walk from store to store, carefully taking notes on price per volume to get the best deal.

   b.  Drive into the closest store and buy the first generic product that approximates what you need.

   c.  Only shop at Taco Bell's drive-up window. All else is donated by your parents, a church charity, and the Salvation Army.

3. **Your hobbies include:**

   a.  Jogging, weight lifting, bicycling, swimming, and translating Shakespeare into Yiddish.

   b.  Strolls on the beach, going to baseball games, surfing the Internet, gardening, and collecting "poodle" skirts.

   c.  TV remote speed-channeling, downloading Internet porn, and collecting disability.

4. **The car you drive is:**

   a.  A high performance driving machine, one of the latest luxury foreign cars that insure at $1000/month.

    b.   A highly reliable and economical foreign car that you hope to keep for five more years.

    c.   On jacks in the driveway.

5.  **Your work philosophy is**:

    a.   Time is money. There are 365 workdays in the year. You carry a cell phone, a beeper, a palm computer, and a portable fax machine.

    b.   You put in 40 hours a week at a job that is not exactly what you wanted to do with your life, but it pays the bills.

    c.   To take jobs only often enough to qualify for unemployment. Then you call in sick.

6.  **Your home**:

    a.   Was studied by the microchip industry as an example of a dust-free work environment.

    b.   Is somewhat cluttered, but could be ready for the in-laws within a week.

    c.   Was named in a lawsuit by the Society for Prevention of Cruelty to Animals as "inhumane," and you don't own a pet.

If you answered "a" to any one of these questions, consider yourself "Type A." If you answered "c" to any of these questions, you are "Type B." (It is genetically impossible for a Type A to answer "c," or a Type B to answer "a" to any of these questions without developing brain cramps.) If your answers were all "b," you are a schizo. You haven't decided what you're going to do when you grow up. You need professional counseling just to choose a hair color. We will call you "Type F."

## Doubles Types

Okay, we have established what type of personality occupies your mind. And no, "sex" is not a personality type. Briefly, this is how scientists define these personality types:

1.  Type A's are obnoxious, overbearing, loud-mouthed jerks. In third world countries, a Type A's typical hobby is global terrorism.

2.  Type B's are lily-livered, wishy-washy, spineless wimps. In many parts of the world, Type B's are eventually euthanized.

3.  Type F's are all of you who are neither A nor B. You require personality lessons from the Colorado School of Mimes.

## Basic Type Styles—Type A

In both doubles and singles, Type A's stand at the baseline just long enough to get the point started. Then aroused, they storm to the net like police to a doughnut shop. In doubles they dart to and fro, slashing and hacking, yelling words in a random manner like "MINE," "YOURS," "SWITCH," and "UP." And that's when they're gathering up the balls between points. Yes, it's fun to watch these types charging back and forth, stabbing and jousting madly like Knights of the "A" Table, untii they both yell "mine" and CLANK; their rackets crash into each other as the ball scoots between them. Point lost.

## Type B Doubles

Type B's are hugely passive. They make Mahatma Gandhi look like an acrimonious mongoose. Type B's stand at the baseline waiting for the next shot. They keep one hand on their rackets and one hand on a cigarette or a beer. If the ball is hit short or wide of where they're standing, the Type B's lurch forward with all the agility of a sumo wrestler with bunions. They eventually arrive just in time to wave their rackets weakly over the ball as if trying to magically turn it into a pumpkin.

## Type F Doubles

No distinguishing characteristics.

## Inter-Type Play:

When all four players are of the same type, their match progresses smoothly because everyone agrees on the correct tempo of the game. But when an A team plays a B team, suspicions run deep because of their genetic feud. Each team thinks the other is using flagrant gamesmanship to annoy and irritate them by altering the pace of a "normal" game.

## A's vs. B's

Let's take a closer look at these inter-type dynamics.

When a Type A team meets a Type B team on the tennis court, the tension is thicker than a bratwurst stand at a PETA convention. The Type A's walk briskly between points to retrieve the balls needed to resume play. Then they begin bouncing the ball impatiently at the baseline as the Type B's amble over to a corner of the court, with all the speed of horticulture, to help a crawling bug leave the court. Type A's hustle over to the other side of the court when changing sides. Type B's frequently sloth over to the bench to inventory the used balls in their bags. Type A's march single-mindedly, taking up their position to resume play and staying loose by bouncing up and down like Ping-Pong balls, while waiting for the Type B's to return from meandering off to the snack bar for a pack of cigarettes.

You can just imagine the happenings when an outside ball rolls onto a court where A's and B's are playing. When a ball rolls onto their court, Type A's always declare a "play two." They then hasten over to roll the ball back to its owners. Type B's on the other hand, not wanting to play the same point twice, ignore the ball until the point is over. In fact, they ignore it until its owner walks over and retrieves it.

Equipment also varies for each type. Type A's always carry at least three rackets, a complete change of clothes, an assortment of grips and racket strings, personal hygiene products, a first aid kit, and an emergency freeze-dried dinner, all in a bag large enough to carry a rototiller. Type B's lug one racket around. If their strings break during an important challenge match they'll ask to borrow their opponent's backup racket.

## Type F Doubles

Luckily for the world, most players are of the Type F variety. This type has the unique ability to not only play too slowly for Type A's, but also too fast for Type B's. Though they are generally despised by A's and B's alike, Type F's are valuable tennis elements.

Type F's act as buffers and catalysts for the other types. They keep the game moving at a comfortable pace. For example: at the changeover, while the frenetic Type A's leap the net to get in a few practice serves into the back fence, and the slow Type B's ooze out the gate to retrieve a nickel somebody dropped on the sidewalk, the steady Type F's quickly towel off, have a drink, and then calmly reassemble the other Types to continue play. Bless their tiny little backhands.

## Doubles Styles:

Doubles, like poker, can be played in more than one way. Since your side of the court, and especially your body, are constant targets, all the doubles styles involve NOT playing like (a) amusement park bumper cars, and (b) shooting gallery targets. Therefore, the first order of business in doubles is to escape head-on collisions with (1) your partner, and (2) those on-rushing balls that emit hissing sounds. In so doing, a team has to weigh the benefits of playing to win versus avoiding being viciously filleted by head-hunting doubles teams.

The USTA-recognized doubles styles are: (1) the *Both-Up*, (2) the *Both-Back*, and (3) the *Up and Back*. It is, coincidentally, evidence of either Darwinism or Creationism that these three styles are practically made to order for the three Personality Types.

## *Both-Up:*

Type A's should always employ the Both-Up style of doubles. When I say "up," I mean "at the net." Type A's can readily play at the net. They are so naturally hyper, it is customary for them to dive for, and occasionally even hit back, balls rocketing down their alleys like woolly torpedoes.

Players of this type eagerly go where whiners fear to tread: the net. They are unusually fearless and don't mind charging forward to intimidate overheaders, or being clobbered by balls that must be surgically removed from their navels.

Yes, volleys are the Type A's legacy. Frenetic Type A's invented them long ago as a way to speed up the game and burn nervous energy. They found that volleying ended points more quickly, which allowed them more time to train for triathlons. Therefore, Type A's should routinely be stationed at the net so that all of their nervous energy can be directed into some practical purpose such as what tennisologists call the *Reflexive Fear Volley* (RFV).

The RFV happens when a ball comes racing at your nose at about the speed of a Formula-1 racecar. You instinctively hold your racket up like a cross to a vampire as you simultaneously execute an emergency duck and cover. (Whereby, you try to protect as many indispensable body parts as one hand can cover.) Those split-second Type A reflexes then spring into action to get your racket in place before the ball knocks you all the way back to Type B.

Type A's hate to stand still. They are so genetically wound up that they compulsively lay in wait for just the right moment, then in an ingenious stroke of ad hoc strategy, they dash along the net to poach the ball away for a deftly placed winner. Frequently, their partners must point out that they just poached away their opponent's serve.

Of course, every type SHOULD play the Both-Up style. This style is the preferred style of all Grand Slam doubles teams. However, my lawyer informs me that I should include the following proviso: *Only those players who can volley without incurring major dental bills should use this method.* Just the same, I realize that more doubles teams would be playing the Both-Up style if it didn't entail so much running back to the baseline to retrieve perfectly placed lobs hit by annoying, leech-like players of the other types.

## Both-Back:

Type B's should mainly stay with the Both-Back Style of doubles. When I say "back," I mean "at the baseline." At the baseline, you are safe from those stinging balls that frenzied Type A's aim at you just in case your mind has drifted off onto those deep intellectual matters that have consumed man since the dawn of time. Matters like lunch.

Spineless cowards and boneless chickens employ the Both-Back technique. However, this style does prove useful against teams whose overheads and volleys are about as threatening as Miss Congeniality.

The Type B formula for success is very simple and very effective. Stay back and lob those attacking Type A opponents until they make a dumb mistake. The average wait is .9 seconds. That's about as long as a Type A can stand around watching, because the Type A creed is: "Do *something*, even if it's stupid!"

Type B's almost never win on talent. Their Standard Operating Procedure (SOP) is to keep hitting balls back until their opponents get cramps in their cheeks from gritting their teeth in frustration and must forfeit the match to go buy an over-the-counter muscle relaxant. First, the Both-Backers clear their schedules for the following 48 hours after the scheduled start of the match because they figure that Type A's actually have lives. They then set up a base camp on their baseline and float lobs until the Type A's have to leave for work, breakfast, or to divorce proceedings. It doesn't matter. Usually, their Type A opponents will drive the ball back deep enough so that it bounces right to them. All the Type B's have to do then is lob again and watch the Type A's race back to the baseline to return it. Type B's keep this up until the Type A's have dashed up and back so often that they collapse on the court clutching their chests.

Of course, if the Type A's can hit overheads, the Type B's have more problems than a Mensa prospect. Overheads are the bane of Type B's. Good overheads make a Type B's day like a rectal probe because Type B's are usually too lethargic to lob them back.

When two Both-Back teams play, they keep drop shotting each other in the attempt to pull their opponents forward so they can attack them with lobs.

## *Up & Back*

The Up and Back style is used by schizo teams consisting of one Type A and one Type B, or by two Type F's. Type F's are true renaissance players. They can play all the doubles styles. This type slips easily into whichever style they feel appropriate for the moment.

The Up and Back style of doubles consists of one player at the net (*up*, to doubles players) and one at the baseline (*back*). As in the Both-Up technique, the player at the net is up there to streak across the net with all the subtlety of a bullet train and intercept their opponent's return for a put-away. If that technique fails, their partner is still in position at the baseline to return the ball, thus giving the net-partner another crack at hitting a glorifying winner.

Actually, the Up and Back style is only useful against a Both-Back team playing on crutches. A competent Both-Back team can lob them until their overheads crack under the slow, methodical lob-torture.

The Up and Back style is entirely useless against a Both-Up team. Not only can the Both-Uppers take advantage of the huge put-away alley that exists between the up partner and the back, but also, the sole player at the net becomes an enticing target the size of a national monument.

When the Up and Back style is the result of a Type A being teamed with a Type B, the focused Type A player understands that "kill or be killed" applies in doubles. The wishful Type B's believe that if their forehand strokes are picked off by the net-person, and sent skipping behind their partner, it's their partner's fault. These players also believe professional wrestling is real. Fortunately for all involved, these hybrid teams break up faster than a beached oil tanker.

You may have already tried the last style of play; it's called the *Both-At-Home* style, and the USTA does not endorse it. People of all personality types occasionally employ this tactic to avoid a humiliating defeat at the hands of unionized club nerds. It's a simple technique: you don't show up. You leave your opponents standing alone on the court at match time scratching their heads. They may strut around the club claiming they forced you into some dubious excuse, like having to paint your garage door. Stick to that story. Years later, after hearing the same frail excuse every week, a few smog-for-brains dweebs will actually begin to believe it and even swear they saw the paint stains on your tennis shoes.

# 14

## *Singles: Sweating for the Fun of It*

Do you have the single-mindedness of a Mr. Coffee? Do you like to run around sweating like a marathon runner? If so, maybe you should stop reading this book and start training for a marathon. It's simple. You just run up and down 20 miles of Alpine roads six days a week. Then on the seventh day you do wind sprints. In practically no time at all you will be ready for your first marathon or intravenous intensive care.

A singles competition is a lot like running a marathon, only more agonizing. In a marathon most runners, especially the best runners, look like half-starved, pencil-armed geeks. Therefore, in contrast to real athletic events, the worse you lose a marathon the better you tend to look. This appearance anomaly exists because marathoners spend so much time scheduling and practicing running that they often forget to eat regularly. Forgetfulness is a common side effect of marathon training. Marathonologists maintain that this forgetfulness is the result of extended *Carbo-Deprivation*, and is largely due to the fact that McDonalds doesn't provide a run-through. Ultimately, a few days before a race, and after months of training and Carbo-Deprivation, runners are overcome by their own deluded vanity. Consequently, they try on their "dress" running clothes and check themselves out in the mirror. In shock, they exclaim, "What a geek!" They then start performing emergency *Carbo-Loading*. Carbo-loading is the process of trying to make up for weeks of starvation by consuming huge quantities of Italian food, every day, immediately before a race. Marathoners exhibit peculiar drinking habits at these races. They splash gallons of liquid all over themselves in an effort to get some into their mouths as they run. They need these drinks, though. These drinks serve to keep them cool and to replenish their sweat supply.

If marathoners don't sweat enough, they get leg cramps the size of car oil filters. How apropos. You've got to hand it to them, though. You have to because they won't stop running long enough for you to so much as ask how they are doing. If you were to run up alongside a marathoner and ask a few insightful questions, the answer would always be the same.

> *You*: "Got any blisters?"
> *Marathoner*: "Uuuuuhhh!"
> *You*: "Want some lasagna?"
> *Marathoner*: "Uuuuuhhh!"
> *You*: "What's the square root of 93?"
> *Marathoner*: "Uuuuuhhh!"

Did you know that marathoners have groupies? I can't believe they have a following just like real athletes. Of course, their groupies are olfactory-impaired sado-voyeurs that voluntarily line the course to get good views of the dripping runners and to hand out the fresh sweat supply.

At the end of the race the winner collects his prize (they are usually intense capitalists), while the throngs of losers sit around on public curbs sweating and comparing anti-fungal creams.

Singles is more agonizing than marathoning because most good players actually LOOK like athletes. This looks differential means an obvious jock could run around on a court for hours (without anyone handing him a drink), and still lose to some doofus-looking geek.

Losing to a geek is agonizing because it entails losing more than a couple of sets and a match. You lose valuable face among your jock peers. This loss of face risk is another reason why doubles is so popular among many tennis players. You only lose half as much face. This is also why the prize money in pro doubles is about a quarter of the singles purse. And then the team has to split that paltry sum. It's clear that the disparity is a result of doubles players being able to save more face by blaming their partners.

| | |
|---|---|
| ***Observer.*** | "You guys LOST to Funk and Wagnalls?!" |
| ***Doubles Player.*** | "Well, my lunatic partner kept hitting their overheads back with his kneecaps!" |

Since singles players play for higher stakes than doubles players—gobs more money and an entire face—they have a lot more riding on a match. Therefore, they have developed numerous ways to keep from losing their faces. For instance, they tend to blame their losses on anything that has been routinely blamed before. Some reliable classics are:

a.   Their opponent's cheating

b.   The elements, (e.g., rain, hail, typhoon)

c.   "Big" tobacco

d.   Microsoft

Can we really blame them? I mean, singles players go out on the court and put their reputations on the line against an immense army of geeks and dweebs in the battle for honor and glory, and sex partners. That road to glory is pitted with the geeky. We really should admire singles players. We should, but we won't.

Singles players are, by definition, egotists. They are the ones that like to stick it to you when they beat you. They like to make sure that all mutual acquaintances and everyone on their year-in-review Christmas letter list know they beat you. They take out ads in the club newsletters, send a strategic fax broadcast, and/or boast of it in a television news editorial reply. They are so wrapped up in winning that cheating is often a far preferable alternative to coming in second, even if they're not playing a geek.

Of course, without singles players, whom would the tennis industry use for their product endorsements? I have never seen a top doubles player that was not also a top singles player endorse a product on television.

Come to think of it, I have not SEEN doubles on television since disco music was considered a possible art form. In fairness, the networks will sometimes show an abridged version of doubles, maybe every other rain delay—after the probing interview with the nutrition coach of the 29th ranked singles player, AND after all the tennis tips on how to hit various shots like the ever-useful "topspin volley."

## *PMS*

Though more people actually play safe, secure, and dry doubles, most people prefer watching those courageous singles players run around, sweat, and throw violent tantrums. Some say the drama of singles is more compelling. I say it's symptomatic of tennis' version of *Puck Mania Syndrome* (PMS).

Puck Mania Syndrome was first recognized in hockey spectators. It was observed that even though it was interesting to watch the players skate around with sticks and bump into each other, it was even more entertaining to watch them comically try to stand upright while raining haymakers on each other's heads.

PMS has been demonstrated to be so intense, this country's leading gynecologists have hijacked this acronym to convey the same raw emotions that women experience on a monthly basis.

(PMS, by the way, may provide an explanation about why marathons are not televised. Simply, the marathoners are just too tired to throw a good tantrum. So, in a way, they also suffer from a form of PMS, specifically: *Pooped-Out Marathoner's Syndrome.*)

In the end, those swashbuckling singles players remain the champions of tennis. As for me, when I play singles, I get it half right. That is,

I don't *swash*, but I do *buckle* a lot. I hope that qualifies me as the aching-head loser in a commercial for an over-the-counter painkiller that 4 out of 5 doctors recommend. Based on a true-life experience, imagine…

**Dave's Big Scene:** A wide-eyed husband bursts through the front door in disheveled tennis clothes, carrying a tennis bag. He charges into the kitchen; his wife looks up. He drops his tennis bag with a loud PLOP:

| | |
|---|---|
| *Wife*: | Lose again, dear? |
| *Husband*: | Yeah baby! But I took some aspirin and I'm feeling GREAT! (Tosses her the bottle.) |
| *Wife*: | (Inspecting the label.) Honey, this is *No Doz*. |

# 15

## *Mixed Doubles: A Form of Birth Control*

Mixed doubles is a peculiar hybrid of doubles. It involves a team consisting of a male and a female playing together against another male/female team. Those of you with mature body parts can sense the exciting possibilities. Yes, it is altogether possible that the man and the woman of a mixed doubles team may indeed experience that exhilarating attraction which leads to the sharing of their most intimate home furniture. But that couple's "honeymoon" is only temporary.

A mixed doubles team's honeymoon lasts only until their first competitive match. This sad reality is due to the one iron-clad rule of mixed doubles: *partners cannot be married to each other, and cannot have engaged in conversation for more than a total of 25 minutes before taking the court.*

Tennisologists have determined that after 25 minutes of talk, a petty husband-wife type of relationship will arise. Specifically, both partners will require remedial marriage counseling due to the inevitable surfacing of marital-like tendencies, and that's just to warm up on the same court. For instance, the tendency exists for one member of the team to NOT approve of the other's court position, shot selection, hair style, shoe size, etc. Eventually, for some reason (that could be discovered simply by sending me enough grant money), the disapprover is seized by an overwhelming urge to play like General Custer at Little Big Court. The disapprover immediately charges in front of the disapprovee in an insane attempt to hit an improbable net-cord winner. The disapprover instead bounces the ball off a nearby light standard, turns to the disapprovee, and yells something like "WILL YOU TAKE OFF THAT STUPID WRISTBAND!" in a voice so loud that airports bring legal action.

Amazingly, there are still a few tournaments offering husband and wife doubles. It is my guess that these teams have their roles strictly defined beforehand, in a Tarzan and Jane sort of way: *Me, backhand. You, deuce court.* Or, they are blissfully married.

Ha ha. Blissful marriage is, obviously, an unnatural state for mixed doubles teams and marriages where neither partner is in a coma. For a married couple to play mixed doubles together, each partner would have to fit the other like an amazingly complex, two-piece, jigsaw puzzle. Get non-fictional. How often do you see couples like that walking around? Maybe once a decade on some daytime talk show like *Operaldo*, when the only two known existing couples are guests on the *Married Mixed Doubles Partners That Still Have Sex* segment. Most husband and wife teams are less pleasant versions of North and South Korea: *Shut up; and play on your own side!*

As a tax-deductible gift, I am magnanimously providing a list of the tennis objectives for each member of each type of mixed doubles team: married partners & single partners. (Dear IRS: The approximate value of this donation is $10,000,000.)

To review, in mono-sexed doubles, the main goal is the same for both men's and women's teams, simply put, to beat your repugnant opponents into clinical dementia.

## *Mixed Doubles Objectives*

Naturally, mixed doubles gets a bit more complicated than the mono-sexed type. This complication is due to the large number of marital status combinations, and the underlying sexual tension regardless of marital status. First, for each member of a mixed doubles team married to each other, the two objectives, in order of importance are: (1) winning the match, and (2) custody of the children.

Second, there are two types of non-married mixed doubles teams: (1) casual and (2) competitive. The objectives of these two types of mixed doubles teams are entirely different. In casual mixed doubles, the men's objective is to sneak as many peeks as possible at the women as they bend over to pickup balls in their short skirts and loose or tight tops (it doesn't matter). Then, driven by their primal urge to impress all females within a quarter-mile radius, men will perform as many animal-like displays of overt masculinity as they can think of, including combing their leg hair at changeovers. However, the most common animalistic display technique of tennis-playing males is to seize every opportunity to hit screaming yellow zingers to and from all areas of the court. The women's objective is to avoid being hit by these hormone-propelled missiles and, of course, to bend over to pick up balls.

In a competitive mixed doubles match, the objectives are pretty much the same as for married partners, except instead of kids, they fight over custody of the blame. The male partners don't care about impressing females. These guys are competitive eunuchs. So, instead of waiting for their partners to bend over to pick up balls, these men stare rigidly ahead, waiting to dash toward and slam anything yellow, round, and within reach. Meanwhile, their heroic partners are gritting their teeth, bobbing and weaving, and hiding behind their rackets everywhere on the court. These women have confessed in therapy to conjuring up various diabolical and inhuman experiments they can inflict upon all men, like (shudder) forced beer deprivation during football season.

Why this immense difference between competitive and casual mixed doubles? Tennisologists now believe that in the fiercely competitive mixed doubles arena, men have learned to enhance their chances of winning by tapping into their higher reasoning capability. This higher reasoning allows men to constructively channel their instinctive urge to display their masculinity toward a higher goal: winning. By utilizing their natural brainpower and educational upbringing, today's competitive male partner employs the *Scientific Method* in an attempt to engineer a victory. (Yes, *the* method you learned about in the science class you took just after you hit puberty.) There are only three steps (so practically any guy can learn it):

**Step 1**: *Hypothesis*:    Can a human-powered tennis ball pierce bone?

**Step 2**: *Experiment*:    Hit all shots directly toward female opponent at speeds approaching that of the Hale-Bopp comet, and then observe results.

**Step 3**: *Conclusion*:    Insufficient data. Repeat steps.

Using this scientific method, males strive to intimidate their female opponents into skittering off the court every time these males draw back their rackets. This "ball-blasting" is why many savvy mixed doubles teams will try to entice "out" balls from vigorously "displaying" opposing males. Their strategy is to use the female partner as a decoy during the point. They'll either station her outside of the actual court or have her scurry back and forth along the baseline.

Certainly, there are many women players who not only stand in there with the best of them, but even thrive on extreme competition. That is, women who can crush (tennis) balls like Xena, the Warrior Poacher. Women, who, yea, though they walk through the Valley of Mixed Doubles, fear no testosterone. Highly competitive males value such women greatly. These desiring males, like the animals they are, strut back and forth in full regalia in the club lounge, striving to attract these women players by performing the ultimate female-attracting behavior: vulgar displays of personal wealth.

All in all, most doubles is played between teams of men and teams of women because it is less convoluted. Men don't feel compelled to display their masculinity by launching tennis balls into hyperspace. And, women don't have to worry about any unsolicited and FDA-unapproved optic yellow breast implants.

# 16

## Challenge Ladder Follies

Tennis challenge matches are modern versions of dueling. These tennis duels serve to determine who is the more skillful player.

Dueling is an ancient male thing. It has been handed down from man to boy through testosterone. The concept involves trying to impale your rival with a foreign object. History is full of these manly duels because men like to keep score. Some legendary duels have been *David vs. Goliath, Hamilton vs. Burr,* and *Skywalker vs. Vader.*

Because people have larger brains than smaller-brained animals and can perform complex extrapolations, men also frequently compete in groups. To promote groupism, groupies often say, "There's no 'i' in 'group.'" I'm not sure what it means, but that's what they say. Some examples of group competitions are the *Packers vs. the Bears, World War II,* and *Microsoft vs. the Justice Department.*

Until recently, women didn't participate in epic group duels. But, they did a lot of dueling. They dueled not only in tennis, but also boxing, and even wrestling where duels are staged and recorded on videocassette, and then sold at adult bookstores. On tennis courts, women hammer it out with each other while the computer decides who is #1 for the week, and who will be the subject of relentless pursuit by the paparazzi.

As a tennis junkie, you are out there dueling, too. You are laying your athletic reputation on the line every week. So, isn't it annoying when tennis wimps decline your challenge and whine about their painful suffering from *Acute Hyperbole,* or some other lame ailment not recognized by the USTA? (See Chapter 47.)

In fact, sometimes the embarrassment of losing to someone lower on the ladder can push some people into extreme efforts to justify postponing their challenge matches until they've purchased enough tennis lessons to dispose of you like used coffee grounds. "Soon," they say, "It'll be soon." Right. Meaning, as *soon* as we achieve world peace, end world hunger, or even longer, like when The Chargers win the Super Bowl.

Of course, challenge matches are your club ladder's engine. Your ladder depends on challenge matches to keep it upright. So challenges should be both issued and accepted at least a few times a year to keep your personal rung attached to the club ladder. Otherwise, the more competitive rungs of the ladder will scoff and ridicule your descent down to that level where they begin avoiding you at church socials.

So, why aren't club courts brimming over with challenge matches? Because every player worth his or her socks knows that, no matter how much better you are than your challenger, the cold sweat-inducing possibility remains that your opponent could have a "good day." That is, a day where your opponent plays so ridiculously well that you would be lucky to hold serve once a set. A day that would drop you so far down the ladder that the only way your peers would play with you would be because it was poker, and you supplied the pizza and beer. (You didn't hear it from me, but a counter-strategy is to threaten to tell their spouse about [club slut or stud's name here]. Who cares if it's not nice, or even true? It works.) The point is, fear of The Challenge runs rampant through tennis clubs. It is a deep instinctual fear. It is a fear similar to the one you experience when you go to the dentist for a probing gum assessment.

Since I brought it up, why are so many dentists the way they are? They make you sit there in a chair inspired by the Spanish Inquisition, with your mouth stretched open to the point where your lips feel as if they are giving birth, just so they can scrape and stab your teeth and gums like a sadistic sculptor.

Um, unless of course your dentist is as good as my dentist! My dentist, Dr. Denny Huston, is so good that patients travel from all over the county to go to him because he doesn't hurt them, painwise. But he is worth every nickel! He is, incidentally, a tennis fan and an accomplished player with whom I play tennis from time to time. Hey Denny, I can't wait to sit in your La-Z-Boy and be treated to one of your soothing denticures. (Whew! I think I dodged an exploratory drilling there.)

The Challenge is especially frightening to players who are not very good, but due to years of ingesting strong hallucinogens, tell everyone that they are quite formidable. These types only play challenges because the club pro arranges it:

*Pro*: Slacker! You and Zoner. Two out of three. On court 2. Go!

Of course, there are many players who are NOT good and DO NOT know it. Do you know? Let's find out with a simple test.

## Dave's Simple Self-Understanding Test:

1.  Do you mistake your innate leadership ability (best demonstrated by such famous historic figures as *Erik the Red, Attila the Hun, J.R. the Ewing,* and *Buffy the Vampire Slayer*) for tennis ability?

2.  Do you tell everyone at the club how good you are even though the club desk clerk (who only knows the name of his favorite heavy-metal band because it is tattooed backwards across his forehead) beats you?

3.  Do you mumble vague threats during changeovers?

4.  Do you carry a concealed weapon in your tennis bag?

5.  Has the club ever asked for a restraining order to prevent you from coming within 100 yards of it?

If you answered 'yes' to any of the above questions, you may be suffering from *Delusional Skills Disorder* (DSD), and you may not be as good as you think. If you're still not sure, answer this: Are you rich? If you answered "yes," you don't have DSD.

A challenge match holds no fear for those of you who are good players and know it. However, you people are rarer than ex-congresspersons. Now, if you think you are a good player and you are right, you are a powerful mental force. You know you will win, somehow. That knowledge means you are able to concentrate on the point at hand instead of taking a mental inventory of every person that will burst a zipper laughing at your incredible geekiness should you lose. You know the humiliation I mean. It's similar to being introduced to the President of the United States with, *Mr. President, this gentleman with his fly open is…*

## It's All Mental

Some tennis mental giants you must have heard of are Chris Evert and Jimmy Connors. They won more tournaments in their careers than most people ever win sets. They were really tough to beat on the court, and impossible to beat mentally—anywhere. If, due to a rogue comet the planets misaligned in a cacophonous divergence, and they somehow did not win, they KNEW their opponent was under the influence of a controlled substance. And, it was only a matter of time before the vermin was discovered and imprisoned with others of that ilk: your basic treasonous, tobacco-smoking, gun-with-no-trigger-lock-owning felons.

If you are anything like I am, you have goldfish-type brains. My brain swims around in circles, looking for a way out of a challenge match, until it goes belly-up. That's because competition leaves me susceptible to my own bleak suggestions. For example, I subconsciously conclude that anyone carrying two or more rackets or wearing a $150 warm-up can handle my best shots like Picasso handled paint.

So, if my opponent hits a scorching backhand down the line for a winner, I instinctively believe that that is his standard everyday backhand. It doesn't matter that he bloops the other 99 out of 100 backhands as short lobs. I know that at any time he can unleash another ultrasonic backhand that could bring down a moose. I also know he is just waiting for me to come to the net to pass me with it. HA! I never give him the satisfaction. I stay back and beat him at his own game! Unfortunately, as I said, that entails hitting shorter lobs than he does.

In preparation for tennis competition, some people try to train their brains to visualize a friendly relationship with tennis balls. They want to befriend tennis balls on a spiritual level. These people will suspend a tennis ball by a string from their living room ceilings, and then wink at it while thinking "friendly" thoughts. Supposedly, word would then spread throughout the tennis ball community about what a swell person he or she is. I guess this type of person feels that tennis balls will then want to do them favors since they have become such good buddies and all. For instance, when a ball sees that its new friend is going to hit a high backhand it would think, "Oh, it's Bev. I'm gonna hit a line for you, Bev." Friends with tennis balls? Oh come on. Now if you could borrow money from them, that would be *totally* different.

In conclusion, even though your club's head pro keeps encouraging the members to get more involved in the ladder, nobody is eager to put his or her rung on the line for some purpose as menial as competition. Therefore, is it really any wonder that most club ladders are pretty much carved in stone?[1]

---

1.   No.

# 17

## *Junior Tennis 101*

Compared to adult tournaments, junior tournaments suck. That's because more immature people generally play and watch junior tournaments. After adults play a match, win or lose, they go back to their lives as stockbrokers, real estate agents, or electrical enginerds. In junior tournaments, not only are hyper-hormonal juvenile players breaking every rule, principle, and spirit of The Code[1], but inevitably their parents show up for support.

Unfortunately, parents not only watch, but they frequently try to subtly assist their children in their matches. This assistance can range from giving their child an energizing candy bar to yelling "Foot fault!" when their child's opponent is serving.

Theoretically, junior players are also developing human beings involved in the slow process of growth and maturation who simply want to take time out along the way to smell the sweat and play a little tennis. Yeah, right. Here in reality, tennis involves peers and competition, which means a junior tennis tournament will typically set a kid's maturity level back five years.

### The Peter-Out Principle

Juniors are constantly trying to find a tennis niche they can fill. All they want is to occupy a higher niche than any of their friends. In finding these elusive niches they instinctively and unwittingly employ the *Peter-Out Principle*.

---

1.   Rules to lose by.

The Peter-Out Principle closely resembles the *Peter Principle* in wording, but not meaning. The Peter Principle states that *everyone rises to the level of his or her own incompetence.* The Peter-Out Principle states that *everyone's estimation of his or her own abilities falls to the level of his or her own incompetence.*

The Peter-Out Principle manifests itself in junior players at tennis tournaments in the following ways: (1) junior players boast that they are better than peer players. And (2) they go out and lose. This cycle continues through puberty and beyond, until they get a career and a mortgage. (**Dave's note**: Telemarketing is not a career.)

In other words, juniors NEVER find their niches in tennis until they grow up! As grown-ups, they are adults by definition and have more mature things to be interested in, such as serial crab grass and the Kama Sutra.

Parents are not immune to the Peter-Out Principle either. They simply ignore it. As a consequence, many parents develop symptoms of acute *Promania.*

Tennisologists warn that Promania is a common mental disorder found in the parents of child athletes of all sports. This disease attacks the parental brain's judgment center. Parents are ordinarily supportive of their child until it comes to the first day their kid competes in a sport. On that day, these otherwise normal parents commit involuntary reality slaughter. They suddenly believe that with the proper instruction and a steady practice regimen their child could become a professional athlete. So, these fevered parents start throwing money around for the finest equipment, instruction, workout groups, and orthopedic mattresses for their future star. Nor does it seem to matter if their kid shows symptoms of advanced *Physical Dyslexia.* Now really, what kind of pro will a kid make if he or she can't buckle a belt without help, or must walk to school with protective knee and shin pads?

Still, junior players' delusions take the cake. Even geekazoid junior players envision themselves in Paris accepting the winner's trophy for the French Open. Any peer claiming superiority is issued a challenging,

"Oh yeah!?" Insults fly faster than ducks in heat. The challenge is accepted and a conclusive match begun. But they will not complete the match. The player coming in second will ultimately accuse the other of flagrant first degree cheating. The accuser will then quit and storm off the court in dramatic indignation.

Unlike juniors, adults crave order and stability in all things. That's why they stake out their niches and cling to them like nervous barnacles. This craving for order also feeds their belief that their niches have been permanently set by the Almighty. This reassuring faith frees them from inconvenient constraints—like the rules.

It stands to this reasoning, therefore, that adults may feel a spiritual obligation to cheat during challenge matches in order to maintain their divine ladder positions. Indeed, if an adult player were to take daily one-hour tennis lessons for a year and actually improve, she would be upsetting the ordained order of the cosmos. The players above her on the ladder would not hesitate to exercise their sacred right to call crucial liners "out" in the holy crusade to maintain their intended rungs.

On the other hand, a junior player will not even acknowledge that the player ranked 20 slots above him could even extend him to three sets. Junior players only know someone is a better player when they don't know the kid that just blew them away 6-1, 6-0. If they know the kid, they will go down in defeat screaming, kicking, and cheating, and that is if the score is 6-0, 6-0. Otherwise, they will go down sweating, too. Regardless of the score, they will swear to mutual friends, acquaintances, and stray dogs, "I had him! I *had* him!"

Yes, it is all too typical at a junior tournament to hear name-calling, threats, crying, screaming, racket-throwing, and other socially unacceptable behavior over a stupid game. And that's just by the vicariously niche-conscious parents!

## *Junior Tournaments*

Junior tennis tournaments exhibit two types of behavior: *Jekyll* and *Hyde*. These are not two separate behaviors. No. They are a twisted dichotomy that weave around each other, feed on each other, and act together in a perverse unity. Family groups consisting of at least one parent and one tennis-playing offspring typically exhibit these types of behaviors.

Tennisologists have determined that two combination sets exist. The first combination is the *Child/Jekyll, Parent/Hyde*; the second is the *Parent/Jekyll, Child/Hyde*. The following illustrations are examples of each combination set.

## *The Child/Jekyll Parent/Hyde Combination:*

Their little darling is playing a tournament match and running all over the court, bravely struggling to hit balls back. Every time she misses a shot, one of her parents buries his face in his hands and loudly proclaims, "How can she miss that shot? She hits it every day in practice!" After another missed shot Hyde yells out, "What the hell are you doing out there? Hey, your lessons cost money. Get with it!"

Some Hydes can become so fed up that they start helping their little Jekylls by suggesting possible line-calls. Tennisologists' studies have determined that the calls most often suggested are:

1.  "Out!"

2.  "Way Out!"

3.  "CALL IT 'OUT,' DAMMIT!"

Now, tournament officials expressly forbid this type of help. Moreover, coaching is illegal during tournament matches. Even so, many Hyde parents will stop at nothing to circumvent this rule. Some parents go so far as to foist an elaborate signaling system upon their children to direct them during matches. The next time you are at a junior tournament take a look around the grounds. You will probably find a distant parent desperately waving hand-held naval aviation lights around his head like a deranged barber.

Of course, encouraging a youngster is not illegal. In fact, encouragement is encouraged. Still, Hyde-type parents confuse encouragement and coaching. You can often hear a Hyde parent, as he follows his little Jekyll from one end of the court to the other, barking such encouragement as, "Hit it to her backhand, you little twit!"

Evidently, Hyde parents are confused about how to encourage their little Jekylls. As a service to these misguided parents, I am providing a few examples of good and bad types of encouragement:

- Yelling "Good shot!" after your child hits a winner is okay.

- Yelling "Nyah, nyah, wimp!" when your child's opponent double faults is not okay.

- Yelling "Good try!" when your child misses a shot is okay.

- Grabbing the fence and yelling, "My grandmother has a better [type of stroke]!" when your child misses a [type of stroke] is not okay.

- Refilling your child's empty drink bottle with a healthy sports drink is okay.

- Substituting your child's opponent's healthy sports drink with mouthwash is not okay.

## *The Parent/Jekyll, Child/Hyde Combination:*

Hyde-kids are easily located, even from distant locations like the next block. Little Hydes throw their rackets, curse, and whine at the injustices in their lives, and that's when they are assigned to play somewhere other than their "lucky" court. On the court they curse and whine, and stomp and cry. They throw rackets, tennis bags, towels, and benches; they smash balls, cups, and small insects—and that's after losing the spin for serve.

Jekyll parents think that this obnoxious behavior is just a phase their little precious is going through. "We've been careful not to damage his self-esteem with parental discipline," they maintain. So, the adoring Jekyll parents encourage their precious 12-year-old Hyde with, "You can do it, Snookums!"

BAM! Snookums blasts a ball into the net. CRASH! Snookums wraps his titanium-alloy racket around the net pole.

"Now honey," Snookums' parents advise, "Try not to get upset. Remember, it's only the warm-up."

"SHUDDUP!" bellows Snookums in a voice dripping with contempt. Snookums' parents smile lovingly, turn to the nearest adult and whisper, "He's a very competitive boy. Probably the result of the hours of quality time we spend with him when we're not at work and when he's not performing his court-ordered hours of community service."

Snookums destroys both of his $250 dollar rackets in the first three games. "Now, now, Snookums," his parents remind him, "money doesn't grow on trees."

"Yeah, yeah," snarls Snookums, "Just go buy me another racket. NOW!"

The Jekyll parent scurries toward the pro shop mumbling, "I'd better buy two."

Now, I have a daughter who is just starting to play tournaments. I sincerely hope to be encouraging without being obsessive. However, if being a tennis parent is anything like a spouse riding shotgun in the car, where aid is rendered to the driver through gentle reminders of the speed limit every 12 seconds, my senses will warp out into hyper-space and my brain waves will fluctuate wildly until the only thing I'll know for certain is: *my little darling is trying to humiliate me by throwing away points by the bushel!*

# 18

## *Bleeping Tennis!*

Have you ever wondered what goes through a tennis player's mind as he or she plays a competitive match? Well I have. I mean, what do they think about out there? Match strategy? Far Eastern relaxation techniques? Socks without holes? Specifically, I wondered what thoughts meander through the stressed-out minds of under-siege baseliners as they dart back and forth along the baseline like a mother hen at an Easter Egg Hunt. I pondered the same question about those swashbuckling serve-and-volleyers as they charged up and slunk back, charge and slunk, charge and slunk, to and from the net. Non-profit thoughts such as these clog my mind like an overdose of Kaopectate.

Even while playing a far-from-stirring match of underwhelming proportions, I am usually thinking fruitless thoughts such as, "Choke, you chickenstick! I *will* you to CHOKE!" and, "I hope bratwurst is the special at the snack bar today." Too often, I find myself thinking of the players on neighboring courts and wondering how their matches are affecting them.

To satisfy my curiosity in the form of an effortless experiment, I borrowed a friend's long distance microphone to covertly eavesdrop in on the strategic comments of players involved in a tournament match.

The microphone looked like those used by television networks at football games. I'm sure you have seen them. They're the jumbo-sized microphones attached by wires to a satellite dish. Little guys wearing earphones run back and forth along the sidelines pointing this device at the players who are engaged in running headfirst into each other's body parts. The audio guys are there to record the exciting sounds of bones

121

breaking and crucial knee ligaments rupturing. Anyway, this microphone looked as if a garbage company contracted the Department of Defense to design its trash can lid.

I conducted my experiment by quietly crouching in some nearby bushes and aiming the microphone at my target court. Here, for the first time in print anywhere, are the thoughts of a harried baseliner while playing a dashing serve-and-volleyer:

> "(Bleeping) volleys!"
> "(Bleep)! Why can't I serve like that?"
> "(Bleep)! He's coming in. Oh (bleep). Gotta get it by him. Yes! (Bleep)! What a (bleeping) lucky volley."
> "(Bleep)! Why does the big (bleep) keep running around his (bleeping) backhand?"
> "Hit like a man, you (bleeping bleep)!"
> "Get that, you pile of…Oh (bleep), he did!"
> "Miss it! Miss it! Oh (bleep)!"

And now the mutterings of a nervous serve-and-volleyer while playing a sure-fire baseliner:

> "(Bleeping) lobs!"
> "Lob, lob, lob, I hate these (bleeping) lobs!"
> "I'm going in. Gotta volley it by him. Yes! (Bleep)! What a (bleeping) lucky lob!"
> "(Bleep)! Why doesn't the little (bleep) run around his (bleeping) backhand?"
> "Hit like a man, you (bleeping bleep)!"
> "Get that, you pile of…Oh (bleep), he did!"
> "Miss it! Miss it! Oh (bleep)!"

This pattern continued for a set.

I'm sure you noticed my editing. I have sagely opted to use terms like "bleep," instead of the immoral and illegal ones actually voiced by those players. After all, I don't want this book rated "X" or even "NC-17" by the USTA. Besides, in my opinion, it expresses the flavor of the actual word(s) better than the other option: *expletive deleted.*

For those of you too young to understand, people in high government offices will euphemistically use the phrase "expletive deleted" when reluctantly describing their phraseology when overheard speaking "off the record." *Expletive* means, 'bleep,' 'bleeped,' and, of course, 'bleeping.' And *deleted* means 'removed for your protection.' So, I chose to use the term that did not also sound like a constitutionally protected right. In so doing, I have done my small part to protect the innocent children that may sneak this book under their covers at night. Yes, it's for the children. However, since the transcript above was taken from a match between 14 year olds, I'm beginning to wonder.

Back to the match. I had no idea so much was bleeped to so few. Those two players sounded like a cross between a National Public Radio (NPR) half-hour report on a day in the life of a Chesapeake Bay clam digger and George Carlin's Seven Words routine. And, except for me, no one was listening.

Again, since time has warped out like the Starship Enterprise, I am sure there are a large number of you who have absolutely no conception about what "George Carlin's Seven Words" means. You probably don't even know who George Carlin is, or why he had a fondness for seven particular words. Well, he is a comedian who at one point annoyed media censors by incorporating into his act the seven filthy, disgusting, and illegal words forbidden on television, radio, and some people's homes. I would disclose those words to you now, but I think only five or six are still considered filthy and disgusting. The other ones are now considered funny and even entertaining. I guess more than just time has warped out.

Meanwhile, after a set of racing around the court like laboratory rats in a maze and whining to their personal tennis gods, both players got extremely tired and winded. The second set sounded more like this:

Scene: Between points, players hunched over, hands on knees, faces red, and dripping sweat.

"Puff, puff, puff, (bleep), puff, puff."
"Puff, puff, (bleeping, puff, bleep), puff, puff..."

Frankly, I was astonished at the similarities of thought between the aggressive in-your-face serve-and-volleyer, and the more passive up-your-(bleep) baseliner. Both players understood the other's strengths. Both players tried to capitalize on the other player's weakness. Both used the language of a truck driver with hemorrhoids.

# 19

## *Little Disasters*

Have you ever taken inventory of the little things that can drive you crazy while playing tennis? I don't mean big things like natural disasters such as earthquakes or root canals. That is, I don't think root canals can be categorized as an *artificial* disaster. After all, stadium playing fields are either natural or artificial grass. Right? And teeth are natural, right? I am guessing, but wouldn't an artificial disaster be one that is not a natural disaster? Therefore, wouldn't a newscast be more accurate if written to reflect this important difference?

> *"An artificial disaster devastated the city today, when Dave's Brewery was bombed by a gang of wine activists, sending millions of gallons of golden beer rushing down the street and into a storm drain."*

Well, that would be a disaster to me.

Specifically, I'm talking about the small disasters that besiege your brain like some loathsome, Communist, bamboo torture while you are immersed up to your earlobes in an epic tennis struggle.

Things like a breeze.

### *Breezes*

A breeze can be a different thing to different people. When you are winning, a breeze is simply a way you become cooler. Or, if the Second Coming of Stephan Edberg is slicing you up like an Adidas blender, a breeze just isn't strong enough to blow him away for you. However, a breeze can take on a demonic disposition if you are losing a hotly-contested match to some nearsighted yo-yo who applies his zinc oxide with a putty knife.

Here's how a breeze becomes sinister. Let's say you are losing to some microchip-brained nerd in a light breeze. Without warning, or any perceptible increase in MPH, the breeze can abruptly grow cyclonic in dimension. You toss the ball up for your serve and it drifts two inches to the left of wherever your pro told you is optimum for you. So, you stop your motion and catch the ball. Then, to let your smug-butt opponent know the level to which your game has been decimated by the raging gale (and not at all by anything he/she is doing) you curse, "'bleeping' WIND!" with all the subtlety of martial law.

Your official recount of the match becomes a gust of embellishments. Balls hit long were "carried" out by the wind. Balls hit in the net were "held up" by the typhoon. Later, you tell friends you lost the match during a tropical storm just before the National Weather Service upgraded it to Hurricane Sergio. Two weeks after that, you inform strangers that you were the real life inspiration for Stephen King's upcoming novel, *Billy Bob and the Zephyr From Hell.*

## Checkered Shade

Sometimes large trees ring a court. Trees can be pleasant enough. But, if those trees are spaced evenly and semi-leafed when the sun is just right, they can deposit a checkerboard of shade and sunlight. This condition has been termed by tennisologists: "Checkered Shade."

As a rule, playing tennis through Checkered Shade, for lack of a printable four-letter word, SUCKS! Why? Because watching a tennis ball as it travels through Checkered Shade requires very high concentration skills. Yes, the same level of skill exhibited by the crack members of the US Department of the Interior's Bureau of Persecuted Species, Marine Life Division, Snail Darter Section, Fin Tagging Team #3.

Under ideal conditions, tennisologists contend that hitting a tennis ball is *a highly complex act of assimilating the non-symbiotic physical nature of interrelated, yet independent, muscle motions involved in striking a tennis ball with a tennis utensil* (racket).

Under Checkered Shade conditions, tennisologists agree the above action is swiftly and diabolically transformed into: *a highly complex act of assimilating the non-symbiotic physical nature of interrelated, yet independent, muscle motions involved in striking a tennis* (I will insert the technical term for 'ball' here) *Distractingly-Blinking, Optic Yellow, Lint-Infested, Hurtling-In-Chaotic-Vectors-Toward-Untanned-Areas-Of-Human-Anatomy, Object with a tennis utensil* (racket).

The official USTA handbook acronym is DBOYLIHICVTUAO-HAO. The street acronym of the USTA's acronym is BYO, which stands for "Blinking Yellow Object" or "Bring Your Own," depending on geography. If you are standing on a tennis court, it is the former. Otherwise, it means you're driving around with a case of beer in your trunk looking for a party.

## The Sun

Yet another annoyance is the sun. There is nothing like that helpless feeling you get when your service toss flies straight up into the blazing sun. There, as if armed with a Romulan cloaking device, it disappears in a blinding flash of cosmic nature. You squint so hard to find the ball your eyebrows leave welts on your cheeks. Through sheer muscle memory you are able to frame-shot the ball over the net with all the effectiveness of the Libertarians. Through salty tears you squint again, straining to detect your opponent's inescapable return. You quickly discover you can't see your opponent. For that matter, you can't see the court. All you see is a bright light before your eyes. Then you see your deceased paternal grandmother beckoning. Wait! That's something else. To buy valuable nanoseconds, you back away from the baseline. At the same time, you hope you are still facing the net and that your eyes can adjust before the ball hits you squarely in the navel, or worse. Your senses heighten. You assume an extreme ready position. You cock your ears for any sound of a normal tennis game: a bounce, a hit, swearing, a racket whistling in the air as it clears a fence. But the ball never comes back! You feel incredibly fortunate that your opponent could flub such an easy serve. Then, you feel like an idiot when you realize your opponent's drop shot is bouncing for the second time on your side of the net.

Now, that is annoying. However, it is unequivocally unfair that your opponent's service toss doesn't go to, through, or anywhere NEAR the sun! Your opponent still blisters his serves while you curse and swear at the lack of divine justice in the universe. You lecture everyone within earshot on the need for more prison space to hold those smug, beefy jerkies who won't "play two" after having aced you the last 12 serves.

What about this lack of divine justice, anyway? Why is it that the sun only ducks behind a cloud on your opponent's serve? For me, it works with overheads as well. Whenever I hit an overhead the sun bursts out from behind a cloud like an opportunistic vulture sensing a discarded meatloaf. Blinded, I bend over and cover my eyes as I slink back to the baseline to take the ball off the bounce. Sure enough, it bounces as the sun goes behind a cloud. Feeling ill, I "throw up" a lob. Finally, a sole pinpoint ray of sunlight needles through the clouds and onto the ball, illuminating it like a laser. With such heavenly guidance, my opponent slam-dunks an overhead over the fence for an eye-popping winner. I want justice, dammit!

Tennisologists say the sun is a constant force to be reckoned with, at least outside during the day. They quietly analyzed the sun phenomenon for over eighteen months and concluded that it is exceedingly bright. They also found that if they did not wear protective eyewear they tended to lose their sight. (Some of the most dedicated lost enough sight that they had to resign as tennisologists and become NFL referees.)

Those intrepid tennisologists also learned that match play was severely affected by how the tennis courts were oriented with respect to the sun. When word leaked out that these brave scientists had discovered this play-altering fact, coupled with the realization that any solution lay in divergent actions subject to influence, powerful political lobbies quickly mobilized their bank account managers. Armies of lobbyists stormed the tennisologists' laboratories, pried open the doors, and plied the scientists with adult beverages and cashier's checks until our valiant tennisologists at last acquiesced and handed over their findings.

Armed with this important information, these competing lobbies strove to impose their own "spin" on the findings. Their subsequent stream of pronouncements ended what had become known in tennis circles as *The Silence of the Labs.*

Predictably, liberal court lobbies demanded that courts be oriented in a North and South fashion. That way, when the sun travels from East to West, the blinding is of minimal duration and equally distributed between players, regardless of their tennis shoe brand names.

These left-wing lobbyists further advocated that players of higher socio-economic privilege should be penalized a point per game for every thousand dollars of income beyond their opponent's. They reasoned that wealthier players are unfairly able to purchase more tennis lessons.

More radical lobbies not only wanted to orient courts in a North-South fashion, they wanted them placed in under-privileged neighborhoods, similar to Afghanistan but more violent. This program, they maintained, would wean street gangs away from their illegal drug incomes. According to their plan, taxpayers would fund a federal program that would pay the gangs to NOT destroy the courts, and to only write their defacing graffiti using federally subsidized spray-cans of disappearing ink.

Conservative lobbyists, on the other hand, pushed for courts to be laid out in an East and West direction. In this way, one player would always be hopelessly blinded. They argued that this would result in a boon to our country's sunglasses industry. Also, the players would learn basic capitalism when they paid each other off to play on the side with the sun at their backs. Claiming it would encourage competition, these right-wingers also argued for the deregulation of matches by "removing umpires and linesmen." (Politically Correct Sic: Everyone knows it's currently "lines-humans.")

The reactionary faction even tried to push through a mandatory prayer before tournament matches and a return to (a) wooden rackets, (b) one-handed backhands, and (c) white tennis balls, clothes, and players. They also favor (d) a ban on all abortions performed on tennis courts.

In the checkered light of these data, I am forming a new lobbying group: The National Association for the Advancement of Tennis Players or NAATP. This group will gratefully accept all soft money contributions for the purpose of lobbying local government officials for nature-free indoor courts! I am generously volunteering myself as treasurer. Come on everybody, money talks! So, let me hear you.

# 20

## *To Play Two or Not to Play Two*

*Play two* is tennis player lingo for, 'replay the point.' Specifically, it means to start the point again with the first serve. *Play one* also means 'replay the point,' but the server must serve like a hopeless dork.

Playing two was implemented long ago to nullify those outside influences that could unfairly bias a match. These influences typically include balls dropping in from neighboring courts and "let" serves. Other unfair events, like breaking a string and "let" strokes, are viewed as not being "play two" worthy. Hey, it's been this way since they devised tennis' scoring system—back in the Bronze Age.

Incidentally, have you ever noticed that only one player on the court ever thinks playing two is a good idea? Well, I once saw a match where BOTH players agreed to play two. It was at the Shady Pines Tennis Club. A gas-guzzling, chainsaw-wielding maniac was clear-cutting the shady pines to make way for a Nature Club regional office. Somehow, he miscalculated the fall of a tree by 180 degrees and a shady pine fell up against the fence surrounding a court where two guys were playing. Both players, understandably shaken, declared, "play two" *at the same time*. Remarkable. Although, I guess the fact that they were warming up their serves at the time somewhat detracts from their otherwise admirable agreement.

## *The Rule*

In the real world, it is possible to get away with "playing two" for more reasons than the official rulebook allows. The rulebook strictly states that you should play two when the game itself is disturbed from the outside. You will notice the rule does not say you should "play two" when the FLOW of the game is disturbed.

Of course, in the real world, most players are like I am. When it suits us, we infuse into this rule some cosmic spirit of intent that incorporates "the flow" of the game. Backed by this convenient outlook, we will do everything in our power to follow the spirit of that mutant rule whenever it would be to our benefit and to hell with "the book."

To illustrate "the flow" angle: You begin the point as you do 59 percent of the time (according to the latest tennisological studies), that is, by slamming your first serve into the net. Then you walk up to the service box to clear the ball from your path in case you experience some hormonal flare-up that compels you to employ the *Banzai Offense*. (The "Banzai Offense" occurs when you think you have your opponent in a defensive situation. Then, flush with predatory instinct, you rush forward to secure the strategic net position like you once did years ago when you thought you saw a dollar bill caught under the net.) Having cleared the ball, you return to the baseline. Unexpectedly, a ball from the next court slowly rolls two inches onto yours. Alleluia! A possible PLAY TWO! Joy leaps into your conniving little heart.

Of course, you and your opponent both know that only *the flow* of play has been disturbed. You also know you cannot unilaterally declare a "play two." So, you must set out to subtly coax one from your suspicious opponent by further disturbing the flow of the game for, with, and by yourself. You wait until the people who own the ball have finished their point so you can personally deliver it. Then you notice one of your shoelaces is a half-inch longer than the other. After retying that shoe you sense it is now a tad tighter than the other shoe. So you retie the loose one. Then you remove an ostensibly irritating piece of leaf from the court that you have been ignoring for a set and a half. Finally, you realize your bullheaded opponent is not going to suggest playing two. So, you must serve with your second serve (the one your pro says you serve with chocolate sprinkles).

Or you may be annoyingly tenacious. You know, the type of person who enjoys running a marathon—backward. If you are such a person, before your second serve you will walk over to your tennis bag to check the strings of your racket by tapping them against the frame of your backup racket. Then you must repeat this action with the rackets reversed. This measurement technique, called the *Ping Test*, produces a ping sound from the strings. From the pitch of the ping, the experienced tennis player can easily determine which racket is more likely to hit winners. You follow the Ping Test with checking the height of the net, and then you call out the wrong score—in your favor. Your opponent must take time to argue. Finally, you feign a momentary heart attack.

If these ploys don't finagle a "play two" from your opponent, check again. That person is either one of your ex-spouses, or worse, their lawyer. However, the chances are still good that your opponent will have gotten a chill. If so, you both will have to warm up again and an automatic "play two" will be awarded! The above stratagems are still within the bounds of the rules, if not propriety (like 95 percent of all tennis players I know).

Let's examine the outright improper use of the "play two" rule. Now here's a somewhat common "play two" gambit that you won't find in the "Play Two" section of the USTA's rulebook. It's the *I don't know where the ball landed–let's play two* gimmick. This scam is practiced by seemingly kind-hearted, syrupy-sweet albeit ruthless, amoral players who prey on your own gracious nature to cut them some unwarranted slack. You know the type: paparazzi and in-laws.

Actually, the official rulebook covers this very situation. But NOT in "Play Two!" The rulebook states that in the event a player cannot make the call, the ball shall be deemed to have landed "in." Yes, IN! As in INside the line! Do not be fooled by those perverts' seemingly reasonable suggestion that if they can't call it (and they certainly couldn't trust a biased person such as yourself or even a casual observer of questionable character, like the Pope), then you should "play two."

Finally, there is the circumstance similar to the "coaxed" play two, yet vastly different. How about the ball that rolls unseen onto your court *during* a point? Remember those sly paparazzi types who beg you to be sympathetic when claiming some dubious eye problem, like "Compound Myopic Line Displacement," on all your liners? They are the first ones to absolutely refuse any rational discussion about the fact that you had just passed them with a brilliantly-placed backhand, when they turned around and spotted an alien ball lying just inside the crack that separates your court from another. They point at the offending ball and excitedly jump up and down squealing, "PLAY TWO! PLAY TWO!" like a helium-sucking pig. When pressed, these misanthropes invariably maintain that they were distracted by the sound of the ball's roll!

How are these vermin permitted to play our noble game when they recognize no code or possess a shadow of personal honor? Where is the CIA, the FBI or the KGB when you need them? Where is the USTA's vaunted secret tennis police? (Answer: out running USTA membership card checks on the players at your local USTA sanctioned tournament. That's how the USTA combats hackerism.)

Let's get tough on this despicable sort of tennis crime! Sleazy players who try to selectively bend the rules currently turn around and run for public office. Instead, these degenerates should be ushered off the court by police dogs and into internment camps for offensive tennis trash. There they would be given only celery and tap water, forced to watch professional bowling on television, and made to listen to the Turkish national anthem over and over until they begged for mercy. If you agree with me, send money.

# 21

## *Choking Happens*

Dateline America: *Mass Choking On Nation's Tennis Courts. Code Blue! Stat!*

Choking happens.

When a player loses a match after having had double match point (as I have), that player is said to have 'gagged' or 'choked.' In my case, I got to choke *again* at breakfast the next morning when I read a headline about it in the newspaper. Page two: "Whitehead Upset In Local Tourney." Great. Just my luck to be upset on a slow sports day.

## *What Is Choking?*

What, precisely, is choking? To answer this question, we asked the world's leading authority on choking, Dr. Heimlich Maneuver. Somehow, he became confused. Instead of an explanation, he regaled us with some odd definition featuring *windpipe obstruction.* Hey Doc, this is a tennis book. Can you say ten-nis? You don't find windpipe obstruction under "choking." It's found under "Handling Cheaters." Get a clue.

By default, the question fell to our little-known, yet underpaid team of tennisologists. These tennis specialists came up with this definition: *Choking—The complete loss of basic motor skills, sometimes even bodily functions, and/or elementary reasoning powers while pre-experiencing a post-match humiliating loss.*

Choking is when everything you do is monumentally stupid. Its symptoms are few, but obvious. First, your opponent wins points by the truckload. And second, you lose. So in a close match, when you hit short lobs to the net-man, it's because your pent-up stress either (1) invokes a brain seizure that causes such a gridlock in your elbow that it makes Congress look diarrheic, or (2) it causes your brain's tennis programming to execute a "choke bug" whereby you literally feel an urgent BODILY NEED to see your opponent's overhead bounced over the back fence.

Choking is the opposite of playing *in the zone*. Playing "in the zone" means 'you temporarily play at a level far greater than your skill.' Whereas most players choke on a weekly, sometimes daily basis, "zoning" occurs about as often as sobriety at frat parties. The best known symptom of zoning is that everything you do turns out amazingly right. All net-cord shots land on the other side of the net. If you lob short, a freak gust of wind pushes it deep. If you fall down, your opponent twists an ankle. Amazing.

Tennisologists have long known that choking occurs at various stages of a match according to each player's individual choke threshold. Some players only choke during crucial, match-teetering points, like during tiebreakers. Other players start choking on important points, like break point. Then, there are those of us who choke whenever the balls come out of the can. Then again, except on a clear day, everybody in Los Angeles chokes just walking to their cars. (Ha, ha. A little choke humor there.)

According to tennisologists' studies, choking manifests itself in only embarrassing and loss-guaranteeing ways. The most frequent type of choke is a second serve that bounces on the server's side—of his or her own service line. Other popular choke shots are (a) blazing overheads. These overheads are blasted so *far out* that awed spectators stand and hold up flaming matches and lighters. And, (b) easy volleys that anxious volleyers pathetically net when confronted by the realization that missing it will cause spectators to laugh so uproariously they'd be invited to perform their volleys at The Comedy Club.

Compared with the other shot types, forehands are hardly ever choked. That's because compared to backhands, forehands are like National Merit Scholars; they don't fail unless they've been drugged. Yes, only a few ultra-accomplished chokers can make a forehand stroke look monstrous enough to resemble a player impersonating a walking body cast.

## Self-Esteem

Choking can initiate a vicious cycle. It can make you feel bad about yourself. If you feel bad about yourself your tennis suffers, which makes you feel bad about yourself. This cycle continues until you ultimately call in your forfeits from bed.

Highly paid psychologists combat low self-esteem via appearances on the world's foremost television talk shows. They remind us that self-esteem is a vital component in handling the stress of losing. This stress is why *Self-Help* and *Self-Esteem* books are a billion dollar a year industry, and that's just in tennis player purchases. Low self-esteem tennis players play to not lose what microscopic bits of self-esteem they still retain after countless losses to geeks and dweebs who are only coordinated enough to drive cars with automatic transmissions.

Players with high self-esteem, on the other hand, are easily pegged. They play tennis with pure undiluted concentration. Then, win or lose and being so secure, they befriend their opponents, drive them to lunch in their Jaguars, and give them stock tips.

Today, many young tennis players suffer from a deplorable lack of self-esteem. At an early age, children often learn that losing tennis matches means that, when compared with their peers, they are inferior, disgusting, and even *bogus*.

Losing tennis matches isn't the problem. Rather, it's that those wacky fun-loving kids use losing as a handy personal value guide for the sole purpose of establishing a tennis pecking order.

Kids love a pecking order. After a tournament, they'll rush out and exercise their latest pecking order in public. Those silly kids higher in the pecking order get to ridicule anyone and everyone below them for any reason. Pecking reasons can range from using a stupid racket string tension to personal hygiene—like not using the "way cool" brand of acne repellent.

Unfortunately, tennisologists have determined that with each loss we incur we add to the ranks of those who can peck on us, not merely by that one person who beat us, but also by EVERYONE who has ever beaten *that* player. So as we lose, the number of people who can peck on us grows "exponentially" (a math term that means 'faster than you realize'). To illustrate, if you were to lay, end to end, all the new people who could peck on you after a single loss, they would stretch from Albuquerque to Omaha or Fargo. The difference depends on various "variables" (another math term meaning, 'I don't know exactly what').

Under such tremendous pressure, is it any wonder our children's self-esteem is so terrifyingly low? And why, therefore, our children drop out of school to spray-paint graffiti on anything that remains stationary for fifteen minutes in some perverted language? Indeed, it is a little known fact, but as a result of their poor graffiti spellings, the original Los Angeles "Creeps" gang unexpectedly became known as the "Crips."

On the bright side, several self-help books exist today that can aid in nurturing a child's self-esteem. For example: *I'm OK; Up Yours!*

## What Can We Do?

So, what can we players do about choking? Once again, we sought the aid of our distinguished panel of tennisologists. According to these tireless tennis scientists, the human brain is no more capable of allowing us to play stressless tennis than choosing the fastest line at McDonalds.

However, these tennisologists observed that after years of torturous practice, a player could achieve a significant increase in what they label *Motor Skill Retention* (MSR). Alas, these same studies indicate that MSR is only achieved with a corresponding decrease in *Rational Thought Capability* (RTC).

The MSR-RTC relationship is called *Loss Assurance Dynamics*, or LAD. Here, briefly, is how LAD works. If you are normal, as your match score becomes closer, your ability to play tennis at the same level as you do in practice decreases. In fact, your skills level decreases to the point that, unless you have burned countless hours practicing in the dark, your game will ultimately resemble The Tin Man on electro-shock therapy. So, if you have a voluntary lobotomy and practice until you develop blisters on your elbows, your MSR will increase—absolutely. However, in response to LAD and via *Murphy's Law of Infinite Fiascoes*, your RTC decreases to the point where you conclude that a satisfactory method of cleaning your car's tires would be public urination.

Here are a couple of examples of LAD. Example #1: Even if you were able to retain a large measure of, say, your service skill during a close match (high MSR), you would then attempt to ace your opponent with second serves (low RTC). Example #2: If you were to retain a high percentage of your volleying skill (high MSR), you would be overcome by the compulsion to mutate your match strategy into one of hitting approach shots off of your opponent's crushing first serves (very low RTC).

In conclusion, if you were to practice laboriously for untold hours and read every self-help article in *Tennis By Osmosis* magazine, you may indeed be able to increase your MSR. However, if you do, LAD will automatically kick in with a corresponding decrease in RTC.

We are left with no choice but to try to find opponents whose LAD is more sensitive than our own. In my case, I like to set up matches with a nervous friend of mine (whom I'll call "Ted," because if I called him "Guy Fritz" he would pop my head like a soap bubble) whose

LAD is jump-started whenever I call. Then, in the days before our match, I know Ted will burn a 12-month supply of deodorant sticks from worrying. Finally, by the time we are scheduled to play, he is sick from anxiety and must forfeit after one set. Add another notch in the "W" column for yours truly.

# 22

## *Gamesmanship Means Never Having to Say You're Cheating*

Gamesmanship is 'the art of competing without playing.' I find this definition of gamesmanship to be puzzling because of its obvious awkward terminology. I say that because I am predisposed to thinking that competing and playing are mutually exclusive terms. When you are competing, do you consider yourself "playing?" No. You consider yourself trying to win, straining to win, willing to trade your mother in for a backhand to win. Playing is what you do with dolls and yo-yos. For that reason, when people ask me, "Do you play tennis?" I answer, "Yes, but only if nobody is keeping score."

Another term in the definition is similarly non-intuitive. The term "art" may be correct, but it's not accurate. "Art" connotes something magnificent, or at least attempted magnificence. Gamesmanship connotes maggots. For that matter, a true tennis competitor should be referred to as a *tennistician* or a *tennisist*.

Okay, let's humor the linguists and say we play tennis (like the IRS plays tax collector). Now, let's spice up our definition with an Oriental martial arts flavor: *Gamesmanship: the art of competing at tennis without playing tennis.*

Gamesmanship is influential and can be found in all forms of competition. From barrel racing to barbecuing, dog obedience to bikini-filling, it permeates them all.

Gamesmanship resembles an infomercial. It is disturbingly common and designed to separate you from your senses. Jerks use it to distract you from playing tennis effectively by causing you to dream about performing a slow appendectomy on them with a pencil.

When playing a gamesmanshipper, the pressure to win stems from knowing that, should you lose, the jerk is going to perform a celebratory dance so elaborate as to be worth millions of dollars in grants from the National Endowment for the Arts. You also know that an unsympathetic third person will videotape it and send copies to the local news channels and the Washington National Archives.

There are degrees of gamesmanship. You have probably lost to someone because of his or her utter gamesmanship. And, the fact is, you may not have realized it. It can be as subtle as a baby's breath. Other times it can reek like a twice-used diaper. Your opponent's gamesmanship tends to be subtle when you look as if you could stuff them into their own tennis bags. Otherwise, if you resemble a bewildered dweeb, their gamesmanship tends to become more flagrant. (**Dave's advice**: If you are dweebic, try a little pre-emptive gamesmanship of your own. Ride up to the courts on a Harley-Davidson with a rifle stock sticking out of a side-bag. Enhance that image with a sleeveless black T-shirt that reads: Insured by Hell's Angels. You may still lose, but your opponents won't be gloating.)

## Sports Purists

Now then, have you ever lost to a sports purist? Did you even know that there are sports purists out there? These are people who just want to compete on skill alone. You know, toe-to-toe, nose-to-nose, lip-to-lip. Wait! Forget kissing; that would be disgusting. Anyway, sports purists are the let's-give-each-other-our-best-shots-until-only-one-is-left-standing types. They don't want any distractions. They just want to determine who is better.

My wife and her father are probably the only two people I have met that are sports purists (although, I'm sure there are more somewhere, perhaps hidden in some Sports Shangri-La in glacial Tibet). My father-in-law, for instance, not only knows the rules of golf; he plays *by the rules!* He also thinks football referees should always use instant replay. He argues that the players on the field should decide the game, not the striped turkeys that routinely get in the way of crack-back blocks. So, if the NFL has the technology to remove third-party errors that can, and do, have game-influencing repercussions they should use it, and by Constitutional Amendment if necessary.

My wife and her father are both excellent athletes. They are undoubtedly in the top ten percent of their respective genders. (He is enshrined in the Nebraska State Football Hall of Fame.) Both are very competitive and very focused. Both will beat you by ignoring all forms of gamesmanship that are not also felonies. If you were to try to mess with their minds during a match, they would hold you in contempt for stooping to devices outside one's own skill and determination. To sports purists such as these, winning with gamesmanship means you have diluted your victory to the point where it becomes meaningless.

Unfortunately, sports purists are as rare as fat-free bacon. Almost everyone else either employs gamesmanship to some degree, or crumbles at the first hint of it. Example: "Boy, it's hot today, huh Dave?" (This comment is my personal cue to wilt.)

To gamesmanshippers, the purist philosophy is nothing but altruistic drivel that only losers and the coaches of losers would espouse. To gamesmanshippers, winning is ALWAYS meaningful. In fact, playing the game is simply the muse from which their devious natures give birth to their obnoxious and unethical plots. To them, the ability to totally distract you with ploys and schemes to the point where you leap the net with your racket raised in a fit of bloodthirsty rage, ready to accept a forfeit and certain jail time, the ultimate. It means they win! They like to win that way. Hell, they PREFER to win that way!

Basically, gamesmanshippers consider all competition to be mental. They believe the game is just a physical manifestation of desire, and that only a pastel-wearing wuss would play without using some form of gamesmanship. Why sweat it out on the court, they reason, when a few unsavory tricks may get the match handed over to them. Gamesman-shippers are frequently also car mechanics and political campaign fund-ing organizers.

## Forms Of Gamesmanship

Some common forms of tennis gamesmanship include: (1) slowing the match down to the speed of a Congressional filibuster by committing ploys such as replacing shoelaces on their opponent's game or set point; (2) trying to speed up the match via *quick serves*[1]; (3) giving the balls to the server by (a) making him or her take long trips back to the fence, or (b) point-blank overheads; (4) questioning an opponent's line calls during the warm-up; or (5) simply wearing a black Oakland Raiders shirt and cap while cleaning an assault rifle with an oily rag during the changeover.

I personally experienced a novel form of gamesmanship. It hap-pened in the first round of a tournament at the local public courts. I introduced myself to my opponent, and he introduced himself and his very attractive, very shapely girlfriend. The only memory I have about the match, besides its outcome, was his girlfriend. She wore a clingy T-shirt and short skirt and sat on the court during the match to watch. No matter which side of the court I was on, she would turn to face me. She would lean forward, resting her chin on her hand, and constantly cross and re-cross her legs. She was very obvious and very effective. (I must have glanced over after every point.) Her boyfriend, however, was altogether ineffective. I would have beaten him even if she had been tap-dancing naked on the bench.

The point is, gamesmanship takes many, many forms. As for me, let's just say I hate being a victim because I'm so sensitive to it. When someone informs me he needs to use the bathroom and then returns

---

1.    To serve while your opponent is toweling off.

having had a beer *without me*, I seethe to the point where my game develops acute apoplexy, and I break out in double faults. So, I now secretly keep score during the warm-up, just in case. That way, I'll know who is REALLY better.

# 23

# *Chart Your Way to a Better Tan!*

Charting is something we players do to uncover unsolicited and unwanted bugs in our competitive *court sense*. "Court sense" is a sense that we athletes develop after years of intense competition. This sense is important because it allows us to be aware of our opponent's court position and to understand how to make their next shot awkward for them. Of course, it helps greatly if your sport is played on a court. No competitive swimmer I know owns a micron of court sense.

Sometimes a player's delicate court sense can get caught in a *loop*. ("Loop" is a technical computer term. In both computers and tennis it means the same thing: 'IDIOT!' Programmers gave it this meaning because sometimes a computer would just sit there performing the same stupid set of instructions until someone came along with a sledge-hammer and told it to stop. Computers are so obsessive/compulsive that way.) Specifically, we players tend to unconsciously slip into kami-kaze match loops. Our opponents don't. Tennis is like that. In fact, our opponent's competitive tendencies are to swiftly identify OUR neon-like, loss-inducing tendencies that are so obvious they are recog-nizable from passing aircraft. Then they feed on them in large carnivo-rous bites like a Great White shark at a Tuna Fish School reunion. Not only that, while we are suffering through these neurotic loops, we have no inkling (literally, "baby ink") about what it is that's sabotaging our otherwise brilliant tennis ability into courtside road-kill.

Now, we could just go ask one of our peers to tell us what our loser tendencies are. But that is considered bad form, and we wouldn't get a straight answer anyway. It's likely that we would, more or less, be advised to go soak our racket strings in a hot tub.

| | |
|---|---|
| *Me*: | "How come I don't get past the second round?" |
| *Buddy*: | "Stop hitting those service returns so low, Dave. You're getting killed by their half volleys." |
| *Translation*: | "Figure it out for yourself or keeping losing, loser!" |

Fortunately, there are a couple of tools that we players use to aid in revealing our loop habits: *capitalism* and *charting*.

## Capitalism

Sometimes you will be fortunate enough to find strategic information for sale. At many tournaments, all you have to do is identify that one weasely individual who knows every player's match tendencies and weaknesses, and who is willing to part with that knowledge for cash.

To learn about your own weaknesses, pretend you are not yourself and offer to buy information on your match tendencies:

| | |
|---|---|
| *You*: | "Pssst. Got anything on Kent C. Strait?" |
| *Weasel*: | "Does gut stink?" |
| *You*: | "How much?" |
| *Weasel*: | "Ten bucks. He always passes down the line. And, watch his line calls." |

## Getting Charted

Other times, like when you are low on cash or the weasel has been run over by a drastically sportsmanship-impaired player, you are forced into doing your own detective work. Therefore, to discover what our opponents have known and manipulated for years, we players get someone to chart us.

The usual method of getting yourself charted is to obtain a pencil, some paper, and a doofus. Draw columns on the paper. In the leftmost column, itemize into rows those elements of your game you wish to chart (forehands, backhands, foot faults, etc.). On the columns across the top, jot down possible outcomes per element (long, wide, netted, whiffed, blisters, etc.). Then, find a doofus who is willing to sit in the blazing sun for hours like a giant jar of sun tea and do nothing but sweat and scrawl prehistoric-looking pencil marks on pieces of paper. To endure such brain-numbing torture, those doing the charting (chartor) require one or more of the following: (1) a sincere concern for the player (chartee), (2) sizable cash payments, or (3) the mental aptitude of peat moss. Most players get a parent or lover to do it.

As the match progresses, the chartor marks down the point-ending shots of the chartee, and/or the chartee's opponent. Don't forget to include that glitzy outcome that's flashed on television screens during telecasts of professional matches: WINNERS. Winners are fabulously fun. They are the types of shots that make your opponents look so pathetic that they sit on the bench holding a towel over their heads during changeovers. At the club level, winners are more like Hercules: heroic and mythical. (**Dave's hint**: Scratch in a few winners to balance out the chart.)

Nobody charts any shot but the point-ending one. You could be playing a marvelously strategic point and confidently position yourself for that sure put-away at the net. However, if your opponent manages to clumsily miss-hit a lob over your head so that you must back-pedal after it, then you trip over your shoestring, swing at the ball while falling on your butt, and still hit your overhead a mere foot out, what does your chart reveal about your overhead? It blurts out, "Hey everybody! I'm a lob-prone geek!"

Charting isn't as easy as it sounds. There are certain tennis situations that are difficult to categorize and should be left to sage tennis philosophers.

Tennis philosophers are a small group of deep thinkers with towel-dried hair and a lot of spare time. They can be found sitting around club lounges and bars, contemplating vague tennis-related questions over adult beverages. Here are just a few of the posers that tennis philosophers ponder at happy hour:

*Philosophical Tennis Question #1*: A player is at the net. The opponent lobs. The player winds up for an overhead and swings like blazing hell. Boink. The ball hits her frame and drops over the net so that her opponent cannot return it on one bounce. Was the overhead a winner?

*Philosophical Tennis Question #2*: What is the sound of one tennis player volleying?

*Philosophical Tennis Question #3*: If a tennis player falls down on a court and nobody sees it, is that player a geek?

The following is a simplified example of charting and how it can help you uncover your match play weaknesses:

## *Dave's Example Chart:*

| Shot | Forced Errors | Unforced Errors | Winners! |
|---|---|---|---|
| *Backhand*: | ///////////// | ////////////// | — |
| *Overhead*: | /// | / | ///// |

With the aid of this chart and a discerning eye, we can draw certain conclusions based on empirical fact. FACT: this player's backhand has a death wish that some fairy godmother is happily granting. However, notice this player's overheads. Here we see some success, and therefore, a foundation on which to formulate a remedy. Because of my years of on-the-court experience, I have solved this player's problem with a mere glance of this chart. Obviously, this player should run around his or her backhands and hit them as overheads. Any trained pro will be equally as insightful.

In today's silicon, high-tech environment, almost anything can be programmed and automated by electrical enginerds—like the hand-held tennis computer, which is sold like a jelly bean distributorship in the back of tennis related magazines.

This tennis computer is actually a small tennis-charting device. Not only does this marvelous instrument give players the freedom from having to haul around a burdensome doofus, but it also has a wonderful bonus feature. This modern tennis miracle includes a built-in tennis advisor. Software experts programmed it utilizing sound tennis logic that was gleaned by professional gleaners from a United States Professional Tennis Association (USPTA) convention's host bar in Tahiti. If any single shot's combination of forced and unforced errors reaches the critical threshold level, as established by some of the world's top tennisologists, this amazing new device issues a piercing series of raucous warbles while the LCD window flashes, IDIOT! IDIOT! until someone depresses its Reset button with a sledgehammer.

# 24

## *Tenofus: The Untold History of Tennis Scoring*

In France, around 200 years ago (give or take a decade or more), a couple of the royalty and certain lofty citizens got together one evening. The conversation turned to the current rage in Paris, just before the guillotine.

Baron Lafite Rothschild, Duke Jean-Luc Picard, Mayor Pierre Chardonnay, and a fellow that history remembers only as Lenny, are meeting at the friends' favorite location–the Baron's renowned wine cellar.

(Four large empty bottles lay strewn across the stone floor.)

**Baron:** What say you all of this new sport that has the Parisian aristocracy positively all abuzz? More wine everyone? (Holding up a half-empty magnum.)

**Duke:** Sport, did you say? The only true sport for bluebloods is the challenge of the hunt, the exhilaration of the kill! (Hands his mug to the Baron.) Yes, thank you.

**Mayor:** They call it ball-hitting, I believe. They employ a flat, frame-like instrument with a handle, the center of which is crisscrossed with the dried intestines of an animal. They then proceed to strike the ball back and forth over a wooden barrier. (Holding out his mug to the Baron.) Yes, very good.

| | |
|---|---|
| **Duke:** | Intestines! Of course, the very viscera of the savage beast, slain in glorious battle for the benefit of civilized play! I sense the sport in this. Come. What fierce beast? What devil's minion? Bear? Or boar perhaps? |
| **Lenny:** | Pussy cats. Like little Fifi over there with the rat in her mouth. More wine did you say? (Presenting his mug for the Baron to fill.) |

The disappointed Duke gulps his wine.

| | |
|---|---|
| **Baron:** | Yes, it is so. (Pouring the wine.) The ball may bounce but once upon a player's side of the barrier before it must be struck back across. Otherwise, that player loses. |
| **Duke:** | *Humpf*, a short sport in duration that. (Holding his mug for the Baron to top off.) No chase. No kill. No glory. No sweat. |
| **Baron:** | Oh, but the players keep track of their point winnings until the victor has accumulated the necessary total. (Pouring the Duke some wine. Others hold forth their mugs also.) |
| **Mayor:** | I say, let us make this sport a sport of the aristocracy, for gentlemen such as ourselves. To that end, let us devise a devilish new scoring system that only we aristocrats could comprehend. (The mayor drinks heartily from his mug.) |
| **Baron:** | Splendid! In fact, I would suggest that instead of counting points beginning with 1, like a common commoner, we should commence scoring with, say, 5. (Drinks from the bottle.) |
| **Duke:** | A duke should begin with no less than 15. (Empties his mug into his mouth.) |
| **Baron:** | Better still, either 5 *or* 15. Shall we then double fifteen for the second point? (Pouring the Duke more wine.) |
| **All:** | YES! (All mugs ring together in agreement. Then all down a mighty draught.) |
| **Baron:** | Shall we then treble 15 for the third point? |
| **All but the Mayor:** | YES! (The Mayor holds his mug back.) |

| | |
|---|---|
| **Mayor:** | But that would surely set a pattern that even the poor and infidel may discern. Wouldn't it better serve our purpose if we do not increase the score by trebling, but lessen the increase by merely adding 10? It is without rhyme. It is devoid of reason. It is inspirational! |
| **All:** | YES! (All mugs ring together in agreement. Again a mighty draught.) |
| **Baron:** | Excellent. I think at this point if we were to dispense with numbers entirely…More wine everyone? |
| **Mayor:** | Brilliant, Baron. At forty apiece we could name that score "deuce." Since it is based on the number 2, the score would be uniquely and incomprehensibly regressing. Imagine the confusion. Yes, more thank you. (Presenting his mug.) |
| **Baron:** | Ahh, the exquisite absurdity. And you must not be able to break the deuce with but one point. I should say two points would be finer. The masses will never fathom a win-by-two concept when one point would clearly suffice. (Pouring wine for the Mayor.) |
| **Mayor:** | Genius! And what shall we name as zero? Zero is so pedestrian, so lowly in stature. It needs a grander name, a name of good breeding, and yet a name that clouds and confuses. (Slouching in his chair, mug on his belly.) |
| **Lenny:** | "Love." Love, I should say. Love is so passionate, so completely splendid; no one could comprehend it as synonymous with 'nothing.' It is not a number. Nor does it make a fifth of sense. |
| **All:** | Bravo, Lenny! (Lifting their mugs.) |
| **Duke:** | A mite tame. Is there nothing of the blueblood's sport in this "sport" of, what is it called again, "ball patting?" |
| **Lenny:** | Hitting. Ball-hitting, my dear Duke. Well, I suppose the barrier could instead be arranged to be made of a hunter's net. |
| **Duke:** | I like that. So it shall be. Gentlemen, I give you Ball-Hitting. (Lifting his glass.) |
| **Baron:** | My friends, a proper, less descriptive name it needs. A name agreed upon by all 4 of us. |
| **Mayor:** | All eight of us, if you see 2 Pierres as I see 2 of each of you. |
| **Lenny:** | Don't forget Fifi and her rat. That makes 10 of us. |

**Baron:**          Wonderful, Lenny. "Tenofus."

**Mayor:**          (Lifting his mug.) To the gentlemanly sport of Tenofus. (All lift their mugs.)

**All:**            *Tenofus!*

Somewhere along the cobblestone roads and back alleyways of tennis history, the name evolved into the modern "tennis." However, its scoring system remains remarkably undisturbed.

# PART III
## The People of Tennis

o o o o o o o o o o o o o o o o o o o o o o o o o o o o o o o o
*"There's a dinker born every minute."*

—*P. T. Barnone*

# 25

## *Dave's Generic Tennis Club*

I have lived around tennis clubs for a long time. Like most people with an ear for gossip and an eye for the absurd, I have been both amused and annoyed by the many characters and interesting personalities that permeate all tennis clubs with what can only be described as CIA efficiency. At least, I hope the CIA is as efficient. The makeup of members of a club is so diverse, yet predictable. It seems almost Darwinian in the way every niche is filled.

The following is an alphabetical list of the members of my Generic Tennis Club along with some of their more distinctive characteristics. Only the names have been changed to accent their idiosyncrasies.

### *Dave's Generic Tennis Club Roster*

**Meg Ahmoner**—Meg is the club complainer. She complains that there are not enough social events. She complains that there should be more children's clinics. She complains that too many children are using the courts. She complains that nobody asks her to play. (She also writes nasty letters to gifted tennis authors.)

**Chip N. Anglum**—Chip likes to jerk his opponents all over the court with his drop shots and sneaky angles, and then he pops lobs over their exasperated heads. Chip plays with a smug grin on his face as you smash your shin into a bench chasing after his cute little angled shots.

**Hal B. Annay**—Hal is a "B" player that competes in "A" tournaments. In this way, he provides proof positive at his workplace that he is an "A" player. After all, "Why else would I play 'A'? Duh." Hal always loses in the first round. He wears his complementary tournament T-shirts to formal functions.

**Jerry Attrick**—Jerry is the club's oldest member. He hasn't actually played since men wore those funny, long, white trousers. Still, he shows up everyday, watches matches, picks up litter other than hackers, and hoarsely yells at the myriad of mindless kids running around puking on each other's shoes.

**Randy Baldown**—Randy is the club jackrabbit. Randy never quits on a point, no matter how, ahem, pointless. He wins a lot of matches though, mainly because his opponents eventually quit with sore arms because of trying to put away yet another one of his returns.

**Olive Baubles**—Olive plays tennis with her face fully made up and wearing two pounds of jewelry that hang from her ears, neck, and arms. She only plays doubles because covering a singles court makes her sound like she is wearing wind chimes.

**Liz Beanne**—Liz is very athletic and one of the best players at the club. She prefers to wear shorts and can bench-press her own body weight.

**Peg Ann Beanum**—Peg Ann is tactless, opinionated, and constantly speaks her mind. It's her opinion that the best way to end a point (and possibly a match) is to smack the ball squarely into one of her opponent's vital organs.

**Karen Boutwales**—Karen the club's leading environmentalist. She pickets every club meeting with placards demanding separate glass, aluminum, plastic, paper, and Styrofoam recycle bins on every court. She rides her bike all around town, and puts flyers on our cars encouraging us to carpool to the club for the sake of the baby geckoes. On the court, she tries to recycle tennis balls–through your colon.

**Dennis Bumm**—Dennis is the Head Pro. Dennis always has a smile and reports to all of his students how well they are playing. Non-students are told that with just a small adjustment they could be his assistant, or maybe on tour.

**Fannie Butkis**—Fannie gushes over the Head Pro, the Assistant Pro, the Club Manager, the Assistant Manager, the number one male player, the number one female player, the club prodigy, and the Clinton administration. Everyone else she pointedly ignores.

**Helena Damwall**—Helena is as steady as a backboard, but more patient. She has no weapons and no shots more threatening than a miss-hit. Her playing style is to push balls back until her opponents drop to their knees imploring God, "PLEASE! I'll go to church. Just let her have butt cramps!"

**Hugh Datt**—Hugh is the new member. Nobody knows if he's any good yet, so no one plays with him because he would embarrass them if he were terrible. Hugh will have to wait until the next club mixed doubles social, so everyone can scope out his skill level.

**Wendy Day**—Wendy is never flat out beaten. That's because every time Wendy loses, she has an excuse. The sun was too bright. Her headband was too tight. The net was too low. She was distracted by her opponent who grunted like a rhino.

**Al Dazzlem**—Al attempts, even practices, trick shots such as spinning the ball to make it bounce back over the net and hitting the ball between his legs. He even tries to hit them in league matches.

Though he's successful only about one in 30 times, Al seems to like the odds.

**Thor DeForce**—Thor's a jock. He played baseball in college and is now taking up tennis. Thor has taken many tennis lessons and watches the pros on television. Unfortunately, the only thing he has learned is that pros hit the ball harder than club players. Not one to settle for second best, Thor emulates the pros. He believes he will be awesome on the day his shots (that he drives through the chain link fence), begin to land in the court.

**Emily Derfuer**—Emily is the perennial club president, captain of the women's team, membership committee chairperson, and social committee chairperson. With her club positions and her regular job as the manager of a Strip-A-Gram company, she seldom actually gets to play tennis.

**Will N. Dowd**—Will is the club stud. He is suave, sophisticated, and successful. The ladies all strive to catch his eye. The guys all strive to catch a castoff or two. He is an average tennis player and scores far better with women than on the tennis court. Still, the better players play with him to stay on his 'A' party list.

**Lou Duncrass**—Lou is the club's dominant male chauvinist pig and the best source of dirty jokes at the club. He took up tennis because the women wear such short skirts. He enjoys off-color comments and innuendoes with women on and off the court. When Lou is not playing tennis, he likes to sit around by the pool. He is also prone to drooling.

**Rich Essoby**—Rich is the club's self-made millionaire. He lives in a mansion and has a tennis court next to his pool. Rich always talks in business-ese. Terms like, *buy third quarter market indicators constraining amortization of the long-term fiscal debt* roll off his tongue while we go broke misinterpreting his advice.

**Stanley Farr-Wright**—Stanley is the club ultra-conservative. He owns a mountain retreat somewhere in Montana. Stanley preaches that the government is intruding into the lives of the poor with forced Federal healthcare and anti-poverty programs. He still plays in all white clothes, and believes there is a United Nations conspiracy to introduce rock music into club locker rooms.

**Erma Geddon**—Erma has a hair-trigger temper. She turns red, curses, and smashes her racket into non-composite fibers when she plays poorly, which she loosely defines as 'missing a shot.' The members can't stand to play with her, but they fear she'll blow up the ball machine if they refuse.

**Nat Goodinoff**—Nat feels that only by playing people better than he is can he improve. He never considers that maybe the very people he pesters to play want to improve, too. He can be observed hanging around the entrance, waving a new can of balls, asking everyone above him on the ladder, "Wanna hit some?"

**Ben Hasbin**—Ben played for his college team. He beats all the other members at the club. Ben gets to partner with the Head Pro in league matches. He enjoys his high status as "member most likely to get a match." He also never brings the balls.

**Robin Hookum**—It doesn't matter who Robin's playing, as soon as someone says, "These go," her vision becomes foggy. Her favorite methods of calling liners out are: (a) sweetness, for friends. "Oh, you just missed," she'll say disappointedly. Or, (b) assertiveness for strangers. "OUT!" she'll bellow, thereby demonstrating her intractability on the subject, in advance of the inevitable question, "Are you *sure?*"

**Bud Imacie**—Bud never excelled as a child. His shrink blames his parents and supply-side economics for Bud's low self-image, and thinks tennis is good for Bud. Bud's a "B" player that plays in

"C" tournaments to win and get trophies so he can display them in his mirror-lined trophy room as self-esteem therapy.

**Bart Kalounger**—Bart enjoys hanging around the courts and socializing. On those rare instances when he plays, he takes 10 minutes at every changeover performing the same routine: toweling off, drinking his sports liquid, snacking on an "energy bar," and trying to lull his opponent into a stupor with boring chitchat.

**Ivanna Kawicki**—Ivanna is the club slut. She has entertained more men than "The Three Stooges." Members refer to her as the "head, head pro." There is no club social get-together that she arrives at with a date, or leaves from alone. She sticks to the single guys though. She knows if she were to trespass, the married women would hunt her down and shave her head with a spatula.

**Guy L'Amour**—The gay guy. Guy mainly plays mixed doubles.

**Bea Lawbiden**—Bea knows every rule in the book and the club. She demonstrates her knowledge by strictly enforcing the rules of tennis with club members during important events such as the Valentine's Day Mixed Doubles Tennis and Potluck.

**Winona Leebucks**—Winona is the club manager. She looks like she could body slam a Coke machine. Winona makes sure the dues come in on time and that guests have paid. To say she is a cross between Genghis Khan and the president of the National Organization of Women is being charitable.

**Skye Lobzalot**—Skye employs lobs against everyone that steps over the baseline or hits more than two shots back in a row. Skye never improves; but then, she doesn't have to. Her opponents usually break down mumbling inanities around the third game or her 12,000th lob, whichever comes first.

**Ginger Lee Malnet**—Ginger makes a pretense of volleying. She is so afraid of being hit by the ball that she'll advance to the net no closer than the service line. Opening a can of balls startles her and bouncing the ball before her serve makes her nervous.

**Andre McEnbecker**—Andre doesn't take lessons. Instead, he imitates the strokes of one or more of the top five players in the world today. After a rankings change, Andre will introduce his new stroke technique to the club, complete with a discourse on why it's made [pro's name here] a top professional.

**Bert Nerny**—Bert is the child prodigy. His parents take him to a big-name pro at another club and to tournaments in neighboring states. Everyone agrees that this kid has the ability to be a pro some day, especially if we disregard his more anti-social tendencies—like arson.

**Anita Nuther**—Anita owns more tennis equipment than the women's tour. Still, she always complains that the racket she is using or the shoes she is wearing are preventing her from playing at her otherwise normal inspired level (a level at which no one has seen her play since she joined the club).

**Herb O'Vore**—Herb is the club health freak. Herb drinks only imported bottled water that he keeps in his cooler, packed in glacial ice, next to his tofu and pumpernickel sandwich and the four-pound bag of daily nutritional supplements. He plays five sets of tennis for fun; then he'll leave to work out or run a 10K.

**Faith Pewpacker**—Faith is the club religious freak. She prays before and after all endeavors such as tennis matches, dinner, and foot massages. Her daily activities include tennis, church, and watching the Religious Zealot Network (RZN). Faith is consumed with starting a club choir, and she believes the club should be closed on Sundays.

**Warren Peace**—Warren likes to talk and has an infinite supply of stories to report. His life reads like a Russian novel. He has endless war stories and has had more romances than Harlequin. He also delights club members with interesting and humorous accounts of every match he's ever played.

**Perry Plegic**—Alas, Perry is the most uncoordinated player at the club. Perry subscribes to every tennis magazine and has taken thousands of dollars worth of tennis lessons, and is still a "C" player. However, he loves tennis and gets more pure enjoyment out of it than anyone else at the club.

**Buzz Poachmore**—Buzz only plays doubles. He positions himself one foot from net on every point. Then, he runs back and forth across the court, his racket flashing like a sword, with the hope of volleying a ball away. Buzz doesn't have a clue about how to be an even average partner. He valiantly tries to pass the net man, and runs smack into his partner when switching sides.

**Eileen Redd**—Eileen is the club radical. Politically, she is to the left of Stalin. She distrusts all businesses and corporations, but especially "Big Tennis." Eileen wants the government to take over and regulate all tennis clubs "so the homeless can join." She advocates government-subsidized room, board, gut string, and home theater systems.

**Art Ritus**—Art is suffering from an acute case of terminal tennis elbow. He ices, heats, wraps, braces, and spreads athletic cream on his tortured elbow before and after playing tennis and poker. Art will try any remedy short of changing his strokes.

**Marvin Skool**—Marvin is the club genius, right down to his Einstein T-shirt and haircut. He knows all sorts of fascinating things, like how flies land upside down on the ceiling, origami, the atomic weight of Telluride, and Alexander the Great's last name. He has a Ph.D. from some leafy college like "Dartford" in some obscure field like *Comparative Invertebrate Mathematics*. The only subjects that stump him are sports, women, and fashion.

**Jess Spinnett**—Jess puts a spin on every shot. His machete slices are so intense that the ball stops dead on the court bleeding lint. His topspin shots are never lower than three stories high. He enjoys watching opponents calmly set up to return his shot only to throw their bodies through the air, in wild desperation, at the ball when it stops dead.

**Hans Stonegrip**—Hans is more powerful than Thor only he would like to be able to hit soft shots like Chip. Poor Hans. His drop shots bounce off the fence, and local air traffic controllers routinely pick up his serves on radar.

**Luke Studley**—Luke always wears the newest Italian fashions and irons each one before going to the club. He carries his four new rackets on court even if it is only to rally for 10 minutes. He drives a European sports car and always takes up two spaces when he parks.

**Diane Tuwynne**—Diane is a very serious, very intense person. She competes at everything, even computer dating partners and grocery coupon clipping. She is deeply offended when she loses the racket spin. However, she usually wins her matches because everyone she plays either plays for fun or would feel guilty if she went broke paying for a therapist.

**Emma Valabelle**—Emma has recently divorced. She was able to join the club with her alimony check. She spends weekends at the club, and she never misses the Friday Night Mixed Doubles. Emma always looks ready for an evening at the opera.

**Les Vegas**—Les is the club gambler. Les likes to make things "interesting." He plays like a comatose zombie if no one will bet with him. But on a wager he springs to life like a just-paid sailor on shore leave.

**Roland Waddle**—Roland took up tennis to lose weight. If he gets the ball back a couple of times per point he figures it's calories well burned. Actually, Roland is a good sport who single-handedly keeps the snack bar viable.

**Ty Wahnon**—Ty never plays without a six-pack of beer on the court. Nor does he sit down without a beer in his hand. His tennis isn't so hot. But then, who cares? Ty is never at a loss for people to play with because he always shares his beer.

**Darlene Wattaboddie**—Darlene is an argument for that old tennis adage that a woman tennis player can rise only to the level of her bra cup size. Guys line the club entrance when she drives up, and jockey for the adjacent courts when she plays tennis in her sports bra and spandex shorts. Although she doesn't play tennis very well, Darlene remains the club's most popular mixed doubles partner.

# 26

## *No Pro Bono*

What about all those tennis professionals? What is a tennis pro, anyway? The prevailing definition is 'a person who plays or teaches tennis for money.' The principle concept here is *money*. After all, there are amateurs out there who can thrash the navel lint out of most teaching pros. But, since they aren't trading on their skill, they cannot be considered pros. They can, however, be considered stupid; otherwise they'd be pulling in the bucks like a Las Vegas casino.

Pros bring diverse attitudes to tennis. The pros that play for money are iron-willed chariots of competitive fire that readily play tension-packed matches for suitcases of institutional prize money. The teaching pros are tin-willed, broken-down scooters of competitive kindling that know how to teach others to play.

Touring pros would beat the sunscreen off the teaching pros. But, at least the teaching pros stay in one place long enough for the local tennis rabble to pick up a backhand from their vast cargo-bays of tennis knowledge. The touring pros are simply too absorbed with either making money now, or jetting somewhere to make it, to assist any player not co-starring in a pro-am charity event as the well-connected amateur. Conversely, teaching pros are tennis' version of the priesthood. They administer to the tennis faithful of *The Flock of Forever Flailing Forehands and Futureless Backhands.*

## Pro Groups

Almost all forms of pros get together in groups to collude. It is a sociological phenomenon that human beings and tennis pros must form groups. This grouping concept was invented long ago and passed down through countless generations in councils and committees, because it was discovered that the easiest way to hunt down and beat up undesirable neighbors was as a pack.

## ATP

One group you may have heard about is the *Association of Tennis Professionals* (ATP). This is a group of male touring pros that gather at various tropical resorts to conspire for more prize money and better playing conditions. For instance, these players can become highly agitated and may even boycott tournaments that refuse to provide complimentary sushi.

The ATP provides something in return, however. They provide good players. That's right. Let's say some Third World country, maybe Antipodes, decides to hold a tennis tournament for the entertainment delight of its starving and illiterate citizens. They call the ATP and promise three chickens and a goat for every player who will come to play in some village that's only accessible by camel. The ATP then mobilizes its contract lawyers to secure an agreement, whereby, every day the Antipodesians must helicopter in fresh sushi from Japan. In return, the ATP fills the tournament with aspiring tour players whose cumulative total of grand prix points is 1. Since players need grand prix points to play for purses greater than domesticated livestock, the ATP awards a few grand prix points to the winner of the Antipodes Open. In this way, tennis is delivered around the globe, and the ATP appears to be a compassionate organization and good world citizen, perhaps worthy of a UN grant.

## *WTA*

The women touring pros have formed their own group for the same reasons as the men. Their group is called the *Women's Tennis Association* (WTA). In it, spitting and scratching are hormonally forbidden. The women have their own tour and, like old sorority rooms, men aren't allowed. Moreover, the two tours typically only intermingle during Grand Slam events.

A large, politically correct corporation, such as Greenpeace, sponsors the women's tour. I don't know the current sponsor, but Virginia Slims (a cigarette company) used to do the underwriting. Then someone who keeps track of politically correct attitudes noted, "Smoking is out, unless it's cigars." So, the WTA snuffed out Virginia Slims (VS). VS has since started looking into sponsoring a professional, female chess tour. Thus far, the women who play chess dress far too conservatively (no visible thighs or cleavage), so VS is still considering its options.

**NEWS FLASH!** A President of the United States has decreed that nicotine (a.k.a. tobacco) is now a federally regulated addictive substance. This means no more cartoons of Joe Camel enticing five-year-olds to buy cigarettes. It also means no pictures of cowboys enticing thirty-five year olds to ride horses. Also, tobacco companies can only display their brand names in the following way: black and white, and only in a foreign language, except the new warning label. This new warning reads:

> *Danger! The Surgeon General has determined that smoking causes you to (1) become addicted to tobacco, and (2) die. Maybe not today. Maybe not tomorrow. But soon, and for the rest of your life.*

Okay, how about the teaching pros, you ask. Do they form groups, too? The answer is, absolutely—a couple of them. Teaching pros divide themselves between the *Professional Tennis Registry* (PTR), and the *United States Professional Tennis Association* (USPTA). These rival groups exist for the same purpose: to promote the sport of tennis throughout the country by holding annual conventions in sun-drenched, exotic locations. Yes, there is nothing like a warm beach filled with shapely sun-tanned bodies to open your eyes to some new-age teaching technique.

## PTR

As advertised on its Internet web page, the newer PTR provides its member pros with a standard method of teaching. With a standard teaching method, students are able to move from club to club and with each new pro pick up where he or she left off. It's like getting the same-tasting Big Mac at each McDonalds. In this way, the PTR pro is a kind of franchised tennis professional.

## USPTA

The USPTA, on the other hand, allows its instructors to use their own teaching methods. However, their pros are compelled to take a competency exam. The pros must demonstrate to the USPTA authorities that their personal teaching techniques fall within the realm of tennis reason.

Incidentally, we do not want to leave out that large gang of group-less pros, those tireless, independent contractors. Many are extremely adept at teaching tennis. However, these pros are usually on their way to careers outside of tennis, like CEO for a Fortune 500 company, neurologist, or ambassador to Uruguay. They don't bother to get certified by tennis group officials who must abandon their Mai Tais and fly in from convention planning at *The Body Shop* in Ft. Lauderdale.

So, which organization do I recommend? Well, since neither group would respond to my requests for support in the form of a money order, I will go on record with this carefully crafted official statement: *either one*. There. I hope I've settled that issue.

Actually, I am a non-dues paying member of the USPTA. Yes, I took their test; I even passed. Here is how they inflicted their tests upon us (there were about eight of us), and how I became a certified, third-rate, teaching professional.

The USPTA officials presented their test in three parts: *Mental*, *Physical*, and *Operational*. The Mental portion of the test consisted of a written test that resembled the SAT, except more important. It measured your tennis knowledge and buzzword vocabulary. Many relevant questions were asked such as, "Name tennis' four musketeers." (Don't make my mistake; D'Artagnan was NOT one.) The test also included questions on court maintenance, tennis history, rules, tennis concepts, and the definition of "loquacious." Wait! I think that last one probably *was* from the SAT.

The Physical portion consisted of a skills test to determine if you, as a pro, could demonstrate to your students the end result of what you were teaching them to do. Or, if you could at least look like a competent player having an off day. We had to execute slice and topspin forehands and backhands to different areas of the court. We had to serve the ball to three different areas of each service box—on demand. We had to hit overheads into the backcourt. We had to hit drop shots that landed within three feet of the net and bounced three times before exiting the service box. We had to hit seven consecutive volleys right back to the tester to demonstrate that we could make a shortage of balls last long enough to approximate a full basket.

The Operational portion was a teaching test to determine whether we could effectively conduct an actual tennis lesson with actual students. To do that, the USPTA testers gathered an assortment of quarrelsome people off the street (customer support personnel, lawyers, the criminally insane, etc.) and assigned them to courts. They then sent us "pros" out to teach them a lesson on some designated part of the game.

After their lesson, the "students" reported to the testers to gripe and complain. The testers assembled them in the formation of a school choir and then aimed a decibel meter at them. The louder the cacophony of complaints, the worse your score.

We received an individual score for each section of the test. The possible scores were '1' (very good), '2' (good), '3' (good enough), and 'X' (would make students quit and take up flower arranging.) Your overall rating was equal to the lowest score of the three sections. So, if you scored a '2' in mental proficiency, a '1' in physical skills, and a '3' in operational competence (as I did), your professional level would be '3' as well.

These ratings mean different things. A professional rating of '1' means you could teach tennis to anyone with the ability to pay. A professional rating of '2' means you may have to provide a few free clinics in order to drum up enough business for yourself. A professional rating of '3' means you would not greatly impede a gifted athlete.

Magnanimously, the USPTA provides certification seminars so that second and third-rate pros can upgrade their pro ratings at approximately the same price as your basic 52-inch large screen, high definition television.

USPTA pros can even be rated higher than '1.' The USPTA also reserves the titles of "Master" and "Grand Master" for those select pros with the knowledge, skill, experience, and courage to charge double and even *triple* their area's going lesson rate.

So, improve your tennis; take a lesson every day. That's my third-rate professional advice.

# 27

## *Tennis Personality Disorders*

People are made up of human beings who have spent dozens of years developing any number of obnoxious personality traits, like running red lights, leaving their mutt's poops in the parks and on your lawn, and letting their *demonic little brats call you names behind your back, like "tennis weenie!"*

Ahem. There are many, many personality types that compose the world's population. For instance, there are extroverts, introverts, redheads, boat people, tuba players, line-dancers, Scandinavian female nudists, etc.

The tennis player group is a loose term because it encompasses a broad collection of aberrant personalities that disregard common decency, and who, for their own personal gain, go out and play some deviant form of tennis. These player personalities are differentiated by their diverse characteristics; and yet they remain connected by the fact that they each exude some ghastly disorder. These disorderly types, *Desperado, Rankist, Hacker, Gucci, Ex-Jock, Scud, Upper* and *Downer* are easily recognizable if you know how. Since you may not, I am providing the following thumbnail descriptions as a guide.

### *The Desperado*

Because some players are so desperate for a hit (I'm speaking of rallying, not any other hit, you mind-altering weed mongers), they will frequently show up at the courts with balls that their dogs have buried and that bounce like giant wads of toothpaste. More often, however, they use a new can of balls as bait to entice a victim onto the court.

Desperadoes have typically been laid up due to illness, sea duty, or an extended prison term. They then go to the public courts in a frantic search for a game. They will beseech everyone standing around to play. I once saw a Desperado stalking a pro shop, and while cleaning his glasses, ask a life size cutout of a cowboy Ronald Reagan to "hit some."

Eventually, so many players complained to the USTA of harassment that most tennis court complexes are now forced to also provide a wall or backboard for the truly desperate. These walls are a kind of self-contained, tennis outreach to the hitless.

## *The Rankist*

There is another type of player who also uses the "new can of balls" ploy. This is the guy who doesn't want to play with anyone he can actually beat. He is out to better his own game. And, for reasons known only to him, he believes he is unable to improve his tennis skills during laborious, 5-minute rallies if, in the end, he wins 51 percent of them.

The Rankist's thought process is somehow this: they can only improve when their opponents are acing them, and stroking winning shots by them, left and right. They figure the worse they are beaten the better they are getting. Therefore, the best practice they can get is to lose 6-0, 6-0, where they can count the number of points they won on one hand. Then they come off the court smiling and high-fiving with other Rankists in celebration of how much better they just became.

The politically correct establishment refers to this corrupt reasoning as *rankism*, that is, discriminating against players not as accomplished as yourself by refusing to play with them. The ACLU (American Civil Lawsuit Union) wants to bring a suit to ban rankism. Let them. The truth is, Rankists are just plain annoying. I mean they keep asking us real players to play! Oh, the inhumanity!

In reality, players better than the Rankists don't want to play with them because the Rankists will not occasionally play down. Sure, Rankists appear blissfully happy to be playing better players, but they're also smugly thinking, "What a fool to play down *with me.*" So, only nice players will relent and play with these selfish types. Maybe that's why nice guys finish last. I mean, if nice guys spend their entire practice time helping to make their opponents better than they are, then yeah, they would eventually finish last. It also follows that once a Rankist has used you to better his game beyond yours, he will toss you aside like used kitty litter.

So unless you're a hacker or a Desperado, steer clear of them.

## The Hacker

Hackers are not players at all. They are fashion-impaired clods. Hackers come in two distasteful flavors: (1) as part of a once-a-year eruption of public tennis enthusiasm, after watching the Wimbledon finals, they stream out onto our nation's public courts to try tennis, but only manage to pollute and defile our holy ground with their incessant miss-hit balls and offensive behavior, like sitting on the nets. Or, (2) they are apprentice torturers for the CIA. This type conducts and re-conducts heinous experiments such as the effects of bad taste and poor personal hygiene on real tennis players. (Wince.)

## The Gucci

Speaking of hygiene, some players would rather look good than play well. These players are immaculately groomed. The First Lady could learn a few fashion tips. Guccis spend hours before their matches in front of mirrors to ensure that every hair on their heads is individually placed and sprayed to stay there, even through small craft warnings (nautical lingo for 'extra windy'). And that's just the men. As a rule, the female Guccis simply will not show up for their tennis dates, unless it's with a male and the chances of actually playing tennis are squat. Otherwise, they call from their beauty salons and reschedule a salad luncheon.

Guccis have expensive tastes in all things. Their homes could pass for museums, and they drive cars that cost more than the average condominium. Guccis buy the most expensive brands of clothes and treat them better than most people treat their kids. They lovingly wash and dry them, fold them, and tuck them into their little drawers by both color and function. Then, on the day of their match, they starch and iron each item of clothing before putting it on. They end up looking like models for some fantasy fashion sport where the players stand around in seductive poses actively not sweating. These players always carry three $250 rackets in an imported tennis bag. They either carry a towel in their shorts, or they place it at the fence behind them. It then serves as a prop for the various poses they assume when pretending to towel off between points.

Guccis bring their own water, not because it tastes better, but rather for the nutritional value of no toxic additives[1]. Then, they indulge in thoughtful remarks such as, "Last spring's rainfall and subsequent percolation into the fluvial groundwater was particularly high in necessary trace elements." Gag.

## The Ex-Jock

Ex-Jocks take up tennis after retiring from one of the brutish team sports. However, they don't want to spend the necessary years developing control over their shots while learning to incrementally increase their pace the way normal people do. They head straight to power like a bull to a china shop.

Ex-Jocks can't help their power urges. They have a gland in their armpits that pit doctors call the *pulver* gland, and the term "pulverized" is derived from it. This gland secretes a hormone that combines a naturally occurring steroid with testosterone. This hormone affects the

---

1.    Like formaldehyde.

brain in such a way that every time they attempt to hit a ball the net and lines disappear from their view, and instead, they see distant foul poles. As a result, their entire body's energy is compulsively focused into trying to separate the ball from its cover.

Very few women have the pulver gland. In fact, I can remember only one I have ever seen that was not playing on television or a body-builder. She was small but powerful, and would race around the court like a militant squirrel, furiously battering balls into lint. Then between points, she would walk around in a conspicuous daze, as if re-enacting the starring role from *The Bimbo from the Planet Valium*.

## The Scud

Scuds are those rare arrogant twits that practice put-away shots during pre-match warm-ups. After dividing the balls up, two for you, one for your unprincipled opponent, you start by hitting the ball right to your opponent. He responds by abruptly zinging a crosscourt winner that leaves an airborne, comet trail of fuzz. You figure he accidentally miss-aimed the ball. So once again, you hit the next ball right to him. This time he rips the ball down the line for another winner. You chalk it up to another freak shot. He then hits his ball to you. You hit it back. You're thinking, "Okay, here we go." But he cracks another crosscourt winner. He warms up his volleys by punching the balls that you fed right to him into alternating corners. Then he starts pressuring you to start the match: "Come on. We've been out here for almost five minutes already!"

Dropping subtle hints about his boorish behavior can sometimes settle your opponent down to the point where he'll warm you up too. A commonly used hint entails walking over and whacking your opponent's ear with your racket.

Who do these people think they are? Professional wrestlers show more respect for each other. You would think that they could pull their brains out of "P" for "punk" and warm up in a civilized fashion. At least we can take comfort in knowing that they are universally regarded as arrogant twits to anyone with a brain the size of a kumquat. I wonder if they have noticed that many of their kind have disappeared under mysterious circumstances. But, being unrepentant drug addicts, I doubt it.

Then there are the players who want to play tournaments in skill levels other than their own. Behavioral tennisologists have identified two scientific categories: (1) Players that play up a division, "Uppers," and (2) players that play down, "Downers."

## The Upper

Players that play a level or two above their own abilities are fundamentally insecure people that over-compensate by way of loud boasts and name-dropping. They tend to be 'B' players with the obsessive desire to be considered an 'A' player by their peers. (If you are more familiar with NTRP ratings, too bad.)

Why play up a level? Because the easiest way to label yourself an 'A' player is, of course, to play 'A' tournaments. It's simple; anyone could do it. You don't have to be an 'A' player, or even a tennis player. But, if you are not an 'A' player and regularly play 'A' tournaments, you are likely to be unfavorably compared to Bozo the Clown.

Uppers can be overheard discussing their last tournament and how they were beaten in the first round by a seeded player. At least they don't lie about their results (mainly because they don't care that they are routinely thrown to the seeds like virgins to fertility gods).

## The Downer

The players that play below their levels are also insecure, except these players compensate, in part, by kicking dirt in the faces of small dogs. These philistines are also usually 'B' level players, but are not a force in 'B' tournaments, where they would stumble forward for a round or two before losing honorably.

All Downers have two things in common: they hate having nothing to show for their modest tennis skill, and they have no honor. The good news is, the longer they go without a winning a trophy, the bigger the dogs they kick dirt on. Inevitably, this practice becomes hazardous to the limbs required to play tennis—like their necks.

Downers are generally ostracized and shunned by 'C' players. However, the slow-to-anger 'C' players eventually become upset and form vigilante groups to burn the Downer's tennis bag or cut all the strings in his rackets. If that doesn't dissuade the offending Downer, a rented large person named "Bubba" will drag him into an alley and explain the situation personally.

# 28

## *Hacker Attack!*

Hackers are not tennis players at all. Hackers are lower forms of life that borrow rackets and balls from Goodwill stores to conduct insulting hack-ins on good tennis courts.

The increasing number of hack-ins has forced the USTA into the unprecedented action of enlisting my help. This chapter is the least I can do to thwart this foul scourge. You can always count on me to do the least that I can do.

As a Public Service Expose' (PSE), I want to alert all you real players to the existence of a devious underground organization called the *American Hacker Association*, or AHA. The sole purpose of the AHA is to take over the world's supply of public tennis courts by geeks, dweebs, dorks, and nerds!

The AHA's depraved purpose has been brought to light by some of the USTA's bravest undercover agents. These daring agents infiltrated the AHA and smuggled a copy of their mission statement out of its secret national convention in Little Rock, Arkansas, by posing as pretzel vendors from Boise.

The AHA's goal is simple: annoy us real tennis players until we throw up our hands in disgust and abandon the courts to those taste-impaired losers, preferably forever.

To help unwary players identify hackers, the Intelligence arm of the USTA, Department 00 (licensed to fold, spindle, *and* mutilate), has asked me to publish a few simple methods to spot these counterfeit athletes. Here goes.

## *Hacker Attack Methods:*

It was always suspected, but it turns out to be an actual policy of the AHA that member hackers must only play tennis while dressed as fashion-handicapped tourists. Hawaiian shirt or old white T-shirt, Bermuda shorts, dark socks, and a pair of ten-year-old running shoes, or even wingtips, are all a part of the hacker's mandatory tennis apparel. Sometimes muscle shirts can be worn, but only by hackers tipping the scales in excess of 250 lbs. and toting a world-class beer belly that should hang out below it.

Other AHA rules state that all hackers must ignore all forms of tennis etiquette and common sense. Some of their most common attack strategies are as follows:

• A hacker must always walk in back of, or through (but never around), as many courts as possible with real players playing.

• A hacker must never close the gate on purpose.

• A hacker must immediately dash onto a court where players are in the middle of a point to retrieve their ball.

• Hackers must ignore all balls that roll onto their court for two points; then they are to claim the strays as "finders, keepers" and play with them as their own.

Yes, unless a player is on his toes, hackers can walk off the court with his three barely used balls. The hackers will act confused and mutter, "Huh? I thought we brought one bali. Now we have four. Oh well. Let's go get a taco."

## *USTA Advice*

To beginning players and those of you with the keen athletic eye of a potato, hackers may seem like innocent dweebs out for a good time. But do not be fooled! They are shrewd and devious. Should you spot a hacker "playing" tennis on good courts, it is important to remain calm. Any show of our customary reaction, such as anger, violence, or puking only encourages them. An anonymous USTA official suggests sounding an alarm by pointing past them and yelling, "Fire! Fire!" She advised that most hackers are, first, pyromaniacs and will race off to go watch the blaze.

Remember that hackers are like a cancer. All they do is take up valuable space and time on perfectly good tennis courts and provide nothing constructive in return. Show them no mercy. Oh, they may say they're having fun. Big deal. To real tennis players, sex is fun. Of course, if you dress like a hacker, you wouldn't know.

As serious tennis players understand, tennis was meant to be exasperating. Serious players go out on the court to work on the crippled and toxic parts of their games. Players work on backhands, serves, slice lobs, you name it. This fruitless practice is frustrating and prepares us for losing.

Losing is highly irritating. So, I think we can forgive all those grim tennis players their frequent lapses into temper tantrums and barrages of four letter words that would make a national shock jock blush, when we think of the tribulations of tennis. We can pardon these players, for instance, as we pause to reflect on the agonies they endure when coping with the inquisition-like tortures of dumping more than one backhand into the net, or double faulting on break point in the semis of a tournament. Have mercy!

Let's face it; tennis players have fun only when they win or when they play well. Interestingly, most players only seem to think they've played well when they were *zoning*. Indeed, independent studies have shown that though they win about 50 percent of the time, players only admit to playing well about once every other Vernal Equinox.

## *Hacker Recognition*

Heaven forbid, but you may find yourself stuck on a court with a hideous hacker who resembles a player because his mother sent him out to play in clothes she bought at a thrift store. If you are still not sure with whom you are dealing, a surefire way of distinguishing hackers from players is the way they react to a ball hit with spin.

## *Spins*

Generally speaking, you can quickly determine a tennis player's playing level by the spins he or she is able to produce. Real tennis players can employ both topspins and slices during play. Hackers accidentally slice, and cannot execute topspin without letting their rackets fly off like a wobbly one-armed Frisbee.

Hackers do not understand spin. They think "spin" is what politicians do. Hackers assume the ball will bounce the same way every time. As tennisologists have expressed it, they have no *Spin Recognition Capability* (SRC) whatsoever. So they stand relaxed as if in a tequila-induced stupor, then they'll lurch after the ball when it spins away. Or, if they recognize a spin is coming, they'll be unsure how it will affect its bounce, meaning they have only *Rudimentary Spin Recognition Capability* (RSRC). They stand motionless and glassy-eyed, their rackets poised like an open bag of potato chips, ready to hop like a toad in any direction.

A review of the main spin types may be useful.

Spins come in two basic varieties: (1) your basic *slice* group, called by eminent tennisologists the "slice group." And, (2) your *topspin* group, called the "topspin group."

**Dave's Note:** Hackers refer to these stroke types as *backspin* and *overspin*, respectively. (Vocabulary is one more way we tennis players publicly expose hackers.)

Slices are hit with a downward stroke that forces the ball to roll up the strings of the racket, thus imparting its spin. Executed by a skilled player, a slice is a long and graceful stroke. You can easily distinguish a hacker's slice because their stroke resembles a farmer with a sore arm chopping cornstalks with a hacksaw. Hence the term "hack."

Topspin is the opposite of a slice. The racket comes from underneath the ball. Thus, the ball rolls down the racket's strings. A ball with topspin tends to dive down in the air, and then to jump up and forward from the ground. You can always tell a hacker's topspin because the ball tends to jump up in the air and dive down into the parking lot.

My personal solution to the hacker menace is to enroll them all in federally funded programs that would hand out coupons redeemable at ice skating rinks. On ice, hackers would wobble, swerve, and drop like crash test dummies right into the sharpened blades of our aspiring Olympic figure skaters and National Hockey League hopefuls. The figure skaters would give them a toe-pick to their shins while the hockey players would perform a few slap shots upside their heads. It may harm our country's chances in the next Olympics, but I think it is worth the risk. After all, it could knock some etiquette into a few ignorant hackers. That would be progress enough. Knocking some common sense into them would require something on the order of a cruise missile; and those are just too expensive.

# 29

# *Mom Was Wrong (Cheaters Prosper)*

Why do some people invest thousands of dollars in tennis lessons just to hit some mealy little backhand over the net? And, why do some players engage in bizarre practice habits whose only result is physical therapy? Simple. They want to *win*.

Everybody wants to win at everything. It doesn't matter what the activity: surfing, number of Girl Scout cookies sold, or previous incarnations. Everyone is trying to be better than you are.

In tennis, no matter how you stack it, only 50 percent of the players can win at any one time. That's why liberals hate traditional sports. Instead, they want us to play non-competitive games so we'll all feel better about ourselves. They want us to believe that if you're a four-star geek and don't win Wimbledon, whoever did win it was, by definition, a jerk anyway. Evidently, liberals don't realize that without competition we would still be protozoa, contented and well-adjusted protozoa, but protozoa nonetheless.

Conservatives, on the other hand, are searching for ways to make tennis a contact sport. They argue that concussions and bruises will enhance competition, which will benefit humanity via the eventual production of nuclear fusion, and the development of a warp drive engine.

Individually, you can increase your winning percentage by decreasing your opponent's. Abraham Lincoln put it best when he said:

*You can win some of your matches all of the time and all of your matches some of the time. But, you can't win all of your matches all of the time without relentless and outrageous cheating.*

Okay, he did not say that *exactly*. But he would have if he had been a tennis player instead of assassinated. He would have been a good player too. He had long arms for a hugely leveraged serve. And, he had great powers of concentration: he taught himself to read by firelight, a feat similar to learning to play tennis with dead balls.

Winners enjoy the good things in life. I'm sure you have noticed this yourself. For instance, the top male tennis players enjoy money, women, travel, money, women, fame, money, and, of course, women. The top female players enjoy money, travel, money, fame, money, and only occasionally, women. As you can see, the male players get FAR more out of the game than their female counterparts, at least from where I sit.

These top players have something else, too. They have something called an *entourage*. An entourage is a group of people, each of whom performs a single function for their pro. One person tells the pro when to practice. One person takes all the pro's money and invests it wisely. One tells the pro which vitamins to take. One drives the car for the pro. One advises the pro on whom to trust and not to trust. One arranges dates. Everyone would like an entourage. As a matter of fact, everyone had one. We all had a very efficient entourage. We called her "Mom."

## *Options For Losers*

If you find yourself losing more matches than you think fair and you fear losing is becoming a way of life, there are a couple of things you can do to remedy this sad, even humiliating situation: quit or cheat.

When the agony of defeat becomes greater than the thrill of victory, many people will quit. Those that don't quit are dedicated masochists who also watch televised shuffleboard matches or listen to Polish opera, or *both*. More often, people prefer to cheat.

Now, there are sincere cheaters and there are dirty rotten cheaters. Sincere cheaters are just so competitively intense and driven by their compulsive need to win that they subconsciously will their eyeballs into an astigmatism whose only manifestation is calling obvious liners "out." These cheaters steadfastly believe they are making the correct calls. They'll even defend their calls in a USTA court against 11 professionally trained lines-humans, led by the Attorney General, all of whom saw the ball hit inside the line. This cheater's intent is not to cheat; it is to win.

Then there are those pus-drooling thieves that know exactly what they're doing when they cheat. The embarrassment of losing to you is so distasteful that they must use immoral line calls to minimize the chances of that wretched occurrence. To them, cheating is only part of the game and always a means to an end. These willful, miserable, rotten cheaters are so nice to you afterwards, too, just when you thought you'd part their hair with your tennis racket. Their intent is strictly to avoid losing—to *you*.

## Sportsmanship

These days, gentlemanly sportsmanship has gone the way of the wooden racket and white tennis balls: extinct. We have become kinder, gentler, more tolerant players, more forgiving players, and, yes, more victimized players. This victimization is due to the dumbing down of sportsmanship. Today, good sportsmanship is recognized as having not committed a felonious assault on an opponent or tournament official within the previous six months.

There still exist stalwarts of sportsmanship: Stephan Edberg (retired), Boris Becker (also retired), the overwhelming majority of the women's tour, and the continent of Australia. But good sportsmanship isn't worth a bottle of *Milk of Magnesia* because the big money endorsements are based on rankings and number of rumored death threats.

Yes, the BIG money is in controversy. If Edberg had called Becker an (expletive deleted), and if Becker had similarly called Edberg a (deleted expletive), a feud would have been declared. The media would have been alerted; press cameras would have followed them both 24 hours a day and the number of their endorsements would have doubled overnight! Unfortunately for the entertainment industry they were friends.

Just wait until the women start becoming bellicose and contentious. They will fill the tennis stadiums. Of course, if they were to incorporate a few elements of female mud wrestling, like apparel, they would need bigger stadiums.

While some old geezers and grizzled veterans still hold up sportsmanship like the Ten Commandments, or at least a good credit report, players as a group are getting in touch with their feelings. They are learning to express themselves and to communicate frankly and openly, both on the court and off. When a gifted and temperamental player smashes his racket in frustration, the public now realizes he is merely releasing his special unique fury at the inequity of making an unforced error to some guy straight off the Florida orange truck with a lowly world ranking of #26.

The truth is, when I lose I want to go berserk in various unsportsman-like ways, too. I want to act out my frustration by launching tennis balls over the fence, running over my rackets with my car, or renting a boat and deliberately fishing over the limit.

In England, they still admire a good sport. In fact, the only thing they enjoy more than a good sport is an exceptionally poor one. But as I said, sportsmanship as demonstrated by a few good men, the women, Australia, et al., has given way to a competitive fervor that today's larger purses only encourage. And England is no exception.

Unsportsmanship has become yet another fact of life, not only on the pro tour, but worldwide. This bare truth is evident even at Wimbledon. In deference to this new fact of life, Wimbledon, that traditional bastion of sportsmanship and fair play, has finally succumbed to this new reality and modified the plaque over the door from the player's room to Centre Court. Kipling now reads:

> *If you can meet triumph and disaster,*
> *And treat those two impostors just the same…*
> *You're a better man than I am, Gunga Din.*

# 30

## *Winners, Losers, and the Lottery*

Winners win; and losers lose. If they didn't, they'd be called something else, like "agoraphobic" or "lanky." Winners have more fun because they get awards, respect, and bragging rights over their loser opponents. Losers get the indignity of losing while having little fun doing it. That is, unless they lose to someone they have heard of and who thrashes them "oh and oh" in about 20 minutes. Then they feel not only good, but also honored.

Does anybody remember that tennis is supposed to be enjoyed by all players regardless of skill level? That time was back when you were a hacker and didn't know how to keep score. Well, there was also another time. It was a time of simplicity. It was a time when dueling was considered sport.

Dueling originated when gentlemen would slap each other's faces with their gloves for emphasis during quarrels. It escalated when the poor, who couldn't afford gloves, used machetes. Today, because dueling is illegal in many areas, tennis has stepped forward as an excellent alternative.

Yes, tennis has taken its place alongside politics and telemarketing as types of cutthroat and ruthless behavior. This behavior is due to the fact that many of today's tennis players ARE cutthroat and ruthless. I am sure you know some. They are the ones who would pour hot cappuccino on your new imported Italian shorts if you took a set from them. (Outside of sports, the IRS and the Strong-Arm Collection Agency best exemplify this cutthroat ruthlessness.)

Citing professional courtesy, tennis' barbarous types have been known to call in anonymous tips to the IRS to report how you were overheard bragging that you have been deceiving the IRS for years. Soon thereafter, armed agents specially trained in suburban assaults and equipped with portable financial calculators and ledger paper burst through your door at 4:30 AM waving a warrant that allows them to search for and inspect everything in your house made of paper or on computer disks. They arrive with either paper-sniffing dogs or the new battery-operated paper detectors that are able to penetrate every known substance except polyester. They wave them mercilessly at your cabinets, walls, and furniture. Confiscating every piece of paper they find, they make you brew coffee and run for doughnuts. Anyway, mean-spirited tennis losers like this can be very annoying to winners.

## *Losing*

Still, losing can be a positive thing, like when the courts order you to take an anger management class to control your road rage. Therefore, losers should remember this: you learn more from a loss than you do from a win. It's like what they say about ice skating and skiing. Only they say it more like *if you're not falling, you're not learning*. In my ice skating experience, this logic is certainly questionable. I mean if that were unfailingly true, my listing sense of balance would have provided me enough falls to make the Olympic team. However, their point is valid.

Losing gives you a great deal of information, but only if you LISTEN. Many players just don't listen! They moan and groan, and whine and complain about how the universe, traveling along its cosmic superhighway of time and dimension, detoured and demonically burped at that very point in time when they were playing the club dork in a vital challenge match. With the universe out of whack, it senselessly fated that they be delivered innumerable bad calls and bad bounces. After their shocking upset, the universe returns to normal (wherein the dork, once again, repeatedly serves his racket into his shin).

The point is, be sure to listen to your game. Listen to your backhand when it repeats shot after shot, *Topspin to the net. Topspin to the net.* Or, *Slice to the fence. Slice to the fence.* It is an outstretched hand, a desperate plea for help.

Your serve, I'm sure, is likewise issuing hysterical screams. Then again, if *you* are smacking your shin with your racket, those screams could be yours. Check your shin for welts and bruises. If your shin is bruised to the point it resembles an angry thunderhead, for goodness sake, influence the universe. Challenge someone.

A player's shot selection can also be a problem. Bad shot selections can make your geeky opponents look like "Smashing" Jack Acer by leaving them abundant court openings the size of a Winnebago. You may not even know that your shot selection is pathetic. It fools many rookies by sending out subtle signals from your own lips. Do you find yourself repeating phrases like, *Good shot,* and *Is that guy lucky or what?* If so, your shot selection may be defective. Therefore, if you're not missing your shots, but you're still losing points in Costco-like bulk, get a doofus to chart you. (Reference Chapter 23.)

Fortunately for you, this moronic condition is temporary. Knowledge happens, even if you don't take lessons, chart yourself, or read *Subliminal Tennis* magazine. After about ten years of repeatedly losing matches, you will find that you have osmotically learned, via constant negative feedback, which of your shots elicit the fewest mortifying winners. It's definitely knowledge worth waiting for.

## Handling Winning

Winning, on the other hand, is easy to take. In fact, it takes an award-winning puke with all the class of an urban crack house to muck it up. But some players sure can, and do. Then, like egotistic pimps, they rub your nose in your efforts. For instance, they are careful to NOT put obvious setups away. Instead, they opt to put the ball just within reach if you run full speed. After they have had their fun and finished you off with the same degree of scorn that French chefs show for Fruit Loops, they slam the gate in your face as you walk off the court. They then issue a special edition newsletter describing your comical attempts to reach their masterfully executed shots. I suppose it only serves them right that after acting like pompous megaphones, the life-expectancy of their gloating, perfect set of teeth, statistically speaking, takes a steep nose-dive.

So the moral is, if you are looking to put some fun in your tennis try winning, or something less competitive, like the lottery. Everybody loses playing the lottery because the odds are approximately 33 *dumbillion* to one. That means you have a better chance of becoming fluent in Swahili today than you do winning the lottery. However, lottery losers get to join that enormous majority of lottery players who lose their money. This repetitive losing makes you "normal." Congratulations! (Of course being a tennis junkie, you are incurably normal that way.) Meanwhile, those occasional winning ticket holders have stepped out of the mainstream and can no longer be considered "normal." Of course, being multi-millionaires, they don't give a fig about being normal, or tennis for that matter. *Tennis matches?* They smugly scoff; *I don't need to win no stinking tennis matches!*

# 31

## *Voluntary Abuse (A Line Judge's Life)*

How do people become linespersons? Forget that. Why would anyone ever *want* to be a linesperson? Admittedly, the job description sounds fabulous:

> *Pacifist wanted to help world-class tennis players from courtside. Watch hours of great tennis. Rub elbows with tennis stars. Occasionally announce 'OUT' while gesturing in obvious fashion.*

Great! Where do we sign up? Right? Well, only if a ball-machine just rocketed a ball off your forehead. The correct answer is, WRONG! At least for everyone with cable television.

It occurred to me that the linespeople we see carefully concentrating on their lines like actors with a headache must not watch much television. If they did, they would never have become linespeople. The linespeople we see on television are embarrassed, harassed, and abused—and that's just by the ball boys and girls. If you didn't know before, I will reveal it now. Being a linesperson drives you to drink. If you already drink, it would drive you to drink MOP & GLOW.

A linesperson's duty is to impartially dispense judgements regarding where balls land on the court. A typical point goes something like this: serve, return, volley, backhand; "OUT!" the lowly linesperson bellows in his best non-partisan voice. "*WHAT?!*" shrieks the player on the losing end of the call. (The linesperson stares fixedly ahead, silently wishing for a double whiskey.) From here, a tense situation deteriorates into a powder keg of exaggerated proportion (what with the player publicly threatening extreme physical discomfort on the body of the linesperson).

The angry player then approaches the umpire's chair like Godzilla approached Tokyo and demands an *overrule*. An overrule means that the linesperson unintentionally blurted out the wrong word (a verbal typo), and the umpire must rectify it. Typically, the unruffled umpire agrees with the linesperson's call and instructs the player to play on. Agreeing with a linesperson is a supremely condescending insult to a player. After all, who is this umpire? Probably some off-duty frozen burrito distributor or Avon rep. What right has he to disagree with arguably the most talented tennis player ever to grace a tennis shoe? So, the player informs the umpire where he can stick his microphone and demands an audience with the next highest authority: the Tournament Director.

The Tournament Director is a veritable King Solomon of tennis wisdom and must be summoned from her buffet to arbitrate the dispute. On one side of the conflict is the umpire and linesperson (both are vested with the power and ability to handle these kinds of dicey calls). On the other side are the player and his entourage of coach, nutritionist, accountant, racket stringer, and personal back-rubber. The earnest Tournament Director listens patiently to the player's complaints at decibel levels that could drown out Woodstock; then she calmly directs the player to continue play.

The player is not mollified and bursts into a string of violent abuses to reveal his mounting contempt. As a first course, he will usually slam a ball into the stands. This action is quickly followed by slamming his racket on the ground. Then, to further demonstrate his scorn, he'll stomp over to the bench and begin slamming his racket into the cups with the sponsor's logo, which showers the sponsor's drink all over the ballkids. Finally, he folds his arms defiantly, plops down in the courtside chair, and refuses to play another point.

In this day and age of The Code, these ill-mannered actions call for a penalty point to be awarded to his opponent under the cumulative weight of the following unsportsmanlike infractions:

1. ball abuse

2. racket abuse

3. sponsor abuse

Ordinarily, losing a point in this manner acts as a powerful prescription that compels these raging players to straighten-up and behave more gentlemanly. However, sometimes a player with more financial assets than the Kennedys will take abuse a step farther, like yelling obscenities down at the linesperson while standing on his chest. This may draw the incredibly strong penalty of, gasp, awarding the opponent an entire game! At this point, these rabidly out of control players will usually repeat abuses one through three. They may even offer up infraction number four. Infraction number four occurs when an irate player uses his racket to slice open a major artery on the side of the linesperson's head, thereby causing blood to spill out onto the court. Infraction number four is, obviously, court abuse.

## Forfeit Rules

Now, Tournament Directors and umpires are empowered to remove players from tournaments for such disagreeable behavior. Really, it's true. All players have heard of this power. Sometimes, on their chartered flights to tropical resorts players have pondered what it would take to provoke a Tournament Director to such a rude action. Most agree that jumping into the stands and hijacking a major sponsor's box seat with a military assault weapon would do it. But, that's merely player speculation.

Realistically, being defaulted depends on the offending player's ranking. If a player's ranking is among the top five in the world, it requires a physical assault on the Tournament Director's mother with an illegal oriental martial arts weapon to trigger a default ruling. For those players ranked in the 6 to 10 range, being defaulted takes the same attack on anyone else. In the range of 11 to 50, The Code is in effect. (If you aren't sure what The Code is, don't worry about it; I can guarantee you that most pros aren't worrying about it either. Basically, it means, Play like a Swede or an Aussie. When was the last time you saw a Swede or Aussie try to impale a linesperson with his racket handle? That's right, never. They play "nice" tennis.) A player with a ranking greater than 50 had better *be* nice to the Tournament Director and umpires, and civil to the ballkids.

You can see why players that move up slowly through the rankings get along well with the tournament powers. Then again, those slow-movers don't have the talent to be in the top 10.

However, players with talent oozing out of their hair follicles that explode onto the scene, explode on the court, and explode in media interviews as regularly as Congressional fact-finding junkets to Aruba, have no respect for Tournament Directors. They figure the tournament powers are there to make life easier for them—as a sort of a lower echelon member of their personal entourage, with powers similar to the tournament-provided limo drivers or the Vice President of the United States.

So, if you were harboring any thoughts about becoming a linesperson, I suggest you think twice. Unless, that is, you are a twisted sick-o who finds deep personal fulfillment in absorbing withering abuse from some red-faced tennis maniac who refuses to play another point unless the tournament immediately replaces its complimentary Gatorade with his favorite flavor of Kool-Aid.

For the majority of us spectators, witnessing these windy tirades leave us dry and unsympathetic. However, I do believe I care to have another beer.

# 32

# *The Tournament Police*

The Tournament Police (TP) manage tennis tournaments. All tournaments use TPs, even tournaments with only two competitors. TPs are there to ensure proper association membership, proper drawing, proper scheduling, refereeing, mediation between disputants, and proper adherence to the rules (and sometimes The Code), but most notably, enforcement of the foot fault rule.

Tennis tournaments, unlike love-at-first-sight and compound interest, do not just happen. Tournaments must be planned and executed by *planners* and *executors*. These executors are normally labeled "Tournament Officials," but behind their backs, "Tournament Police."

Note: Tennis tournaments are, basically, tennis conventions where we players go to exhibit our latest state of the art losing techniques. For instance, you may dedicate months of hours of practice in an effort to forge your feeble first volley into a high percentage shot. You may even dedicate so much time on your volley that you neglect your first serve and career. As a result, your first serve percentage drops to nine percent! You can't even get a point to include a first volley! Your chances of being fired, however, are excellent.

## *Making A Tournament*

Like any living thing tournaments have a lifecycle. In the beginning, a group of local tennis movers and shakers assembles in pager-filled rooms, lined with pictures of deceased tennis players and officials, and resolve to (a) call themselves a "committee," and (b) hold a tournament.

Why hold a tournament? Let's see. To aid and abet the development of the local talent pool? Maybe. But more than likely the reason is, if you do it right, when all is said and done there is money left over. And, that money can be put to use for just about any worthwhile cause: court maintenance, new squeegees, even a vaccine for polio. If it is determined that polio already has a vaccine, then that money is available to purchase trips to Monte Carlo to meet and decide how next year's tournament revenues can be used to benefit the community.

Okay, the tournament committee has checked hotel accommodations in Monte Carlo and determined that there is a pressing need for a tournament. The next question is, when shall it be held? Some tennis-ambitious communities have a tournament almost every weekend and you must sneak a new one in between them. Then there are some dates that should be avoided altogether because, otherwise, nobody would show up. Even more alarming, nobody would pay to enter them. Christmas day, New Year's Day, and (unless it's a women's tournament) Super Bowl Sunday are examples. Therefore, committees work tournaments around these important dates.

Now, let's pretend the dates are determined. (We'll assume the committee's club will supply the courts.) So, which tennis players will play in the tournament? The best players in town? Or, perhaps in the state? The hobbyists? The hacks? All the above?

If only the best players are preferred, they will need to be enticed to play your tournament with some stiff competition, which means offering some sort of battery-operated trophies. If the hobbyists are targeted, they can be enticed to play with complimentary T-shirts. However, if all levels are selected, there will be enough players in each division (i.e., the Men's 55 With Pattern Baldness Division) to get away with supplying small plastic trophies and make a tidy profit.

Now then, we know who, where, when, and why. The entries have been sent out to the usual clubs and e-mail spam companies; and they've come back complete with personal checks that have been safely deposited somewhere in the Cayman Islands. It is time to draw up the tournament.

## *The Draw*

The first step in setting up the draw is to *seed* the players. Seeding players is the process of determining whom Las Vegas oddsmakers would pick to win the tournament, who should come in second, third, etc. To do this, the committee ranks the top players in each division according to previous tournament results. The first ranked player is seeded number one and placed at the top of the draw (although some backward communities considered it "cool" to place them at the bottom). The second seed gets the opposite slot. Then the names of the third and fourth seeds are placed in a bowl and drawn for the top and bottom semi-final slots. The quarter-finalists are drawn and so on until only the unseeded players remain. The committee then selectively places those entrants whose checks are substantially in excess of their entry fees. Finally, the unseeded players get sprinkled around in the draw like that legendary loser, Thompson Seedless.

Finally, the draw is set and the seeds have byes. A "bye" means that a player begins the tournament in the second round. If there aren't an even 8, 16, 32, or 64 entrants, some players will have to wait until the second round to begin play. Those players are seeded.

Seeds are so good, instead of letting them skewer plain vanilla hobbyists or hackers (who wouldn't know a "bye" if it waved to them), good tournament officials will let them practice an extra day with their personal coaches.

The hobbyists, meanwhile, engage in epic, three-hour battles to see who gets to be slaughtered in the next round by a seed. This is good because the two hobbyists get to play a competitive match. A tough match leaves the losing hobbyist feeling good about the tournament and willing to pay an even larger entry fee for the next year's event. The winning hobbyist then gets to see how the other half plays—up close and personal. They get to proclaim, "Nice shot" and "Love-forty," a lot.

## Running A Tournament

The day of the tournament is at hand. The Tournament Police are sitting in place behind the tournament desk playing with colored push-pins and magic markers. Their top ten priorities are:

1. check in players

2. eat doughnuts

3. assign matches to courts

4. drink coffee

5. call foot faults

6. go to lunch

7. arbitrate disputes

8. record match results

9. dust the trophies

10. ensure the tournament runs on schedule

That's right. Making the tournament run on time is last AND least. In fact, it's a ruse. If a tournament inadvertently runs on schedule its director is often hauled before the local chapter of the USTA, fiercely interrogated and ultimately accused of being a "player sympathizer." Before long, the tournament director usually sees the light (of a 300-watt halogen bulb inches from her brow), and vows to clean up her act next time by scheduling twice the number of matches as courts available. As a scheduling aid, USTA counselors strongly encourage the use of the First Seed.

The First Seed philosophy is that he/she has earned special privileges on account of being the pre-tournament favorite. For instance, the average player must report for his or her match within fifteen minutes of the scheduled time or forfeit (i.e., be discarded from the draw like used dental floss). The first seed, however, can show up hours late, intoxicated, handing out cartons of cigarettes to children, and still the tournament director will order his or her match to center court. If you are playing this seed and after waiting need to use the bathroom, the tournament director will threaten to forfeit you right then and there because, "What if everyone wanted to go to the bathroom? CHAOS!"

Seeds always play at the club or wherever the tournament is being conducted. As tournaments become more successful (e.g., more paying entrants), more courts are required to accommodate the burgeoning number of players. So, tournament officials will conspire to schedule some matches at off-site courts.

## Off-Site Courts

Off-site courts are always in bad neighborhoods where *grand theft auto* is considered legitimate job training. Courts in these areas have more cracks than a California sidewalk, and whose nets have more unintentional holes than my sock drawer. These courts are frequently made of an often gooey, always filthy, substance called *asphalt*. "Asphalt" is a word derived from the early Native American *as*, meaning 'black,' and *phalt*, meaning 'death.' The first known tennis courts of this type were unearthed in La Brea, California. Early settlers aptly called them "tar pits."

Most civilized cities have strict ordinances relegating asphalt to the streets where it belongs. Unfortunately, some uncouth and ignorant communities have constructed tennis courts with this appalling and toxic substance. And, if that was not enough, they paint lines on them in seemingly random patterns that veteran middle school coaches swear under oath are not only tennis, but also basketball and volleyball court lines. These lines radiate in all directions so that even distinguished cheaters get confused and often end up cheating themselves. "OUT!" they bellow confidently, pointing at the ball as it skips off a line. "That's the basketball free-throw line, you dipstick!"

Often you will find steel nets on these courts. The good news is they have no holes in them, unless terrorist-grade vandals have attacked them with The Jaws of Life. The bad news is every "net" ball becomes a short lob.

Steel nets are manufactured by the infamous Lob-O-Matic cartel. If a normal, ferocious stroke just ticks the top of the net, the ball will float straight up into the air like a wafting dust bunny. Obviously, players whose shots routinely clear the net by 14 feet have no problem. However, players who hit a flatter ball are often dismayed when their blurred passing shots clip the net and float that same 14 feet up in the air. These shots would probably land a mere five feet beyond the net as setups, except that your opponent has already SMASHED them away, laughing.

## *TPs As Arbiters*

Sometimes Tournament Police must act as arbiters. During a hotly contested match, disagreements can arise over the some of the rule's finer points. For example, is it legal to declare a "play two" during a point if a passing bird drops a guano on your head? Or, can you legitimately let a ball bounce twice before hitting it if you proclaim in a loud voice beforehand, "TWOSIES!?" TPs must rule on delicate matters such as these.

Some issues are tougher. Let's say you are playing a match on some obscure court and you are winning by the score 6-2, 5-0; then you win the next game. You advance to the net to shake hands. Your opponent acts stunned and insists the score is 3-3. You both yell, kick, and spit in fierce paranoia. Finally, because there are no witnesses and you can't even agree on who won the first game of the set, you call in the Tournament Police. The TP listens intently to each side's case. Since the TP cannot simply award you the match, with his best Solomon-like expression he declares the score to be 3-3. His TP reasoning is, if you had really won 6-0; you would simply run out the set again. Tournament Police do not believe in what tennisologists call *Rampaging Tank Syndrome* (RTS).

## RTS

As tennisologists define it, RTS is: *A player's manifestation of complete and utter loss of competitive effort through the application of farcical power levels while attempting the lowest percentage shots outside his or her repertoire.*

RTS manifests itself in players who are victims of unfair circumstances. Just about anything can set off RTS: a wrong line call, a broken string, a bad hair day, PMS. If I were you, I'd keep a written record of the score as you play, and have your opponent sign-off on it at changeovers.

Most tournaments cannot provide a TP for each match, so you must play by the time-honored "honor" method, meaning, you call your own lines. Obviously, some players are less honorable than others. These players are well known in player circles as "cheaters," and by TPs as "winners."

When two of these "winners" meet in a match, the result is often arguments. They won't be able to agree on the day of the week, much less line calls in the range of six inches inside the line to six inches outside the line. (Curious tennisologists are currently studying this phenomenon for publication under the working title: <u>The Effects of Straight, White Lines on Retinal-Initiated Response Mechanisms in Tennis Players</u>. Until all their data are gathered and shrewd conclusions drawn, I will be dutifully lounging poolside, ready to break their important findings to you the tennis public.)

Often, when one of these winners begins losing he or she will resort to extreme measures, like calling for a linesmon. (In this instance, to coin yet another gender-neutral term for my more sensitive readers, I have performed an a-ectomy on "linesman," and a subsequent o-graft using the "o" from "lineswoman." I then transplanted it back in to the body of "linesm_n" to refer to the unisexual TP, "linesmon.") A linesmon is endowed with great power. That power is the capability to overrule line calls by unscrupulous winners.

Around lunchtime, the supply of TPs tends to disappear. So, TPs must deputize other players or innocent passers-by to be linesmons. A sneaky opponent can ultimately take advantage of this practice in a number of underhanded ways. For instance, unless diligent, a player may find that the lines of his or her match are being called by his or her opponent's cousin or stockbroker.

## *Foot Fault Fiends*

The Tournament Police include a roving foot fault judge. These TP types stroll around the courts searching for foot fault infractions. They waltz up to your court shouting, "FOOT FAULT!" at your game-winning ace in the same tone of voice that tobacco companies are convicted. Then they walk away. Two games later, they show up again. "FOOT FAULT!" they bellow, and again walk away.

Meanwhile, your opponent is stepping into the court on HIS serve like Fred Astaire in shorts! Where is the justice? Where is the foot fault judge when he can actually be useful? Answer: watching the legs of the Women's 21 and under division players. Why? Because they can, and because justice is only a vague mind-numbing concept to TPs, not a goal.

What can a player do when this kind of injustice strikes? Well, you can bravely step up and stand back on your serve. Or, you can give the more customary response: launch into a historic case of Rampaging Tank Syndrome. It works for me.

# 33

## *Analyzing TV Experts*

How many of you watch tennis on television: Wimbledon, the US Open, the French Open? Since you are reading this book, you are obviously a hardcore tennis junkie. You probably call in sick to stay at home to watch the Bakersfield Invitational on CCSN (Country Club Sports Network), and read everything published on tennis including *Tennis Biz* magazine's annual "Sweatband Issue."

I like tennis on television. The parking couldn't be better; I'm always in the shade; I don't walk far to get something to drink; and the price is right. Hey, we under-employed tennis instructors don't receive free tickets like you megawatt CEOs. That's why so many of us campaign for politicians in favor of creating the *National Endowment for the Racket-Derived Sports* (NERDS). This organization would redistribute federal tax dollars to suffering tennis, badminton, racquetball, and squash players who make less than $68,000 a year.

Another possible program is *Sports-Stamps*. Sports-Stamps would be another federally funded, sports welfare program and would be modeled after our exemplary Food-Stamp program. This government program would provide stamps to under-privileged persons who, in turn, would exchange them for lessons or tickets to professional sporting events.

## *Television Experts*

To bring us the finest tennis coverage possible, television networks employ expert commentators who either have actual telecommunications talent or an impressive array of Grand Slam titles (rarely both). These experts take us down onto the court, over the net, and into the minds of the players to help us understand the ebb and flow of the individual dramatic moments that compose a professional match. They are there to interpret for us the many uniquely professional tennis actions, like raving uncontrollably and threatening a linesperson with used socks. It is precisely at competitive junctures such as these that the expert earns his or her pay. The expert will lean forward and expertly share with us, "He disagrees with that line call, Bob."

Aside: How many sports allow its players to intimidate the umpires? Admittedly, most other sports are team sports, so the umpire just makes the team replace the offending player and play continues. In tennis, no can do. If the umpire throws a player out, the match is over, kaput. Ticket stub-wielding fans may feel cheated and demand a compensatory souvenir, like the umpire's underwear or a bicuspid.

As I was saying, the ex-pro expert is there to give us insight into the underlying meanings during play. "Her serve is a little off today," the expert shrewdly observes after that player's ninth double fault of the first set. Or, at 6-1, 5-0, we get profound comments like, "He needs to win this game to stay alive in the match, Bob." This keen expert insight ranks up there with an expert sky-diving commentator advising the professional announcer as a sky-diver plummets toward the earth at speeds approaching *hurtling*, "He needs to get his 'chute open, Bob, to stay alive in this, uh, lifetime."

Now, these experts can't do it alone. Well, they could; but they aren't allowed. Can you imagine some well-known ex-players doing tennis play-by-play? (They will remain nameless because they have attorneys with more legal power than AT&T and just as many connections.) "Whadaya mean 'break for commercial?' I got somethin' important to say here! Stuff your commercial!" So, professional announcers who know how to go to commercial are put in the booth to guide these expert commentators. The professional announcers know a lot about talking and just enough about tennis to report which player is serving and who is ahead. Of course, our expert must remind us that the players are actually *on serve.*

## On Serve

"On serve" means that even though one player is clearly ahead by one game, they are 'virtually tied.' This tied condition occurs when players take turns winning the games in which they serve. Therefore, on the odd numbered games when they change ends of the court, one player is always ahead. "Big deal," yawns the expert. "The player trailing will be serving."

Being the server is always an important distinction, even at your club, because the server's chances of winning that game are understood to be all but assured. Moreover, only a freak accident, like the server being hit by a stray bus, could alter that inevitable outcome. In fact, it is universally assumed that no matter who the server is, he or she will sink into a deep trance, tap into that mysterious power that allows some people to understand modern art, and serve with more explosive power than weapons grade plutonium. You could be watching the girls 14 and under, and when you are told they are "on serve," you are led to believe that each girl is forcing errors from the other with her service weapon assembled by General Dynamics. More than likely, it means each girl has LOST every game she has served.

Most players don't serve 120 mph without faulting. Still, many players voluntarily smash their first 850 first serves straight into the net or back fence while attempting to hit a supersonic ace. These types of players also spend an inordinate amount of time stalking supermodels. They are of the *schizo* player type. Schizos end up putting the ball in play with a putz second serve after routinely disregarding their astrologist's advice against slamming their first serves: "Wait, young Ballhopper," they advise, "until the stars are more favorable, like in the Chinese Year of the Fruit Bat."

I prefer the experts that detail a player's match preparation: "She was out last night at Club Fabio, drinking and dancing on tables." These experts are always just-retired players. They have good national audience recognition (meaning similar to that of the Mayor of New York).

These ex-perts know the intimate scoop on the current players. Networks hire them to spice up the telecast by adding personal tidbits like, "And did you know, Bob, that Stephan's favorite color is green? I don't know many players whose favorite color is green—until payday that is. Ha, ha." Any ex-pert humor is always welcome.

After about five years or so, these ex-perts are no longer providing the intimate details of the pros' private lives. This lack of detail is the result of spending too much time in the booth with the announcers explaining the "on serve" phenomenon. Too often, they end up missing out on vital info-gathering sessions that would enable them to learn, and share with us, the sexual preferences of the latest top twenty pros. Accordingly, unless the analyst is currently popular tabloid fodder, the networks re-cast these ex-pert commentators as ex-ex-perts. The networks then quickly find themselves another just-retired player who knows the locations of peculiar birthmarks on the current crop of top pros.

The bottom line is, tennis on television is a function of its player's personalities. If the top pros are dullards with sleepy eyes, you will never know it because the television networks avoid them like real players avoid hackers. On the other hand, if a player has a sizzling personality, television cameras will follow them to the corners of the globe, including the bathroom. So, if you are a tennis player aspiring to become a professional, do us television viewers a favor and take personality lessons.

# 34

## *Dave's Guide to Cossack Tennis*

Although millions of people play tennis, a scant few can be considered *Cossack* Tennis Players. Cossack Tennis Players are a breed apart—tough and uncompromising. Cossack Tennis Players meet every obstacle head-on because they believe in overcoming them by force. These insolent players are drawn to the serve-and-volley power style of play while turning up their noses at the myriad of mere tennis-playing wimps.

Cossack Tennis Players bring to the game an assortment of deep convictions, a philosophy of morality and ethics that transcends mere winning. Often times a Cossack Tennis Player will walk off the court after losing to some runny-nose dinker, secure in the knowledge that he or she is the superior player. Why? Because Cossack players play by the Cossack code–not "The Code" that wimpifies the sport by specifying "nice" tennis. The Cossack Tennis Player's code is visceral and defines the very essence of his or her game. That code is: *destroy the enemy with repeated and uncompromising thrusts of attacking power.*

### *Early Cossacks*

Cossack tennis players are aptly named. Cossacks were an intensely independent group of like-minded people living in Russia. They lived life by their own indefinable rules—because they made them up as they went along. Is it mere coincidence that the words "Cossack" and "chaos" both begin with the letter "c"? I think not.

Cossack hobbies included shopping and riding around Russia on horseback carrying long heavy mallets and swinging them at the heads of everyone that suggested they should obey the local ordinances. If someone were to post a sign such as, "Please keep horses on trails," the Cossacks would boldly graffiti it to read, "Please keep horses oFF trails." Then they would go off-trail riding. This blatant disregard of official signs incensed the local authorities. Of course, if a community delegate attempted to confront the Cossacks about their independent riding habits, the Cossacks would respond by erupting into an invigorating polo match using the delegate's head as the ball.

After his horse, the Cossack's best friend was his mallet. Mallets were not only used for polo, but as crutches, hammers, bargaining tools on their shopping trips (that today we call *plundering*), and discouraging orderly strangers.

Cossacks didn't trust strangers. They thought strangers were far too pre-occupied with hatching new rules for some constricting *system*, like a government. Cossack always fought "the system." Whenever government officials tried to civilize them with taxes, the Cossacks convened polo tournaments.

To this day, many subgroups still exhibit Cossack-like tendencies: defiant jaywalkers, computer hackers, every small town in Montana, and even a small minority of tennis players.

You may unknowingly be a Cossack Tennis Player (CTP). Or, you may know someone who is a CTP. To finally acknowledge these unsung heroes and guardians of the Art of Tennis, I have provided a list of the behavior manifestations of the Cossack Tennis Player's philosophical code.

## Dave's Guide to Cossack Tennis Players:

**Cossack Tennis Players don't use two-handed backhands**. Two-handed backhands are for pencil-armed geeks with insecurities the size of a Peterbilt. Cossack Tennis Players would blow these geeks off the court if they didn't use both anorexic arms to hit their backhands.

**Cossack Tennis Players serve and volley**. CTPs use a powerful serve and volley to dominate and devastate their feeble-armed opponent's pitiful attempts to keep the ball in play. CTPs continually attack until the point is finished.

**Cossack Tennis Players don't play with less than three balls**. Only delusional masochistic hackers, who think they are "players," play with two, one, or no balls. CTPs often back their sport utility vehicles over players without three balls.

**Cossack Tennis Players don't wear junk brand clothes**. Only tasteless hackers wear any brand available at Scrooge-Mart or any other store where members of obscure religions pass the plate at the entrance. CTPs are on the leading edge of Italian tennis fashions. If you cannot pronounce the brand name of the clothes you wear, you are not a CTP.

**Cossack Tennis Players carry a minimum of three rackets**. Because power is the very nature of their games, CTPs must be prepared for any eventuality, such as breaking a string while hitting an overhead or breaking a frame after missing one.

**Cossack Tennis Players smash their first serves**. They know that the harder they serve, the easier the return they get to volley away while sneering. CTPs also know that if they serve hard enough, they can go weeks without having to volley at all.

**Cossack Tennis Players don't rely on slice shots**. Constant slicing is for pussyfoot pansies who can't hide their compulsive need to keep the ball in play. CTPs only slice as an approach shot or to demean their whiny opponents by making the ball bounce back to their own side of the net.

**Cossack Tennis Players bounce their overheads over the fence**. Power is the backbone of the CTP's game. CTPs demonstrate their power by trying to bounce all overheads over a fence.

**Cossack Tennis Players don't hit tactical drop shots**. The only time a CTP uses a drop shot is to completely humiliate some slack-jawed, wuss opponent with Dumbo thighs.

**Cossack Tennis Players aim shots at their opponents**. This tactic is always used as a demonstration of their utter disdain for their sniveling opponent. It is not uncommon for a CTP to launch a fuzzy yellow missile into the forehead of a wormy opponent with his second serve.

**Cossack Tennis Players go for the lines**. "Keeping the ball in play" is the hallmark of the novice and the cowardly. The only time CTPs don't aim for the lines is when they have the chance to put a hole in their cowering opponent's Child-Labor-Mart brand shirt.

**Cossack Tennis Players carry a tennis bag**. A tennis bag indicates more equipment to carry, which indicates the grim attitude with which the CTP takes the game. This means the CTP probably takes three one-hour lessons a week. More lessons means he/she knows more about the game than you, which means you are a loser with more questions than skill.

**Cossack Tennis Players don't take doubles seriously**. Doubles is for insecure momma's boys and girls who recoil from head to head competition. CTPs use doubles as a vehicle to show off their serve, overhead, poaching, and Italian designer wardrobe.

**Cossack Tennis Players don't share towels, drinks, etc.** Sharing is tantamount to aiding and comforting an opponent. CTPs scoff at their opponents. After an opponent sprains an ankle or tears knee ligaments, CTPs remind the loathsome, groveling weenie that play is continuous.

**Cossack Tennis Players don't use aluminum rackets**. Aluminum rackets are made for dullard beginning players with no imaginations. CTPs use the newest, most expensive, high-tech graphite, kevlar, and ceramic-titanium composite rackets.

**Cossack Tennis Players don't use nylon strings**. In fact, no conscious tennis player uses nylon strings after reaching puberty. Hackers use factory-installed nylon strings that are strung looser than a lace doily.

**Cossack Tennis Players don't lob**. Lobs are for wimpy baseliners who can't handle the power of a Cossack's shot. CTPs always rip passing shots, even from the back fence.

**Cossack Tennis Players don't play mixed doubles**. Mixed doubles means they must play a little *easier*. By definition, "playing easier" is for abject geeks. CTPs avoid mixed doubles unless they think they can score on their partners.

**Cossack Tennis Players never play "B" tournaments**. "B" tournaments are for wimpy neurotics that love to tell others how far they got in the draw. Cossack Tennis Players play the "A" division even if they are only "C" players. CTPs use "B" tournament entry forms to start fires or clean mud from their tennis shoes.

**Cossack Tennis Players don't say, "good shot."** The only good shots hit on the court are their own. The others are just dumb-luck shots hit by dumb-luck dinkers and deserve no comment beyond "the finger."

**Cossack Tennis Players grunt when they hit the ball**. CTPs grunt under the effort to transform the ball into a yellow cloud of sub-atomic particles. Other players utter whiny gruntettes while agonizing over keeping the ball in play.

**Cossack Tennis Players keep towels at their end of the court.** CTPs use these towels to punctuate their latest put-away by pausing to towel off, then vigorously throwing it down before smugly resuming play.

**Cossack Tennis Players complain when they miss a shot.** Every Cossack Tennis Player knows that no weaselly backcourt bozo can hit an attacking tennis shot on purpose. Therefore, the clown's shot was either a nerdy gross miscalculation, or just as likely—satanic intervention.

**Cossack Tennis Players ignore "Inner Game" techniques.** Inner game techniques are a crutch for players with weak minds and linguini serves.

**Cossack Tennis Players don't drink tap water.** CTPs always drink a commercially available sports drink, fresh-squeezed orange juice, or bottled French water with a twist of steroids.

**Cossack Tennis Players never play with strangers.** Most strange players are beginners who wouldn't know a Cossack Tennis Player if they were beaned on the forehead by his or her serve.

**Cossack Tennis Players carry extra clothes.** Extra shirts allow CTPs to look fresh and ready to whip their Salvation Army poster child opponent no matter how tired they really are.

**Cossack Tennis Players don't use the Continental grip.** The Continental grip was invented for uncoordinated nerds with obvious learning disabilities. CTPs switch grips.

**Cossack Tennis Players take all warm-up serves before the match.** All the big tournaments use this format. If it's good enough for the pros, it's good enough for the dorks and dweebs.

**Cossack Tennis Players don't play "percentage tennis."** Percentage tennis was invented by timid pseudo-intellectual geeks who are unable to "think big."

**Cossack Tennis Players know the precise string tension of their rackets.** They also know three reasons why it helps their games. This level of understanding demonstrates their superior knowledge of the game over the mental defectives who think they are tennis players just because they haven't quit yet.

**Cossack Tennis Players hate backcourt specialists.** Backcourt players are gutless cowards with parasitical strokes and an innate fear of being hit by the ball if they were to step past the "big bad" baseline.

**Cossack Tennis Players hate long rallies.** Long rallies are the stock and trade of the girl's 12 and under division and cowardly baseliners. CTPs end rallies before they start.

**Cossack Tennis Players hate clay courts.** Clay courts were devised by wimpy baseliners to handle the incoming pace of a CTP's shot for them. The only clay courts CTPs play on are the ones in Paris, Rome, or Maui.

**Cossack Tennis Players don't play on obscure courts.** Out of the way courts are for hackers and tennis twerps that prostitute all that CTPs hold dear just for the expediency of getting in some practice. CTPs strut their stuff.

**Cossack Tennis Players play with new balls.** New balls mean "power." Old balls are used by dorky hackers in hole-ridden T-shirts, plaid Bermuda shorts, and black socks to entertain their dogs.

**Cossack Tennis Players know the rules and enforce them.** If a CTP's vacuum tube-brained opponent doesn't take the time to learn the rules, he or she shouldn't be on the court. CTPs claim points when flaky opponents stop "out" balls in the air.

**Cossack Tennis Players don't believe in tournament schedules.** Wishy-washy tournament committees draw up hopeful schedules. Power-drunk tournament directors try to run on schedule. Frightened tennis wimps strive to meet tournament schedules. CTPs ignore schedules.

# 35

## *Dear Dave (Advice To The Tennislorn)*

Many tennis fans mail me asking for advice, or they simply come up to me and blurt out questions. "Dave!" they blurt, "what about blah, blah?" Or, "How do I yada, yada?" I tell them to look it up. That's the technique my mother used so often on me.

*Me*: "Mom, where do babies come from?"
*Mom*: "You're 19 years old. Look it up!"

Many of the questions I get are about tennis, and of those there are some I can answer. The following are some samples.

**Tennis Hopeful**: How do I tell my partner to move forward beyond the service line when going to the net?
—*Irritated in Illinois*
**Answer**: Dear Irritable,
Where did this worm learn to play tennis, the Institute of Consummate Paranoids? Seriously, the fear of *death by tennis ball* is a common psychosis that pervades many tennis clubs. When these poor psychotic dim bulbs see the little yellow fuzzy ball zoom toward them at speeds approaching "soil erosion," their paranoid little brains translate the sight into a savage and dreadful monstrosity. For psychos, it's simple: stand behind the service line and they see a cute ball of fuzz. Inside the

service line they see something akin to flesh-eating, blood-drooling killer bees. Hey, that's why they're psychotics.

Tennisologists have conducted several experiments to find a remedy for this debilitating fear of being struck by a fuzzy tennis ball. So far, in their efforts to desensitize the volley-phobic, tennisologists have tried tying them to stakes erected inside the service line and asking a dozen hormone-charged teenage boys to practice serving at them. The only result was that the teenage boys became tired.

Tennisologists then tried plying these poor dysfunctional volleyers with adult beverages. This technique got the players inside the service area all right, but many side affects were observed, such as the test subjects failed to stop approaching the net until they had tripped over it. Other subjects failed to contact the ball entirely, even when they could find it. Some even seemed unsure of where they were and what they were doing. Still others began making passes at the dedicated tennisologists. Follow-up tests are being planned.

Until our esteemed tennisologists have solved this riddle, move to another state and join a club there.


**Tennis Hopeful**: Why do I always lose?—*Larry in Louisville*
**Answer**: Dear Larry,

A profound question. A question of both breadth and depth. A question that swims in a sea of questions: Who am I? Why am I here? Why are there gophers?

To seek the answers to these questions is to seek one's self. To know one's self is to be one with one's self. To be one with one's self is to be alone. Why do you want to be alone? What dark, loathsome secret do you hide? I ran a routine check with the police. You are clean except for the unpaid parking tickets. I think you should see a shrink. Or, you might consider some other fruitful activity, like truck farming.

**Tennis Hopeful**: How do I tell my doubles partner her game stinks?
—*Annoyed*

**Answer**: Dear Ann,

There are several ways to get your opinion of her game across to your partner. Gift certificates for tennis lessons have been known to convey this delicate message. However, the price of lessons may be more than you are willing to spend. If you are like I am, 10 cents is more than you are willing to shell out.

The next most accepted method is to undertake hitting as many of her shots as humanly possible. Poach on her every serve. Cut across on every ball hit to her side of the court. This method tends to break down, however, when used on a partner with an IQ approaching latex paint.

Stronger arguments may be required. If so, at the start of your match, declare an *emergency democracy*; then try to arrange with your confused opponents to perform all of your team's service returning. Or, if your partner is a little sluggish moving to the proper area of the court, you can bean her with the ball from behind. This type of negative reinforcement definitely works well on dogs.

**Tennis Hopeful**: Why can't I get my first serve in?—*Serveless In Seattle*

**Answer**: Dear SIS,

First, let's make sure you know WHERE to serve the ball. Many people just throw the ball up and swat it. If the ball lands anywhere inside any of the lines they figure it's good. Subsequently, they are surprised and sometimes hurt when their hysterical opponents signal their serve was "out" while rolling on the court laughing.

If you think you know where to serve, then you may be doing the "how" part wrong. The next time you play, take a look around. If everyone but you is holding the skinny part of the racket and hitting with the flat stringy part, try it their way.

I suspected another reason you miss your first serve could be a medical tennis condition commonly called *Geekosis*. Therefore, I consulted with a pricey tennisologist. He agreed with me and suggested you may, indeed, be suffering from *Terminal Geek Syndrome* (TGS) or Geekosis. TGS is a congenital disease with no known cure. However, a few teaching professionals are claiming some remedial success with an intense program of lessons, practice, and back rubs. They report that after years of this regimen, TGS sufferers can lead a relatively normal tennis life.

Since we're wondering if TGS is the reason that you can't get your serve in. Let's administer a little self-test and see.

## *Dave's TGS Self-Test:*

You may have TGS if:

1.   You not only miss your first serve, but your second serve, and every other shot that involves hitting the ball with your racket.

2.   You cannot open a can of tennis balls without having to apply a tourniquet to stop the bleeding.

3.   You walk into the net pole when you change ends of the court.

4.   When you bend over to put on your socks, you miss.

5.   You poke yourself in the eye with your toothbrush while brushing your teeth.

If you suspect you may be a sufferer, see your tennis pro immediately! He or she can set up a program of regular lessons and automatic bank withdrawals that will help you become a normal functioning member of your club's 3.0 ladder, or a destitute homeless person, whichever comes first.

There is absolutely no shame in having TGS. Some of the finest people to have ever quit the game suffered from it. I'm sure you have never heard of Leonard "Le'Nerd" Claude. That's because he quit. Mr. Claude is best known for establishing *Geeks Anonymous* (GA).

Geeks Anonymous is a support group dedicated to helping geeks live with their geekiness. They meet to support each other in a room of beanbag chairs.

If you're a geek, remember: you're not alone. Everyday, thousands of geeks, just like you, eat their meals with plastic spoons. So, walk carefully over to the phone and call GA at 1-800-IM-A-GEEK.

Sometimes I don't get questions at all. Occasionally, I get progress reports, or a revelation such as this one:

*Dear Guru Dave,*

Hello. My name is Asis Hartusi Platoo. People call me "Ace." I have been the last eight months in Tibet, Kansas, sitting atop a silo, thinking. What about, you may ask, was I thinking there atop a silo in Tibet? I was thinking that I was requiring more than a loincloth only. Also, I contemplated the tennis. I studied its every facet, from the simplicity of the rally to the mystery of the shock damper. I became one with the spirithead of the game. I looked at the tennis from both sides now, from yin and yang, and still somehow it's the tennis' illusion. Wait! I am thinking I am channeling Judy Collins.

Now I continue. I was seeking for the tennis' irreducible meaning. Well, I have noticed it! Yes, it is true. Oh, happy day! It was descended upon my brain during an evening storm of hail. Now, I give to the players of the tennis through you, my guru, free with no obligation, the meaning. Here it is: winning. Yes, WINNING!

Is this not most surprising? My country-peoples have always thought that it was "the struggle" from which glorious enlightenment was obtained and poverty strengthened. But, I see they have been misled by the followers of Tayktoo, Giver of Gamesmanship.

I am saying that winning IS the path to enlightenment; and enlightenment, once achieved, can bring upon one's self much commercial endorsements.

What then, precisely, is winning? Winning is to fail to lose! Losing is a negative that has itself been negated in a reversal to great fortune! Simply, winning is beating your eel-like opponent into so much ash of the incense!

How then to win? Winning comes with much sacrifice of one's sweat to Perspira, Goddess of Muscle Cramps. Winning requires gallons of patient sacrifice to obtain enlightenment and endorsement. However, enlightenment without endorsement can be self-realized by entering into competition with a player of the tennis who has sacrificed less than yourself.

I am saying to you and the readers about the tennis, when you go onto the court to play the tennis, winning should be upon your brain like stripes upon the tiger.

Go now, with yourselves. Contemplate the tennis. Look at it from both sides now, from yin and yang, and...Hello? Good-bye. I am thinking I must go now to Judy on channel waiting.

"Ace"


Dear "Ace,"

Thanks for the insight. Winning is a quaint secret only a few million players know. As for me, instead of endorsements via winning, I went the self-subsidized book-writing route. Consequently, my poverty is strengthening daily.

# 36

## *Tennis & Engineers?*

Often, teaching members of your own family is like cutting off your nose with a chainsaw: it's loud and it's painful. I am currently teaching my 12-year-old daughter to play tennis. Being young, she is still largely coachable. Thank goodness.

I also try, once a year or so (when the urge to be selfless overwhelms me), to help my wife in some of the finer points of tennis. I say "finer points" because she is a good player. As an outline, my wife, Molly, is a 4.5-5.0 on the NTRP scale of tennis skill. (NTRP is a rating system that helps better players identify those geeks and dweebs that they wouldn't be caught dead playing.) Here in Southern California, my wife plays in the "A" and 5.0 leagues. She has only been playing tennis since college and has only modest match play experience. Still, she is an excellent athlete and a determined competitor with an insatiable desire to improve. She is also a natural-born and university-trained engineer.

Of all the qualities about my wife and her game that I have profiled, being an engineer is the most pertinent.

### *Engineers*

Engineers are straightforward and task-oriented. If you were to perform a task that did not contribute in any measurable way toward accomplishing your goal, even a goal as ordinary as eating a bowl of cereal, they would roll their eyes and throw up their hands. They would think you had just embarked down a path of such inexcusable naiveté, even outright stupidity, that you required a corrective lobotomy.

Engineers are very thorough, as any engineer will assert in an earnest ad hoc lecture complete with impromptu visual aids. You do not just "have a bowl of cereal." That concept is shallow, shallow, *shallow*. What you have is a *problem*. You must, therefore, employ a methodology that engineers call *problem solving*.

"Problem solving" was contrived by ancient engineers way back when forced labor was fashionable in order to maximize results (goals) while minimizing unnecessary actions (fun). The people who built the great pyramids in Egypt were wonderfully efficient engineers. In fact, instead of taking up valuable time to let the workers file out of a finished pyramid, they found they could save time if they just sealed them in.

So, how do engineers function outside of the workplace? Well, let's examine the bowl of cereal example. First, let me describe my old way of eating cereal: I would go into the kitchen and, (1) grab the first clean-looking bowl around. (2) Put it down on the nearest flat surface. (3) Pour cereal in the bowl. (4) Open the refrigerator; discover we didn't have any milk; and (5) pour the cereal back into the box (spilling some cereal parts between the counter and the stove). Or, if I had the milk, I would (4) pour the milk in the cereal. And, (5) fish around in the box for 45 seconds trying to find the neat little toy (that my cereals contain) until my cereal soaked up the milk supply and turned into a squishy mush.

Now, since my wife's many lectures on Kitchen Engineering Principles for the Complete Boob, I have learned the engineer's approach to having a bowl of cereal. Here it is for you lay types:

*First*, define your problem:

Problem: You are hungry.

*Second*, define the objective:

Objective: Eat a bowl of cereal.

*Third*, map out the solution:

Solution: (1) Measure milk and cereal supplies to ascertain if sufficient quantities of both exist to make a "bowl." (2) Determine cleanliness of cereal tools (bowl and spoon to artists and laypersons). If your tools are clean, continue at Step 4. If not, (3) clean your cereal tools. (4) Pour cereal into bowl. (5) Determine impermeability of all flat kitchen surfaces.

Now, here is where it gets tricky. Let's say your kitchen is like mine. It has tile counters, a wooden cutting board drawer, and a couple of glass or plastic cutting boards. You must now set your bowl down on the proper surface. That surface must be one that resists liquid spills. I don't mean just any liquid-resistant surface in your kitchen. I mean the MOST resistant.

Do you understand the danger involved in pouring a liquid over a tile-covered countertop? I didn't. Now I know. The tiles have grout between them! House builders secretly use cheap, milk-absorbing grout between their nuclear bombproof ceramic tiles to pad their already scandalous profits! Therefore, the correct pouring surface is (immediately apparent to any engineer): the glass and plastic cutting boards.

You engineers may not realize this, but impermeability is not a relevant notion to laypersons. Lay people think, "Hey, it's hard. It's a countertop. It's made to put things on. What's the big deal?" Poor, ignorant lay people. To engineers, impermeability is much more than an idea. It is an *Engineering Principle.* It's also an Engineering Principle that all Engineering Principles trump all Lay Concepts. Happily, after a couple of years of intense Kitchen Engineering therapy, under the charge of any engineer, a layperson may be able to care that a wooden cutting board absorbs liquids faster than the other flat surfaces in the kitchen.

For those of you with Formica or other type of solid countertop, there is another Engineering Principle. It states that it is easier and cheaper to replace the liquid-stained cutting boards than it is to replace a liquid-stained Formica countertop. Never mind that milk will stain neither. What if you were pouring sulfuric acid? It's the Engineering Principle that's involved here.

Where was I? Oh yes, step (6) pour milk into cereal tool, then (7) eat promptly and efficiently (without reading the cereal box), thereby minimizing any unnecessary cereal transition into *crisplessness*. To you lay people that means, 'get soggy.' This method requires more steps, but that's what engineers are good at: creating more work.

Incidentally, my wife is holding my chocolate chip cookies hostage until I perform the public service of informing everyone that she is starting a group called, *Engineeranon*. It's a support group for engineers with non-engineering type spouses. Their toll-free number is 1-800-WHY-ME-GOD.

## *Tennis Playing Engineers*

Which brings me back to my wife, the tennis player. When my wife asks questions about tennis, I now know they are actually engineering inquiries disguised as tennis questions. For instance, she may ask, "What do I do with a forehand just inside the baseline?" If I try to answer that question as a layperson, I quickly learn through her unsolicited qualifying data that she was really asking something else. Something like, "What do I do when I have to hit a 4.2 foot high forehand, from 1.6 feet inside the baseline, and my opponent is standing on a diagonal vector toward the cross-court corner, 3.5 feet from the center?"

Having used the traditional lay methodology of trial-and-error-until-something-works, I have learned that she does not understand broad and ambiguous terms such as *deep* and *high*. After all, mathematically speaking, there are an infinite number of discrete points between "ankle high" and "knee high." For that matter, it is only her selfless benevolence that allows her to compromise from the obvious reality of these innumerable points to the less definitive finite set of heights:

*waist high, elbow high, shoulder high, head high, over-your-head,* and *Robert Downy Jr. high.*

In short, she wants to hear me answer her tennis questions like an engineer: in terms of angles of trajectory, stroke vectors, velocities in MPH, and success percentages. Me. Yeah, right. I'm the guy she had to train to eat a bowl of cereal.

P.S., After a few years of teaching my daughter the various strokes, the one thing that sticks out in her mind is: "I can't learn from Dad." She could be walking out the door to play the finals of a televised tournament in high heels and I have learned to bite my tongue. Still, it's better than a nose-ectomy with a chainsaw.

# PART IV
## Tennis Ads & Ins

o o o o o o o o o o o o o o o o o o o o o o o o o o o o

"May the lines be with you"

—*Luke Linewalker*

# 37

## Courting Disaster (Indoors & Out)

There are two major types of club tennis players, *outdoor* and *indoor*. These two types of players, sometimes called "outies" and "innies," require a couple of differing abilities to be successful. To succeed as a tennis player in and out of doors, players must harness them both as they would a pair of charging yaks.

### Outies:

The ability that an outdoor player requires most is the ability to be lucky. "The Great Outdoors" is absolutely brimming with what meteorologists call *elements*. These elements, such as rain, sleet, cyclones, molybdenum, and monosodium glutamate can have a deleterious affect on a tennis match. The sun can be blinding. The wind can come howling over the court. (And if the court is missing its windscreens, the local tennis snobs will gawk and further mock your richly maligned backhand.) Temperatures can vary wildly from unbearably tropical to bone-chillingly arctic, thereby causing dyslexic fashion statements.

Outdoor tennis is a crapshoot. You don't know what's going to happen. Therefore, outdoor players depend on information groups like Weather 'R' Us (WRU). Originally started by failed members of Gamblers Anonymous, this organization was established to warn suburban gardeners of impending hailstorms in the form of the newsletter, *Hail To The Cheap*. The group has expanded and now also serves to warn working people of impending lost weekends. Tennis players use it to track looming lost matches.

Outdoor courts can become unmercifully weathered. Cracks wreak havoc on bounces. Weeds sprout up like, well, weeds. Sand gets blown under foot and tennis ball lint flies into searching eyes. Rain leaves puddles so enormous Moses couldn't part them with The Holy Squeegee.

Yes sir, outdoor tennis is hell. There are just too many ways that Mother Nature can take your opponent's side and cause you to lose your concentration, your backhand, and your electrolytes. For instance, mosquitoes. Mosquitoes are rapacious, blood-sucking insects that leave itchy welterous knots on your legs, arms, and neck. They frequent tennis courts because evolution has taught them that sweaty human beings issuing loud, angry words, while chasing what appears to be a Godzilla-sized pollen spore, will not notice as they are being systematically depleted of blood until they pass out while lobbing.

Other insects don't mind a distracted tennis player either, like flies. Flies love flowing sweat. They quickly abandon whatever pile of disgusting filth they are reveling in whenever they whiff that musky blend of gut string and sweat. And bees. Bees are highly attracted to yellow balls of fluff and become enraged, slavering, stinging beasts when you swat the object of their ardent desire ten bee-miles away.

Often fallen leaves will litter your outdoor court. Leaves have a dual effect. They cause all moving objects to skid, like the ball you were about to stroke for a winner or the foot you just planted to change direction. They also cause sincere tennis players to hand over points. These earnest dupes stop play in the middle of a point because they thought they saw, in the corner of their eye, the neighboring court's ball maliciously poised on their baseline like a shadowy gargoyle.

Sometimes native wildlife present hindrances to players. In Florida, alligators lurk silently in the lush underbrush, ready to hinder those tasty tennis players as they dash for an open court. In Washington, returning salmon leap from rivers onto riverside courts with utter disregard for the score.

On urban and suburban courts it's even rougher. Urban/suburban courts are located in the natural habitat of wild roving packs of teenagers. These gangs (slogan: "If it moves, destroy it. If it doesn't move, destroy it. If it's still standing after that, spray paint it."), do not specifically target tennis courts. I mean, they don't hold organized meetings:

*Gangster #1*: "Mr. Gangleader. I move that tonight, after the Tonight Show, we trash and vandalize the city tennis courts on the corner of Che and Guevara."

*Gangleader*: "Motion to trash and vandalize the city tennis courts on the corner of Che and Guevara. Do I hear a second?"

*Gangster #2*: "I second; and I further move that we knock over the 7-11 across the street for dessert and petty cash."

*Gangleader*: "All in favor of trashing the tennis courts and knocking over the 7-11 signify by saying 'aye'."

*Gang*: "Aye!"

*Gangleader*: "Motion is carried. Members will reconvene at the corner of Che and Guevara at thirteen hundred hours with implements of destruction. If anyone requires a new implement, please stop by a hardware store and 'liberate' one."

So, these packs of adolescents, that deal in drugs and black market acne cream, wander mindlessly onto public courts and, as frequently happens, the soberest one announces that the court does not appear to be moving. With this revelation, they strive for five minutes to pull the net posts out of the ground. Exhausted, they then look at each other and grin. As one, they quickly whip out cans of spray paint from under their bandannas and begin writing the name of their gang in the service boxes and on windscreens. Of course, since they haven't been to school since the third grade, no one knows how to spell it. And, since all are experiencing the first-hand effects of substance abuse, it looks like cursive Korean. So no one can read what they "tagged." (**Dave's note**: That's probably why gangs use colors. They learn colors in *first* grade.)

Finally, the guy with the glassiest eyes stares at the court thoughtfully and concludes that, yes, the court is, in fact, moving. In a stroke of accidental empiricism, one of the dropouts suggests they conduct an experiment to determine what is moving underneath the court. So, after hammering away at the court surface for ten minutes with the biggest rock they can successfully lift, the gang decides it would be easier to simply go to the edge of the court and look. "Dirt!" they answer proudly, and walk out the gate wondering what the question was. On the way out they lob empty beer bottles onto the court in a contest to determine who can form the largest splash of broken glass.

**Dave's Additional Note of Social Concern**: If we, as a society, were only compassionate enough, we could redirect illegal gang activities into a kinder, gentler madness. We could pass a special spray paint tax that would fund The Gang Olympics. Gangsters representing various "turfs" would assemble from all over the country to compete in diverse events. After the traditional opening ceremonies of lighting a liquor store ablaze with the traditional Molotov Cocktail, events would include: the previously described *Glass Splash Competition*, *Shoplifting*, *Breaking and Entering*, *Team Looting*, *Interstate Flight*, *Free-Style Tagging*, *Cross-Country Car-Jacking*, and *Drive-by Shooting* (wherein the more non-targets you hit, the more you score).

Playing tennis in "the great outdoors" isn't so great.

## Innies:

Indoor courts are considerably more civilized. Indoor courts are cared for by conscientious housekeeping professionals toting whisk-brooms and dustpans. Indoor courts never have cracks, weeds, puddles, or insects more threatening than ants. And, these courts always have drinking water readily available. Why? Because people pay sizable amounts of disposable income to play on indoor courts, and they insist on having them in prime shape. No weeds. No puddles. The only thing these players want that the club does not provide is a lob.

Because indoor courts are by definition 'under a roof,' indoor tennis players must demonstrate the ability to aim their shots a smidgen finer than their outdoor counterparts. Specifically, tennis courts with roofs mean those tennis players with lobs must place the ball between the ceiling and their opponent's overhead. Indoor lobs must be performed with the same meticulous skill that those in the US Congress demonstrate regularly by raising our taxes and then convincing us to re-elect them.

Interestingly, indoor courts have been proven to have psychological benefits. When you first hit a ball on an indoor court, the sound of that impact reverberating powerfully off the walls reminds you of the sounds heard at Wimbledon's Centre Court: BAM. You swing proudly and hear that intoxicating BAM as the ball zips off your racket strings. You feel good. You feel strong. Your self-esteem builds with each sound of a shot magnificently struck. You hurry to pick up balls and to change sides. You are pumped. "Damn the game plan," you say. "I'll serve and volley!" Then, Wham! BAM! Shake their hand. You lose as usual. The snobs chortle. Then you realize that indoors may sound good, but outdoors has all the really good excuses.

# 38

## *Fast Times on Fast Courts*

Fast courts are annoying. They are totally unlike women and cars where "fast" means you drive to a quickie quickly. Balls don't bounce off fast courts; they skid. That means balls must be scraped off the court surface like warm chewing gum. Very irritating.

If you regularly play on nice, normal-surfaced courts, and then due to an unruly brain spasm decide to play on a fast court, you are guaranteed to look and hit like a black-belt geek. You will be hitting balls into the nets of the adjacent courts, if you're lucky. Frequently, the ball will go scooting under your racket like a cockroach late for curfew.

By the way, it's the same for those of you who climb to mountain resorts like Upper Klass to play at altitude. There is simply no way to prepare yourself for a ball that is traveling an order of magnitude faster toward your sensitive and delicate bodily areas. Even if your brain keeps reminding your body to be ready to react early, your body just yawns, "Hey, tennis is tennis. Don't be such a wimp."

Where did fast courts come from? They came from the same people who institutionalized "taxation without representation." Members of the All England Club at Wimbledon invented fast courts. Instead of subjecting themselves to the random bounces of the then state of the art hardcourt surface, cobblestone, or common dirt with its obtrusive weeds and clods, Wimbledonians realized that balls bounced truer on a smartly cut lawn. Of course, to cut the grass that finely they had to turn a herd of goats loose on the courts. After that, bad bounces only occurred when balls landed on one of the goat's droppings. Satisfied, England then embarked on a campaign to create an empire of grass courts. In just a few decades, England could proudly boast, "The grass is always greener on the English Empire."

When I think of fast-court players I think of those tall, bazooka-armed, boom boxes of muscle types. You know, those Mr. Universe sorts that can drive tennis balls through their opponent's strings like a motorcycle through a car wash. They then charge the net like a pit bull to a poodle so they can bounce thunderous overheads over the back fence and into puddles of standing water. I hate that.

At the same time, I admire those power players and frequently like them. It's not their fault that their serves make mine look like I'm playing backyard badminton. (Note to all of you bird-bashing badminton players who own enough rackets to sacrifice one over the top of a blasphemer's head, I said *backyard*. That's because *real* badminton players play indoors. They power the bird back and forth like some feathered, heat-seeking missilette. Then they intersperse their smash rallies with copious dinks that are designed to drain their opponent's strength down to the point where a strong breeze can topple them onto the floor. However, since they play indoors and out of the wind, either the first player to reach 15 points wins or the first player to fall into the net, without the strength to get free, loses.)

I always wanted to play like those steroid-laced, yogurt-powered players do—with a big serve and a strong volley. Only two things keep me from it: a big serve and a strong volley.

Oh sure, I have volleys. They're perky little volleys that bounce straight up like Tinkerbell with a boob-job just past the service line. My sprite little volleys allow my opponents to rush forward like a starving car salesman and crack passing shots down the line before I can even *split-step*. (The "split-step" is a technique devised by compassionate tennis pros for the terminally geeky. It allows the maximum reaction time, from the instant your opponent rockets his forehand at your chest, to the moment you should have been able to hit the ball. Unfortunately, the terminally geeky are unable to comprehend it or its benefit and so they don't execute this maneuver in a timely fashion. Rather, geeks seem to hold an internal debate about whether the ball should be hit as a forehand, a backhand, with their free hand, or whether an instant forfeit is still possible. The debate soon ends, however, when the ball forces the air from their lungs.)

The other thing I lack, the major thing, is a powerful serve. With my incredible eye for the conspicuous (my wife informs me I would only notice her new haircut if it were on the cover of *Playboy*), I noticed that the better serves elicit the weaker returns. I have even witnessed players with serves so enormous they could go entire tournaments without volleying. Most of those servers were strapping dudes over six feet. Since I was almost 5'10" I deluded myself into thinking my weenie serve was a function of my shorter height. I ignored, as runaway sideshow freaks, those smaller players who could serve balls through plexi-glass. So, instead of dueling the big servers with my hardest first serves (which brought smirks of bemusement to their steroid-induced, five o'clock-shadowed faces), I used my "power" slice serve.

It didn't take long for me to figure out that my power slice serve wasn't powerful enough. Following it to the net meant being passed quickly and consistently. The experience was similar to running out of gas at rush hour on an eight-lane freeway. Cars go zipping past your doors like a stampede of spooked bison around a lone tree, daring you to safely reach the shoulder of the road. Therefore, I opted to stay back and delay the end of the point by meekly setting up my opponent for his inevitable aggressive return of serve. I would serve and wait in my ready position, hoping to get a good jump on the return so I could run down the ball, pick it up, and use it to serve with again the next point.

I was able to hold my own with average baseliners and with those serve-and-volleyers that volleyed by moving to the ball in violent uncoordinated spasms. I usually lasted a couple or more rounds in tournaments. Eventually, I would run into someone who knew how to serve and volley effectively. Wham! Bam! Overhead SLAM! Dazed, I would mumble, "Am I still in the doubles?"

In the end, I could read the writing on the windscreen. Serve and volley was the style the good players played and they played it best on fast courts. I was a serve and volley wannabe on the outside peering in through the holes in the windscreen of tennis.

## Connors And Borg

Then Jimmy Connors and Bjorn Borg came along. Suddenly, those two guys demonstrated that any player with surgically precise strokes, gifted foot-speed, boa constrictor concentration, and alas, a two-handed backhand, could beat world-class serve-and-volleyers. More-over, those two guys absolutely dismantled the serve-and-volley pros and at the same time made them look as if they were playing in ortho-pedic shorts.

Connors crushed the opposition with the above-mentioned game and by intimidating opponents with his indomitable spirit. Borg did it by quietly pounding topspin strokes by his opponents until their games turned into pulp.

Connors and Borg had an interesting relationship: silent. During interviews, reporters would ask Connors, "What do you think of Borg's chances in his next match?" Annoyed, his answer was always the same: "Borg is Borg." How profound. You may be wondering what he meant. You are not alone; mental health experts do too.

Here, revealed now, for the first time, is what Connors actually meant when he said, "Borg is Borg." Essentially, it means, "Borg is Swedish" or "Borg likes pizza." I don't think he meant it as an indict-ment in the same way as that old, chicken sandwich commercial, "Parts is parts." And, it certainly couldn't be construed as a compliment. Therefore, he was simply and safely stating the obvious.

Stating the obvious is easy to do. Anyone can do it. But, who wants to risk a tongue sprain?

On second thought, I suppose it could prove useful in airports and at theme park entrances. You know, where robed people with painted faces and very short hair thrust themselves in your path and threaten you with several hours of small talk in the hope that you will pay them to leave you alone. Flatly stating the obvious may disarm them. The following are a couple of illustrations:

*Robed Person:*      "Hello. Would you like a flower?"

*You:*      "Squirrels climb trees."

Or when stopped for speeding...

*Police Officer:*      "Hey, chief, do you know how fast you were going?"

*You:*      "Cars have doors."

You get the picture. However, if you have fallen on your head, dislocated your brain, and somehow feel compelled to experiment with this sort of response technique, mind my caution:

**Dave's Caution**: Use this response technique with close friends and family only. (Note: In-laws are not considered family.) Never attempt this during a job interview, and positively never, *ever*, at a sanity hearing.

# 39

## *Slow Courts (Make Me Tired)*

I am not fond of slow courts either. Slow courts were devised by people with insignificant serves to help them compete against the blitzkrieging serve-and-volley types. When the hordes of serveless little dweebs (whom you used to be able to overpower) discovered slow courts, they moved in faster than a foul neighbor with lice-breeding teenage felons.

Slow courts transform an otherwise perfectly good tennis ball by expanding its fuzz frontier until it resembles an extremely moldy grapefruit. Worst of all, slow courts have aided and abetted the infestation of two-handed backhands.

Now I realize some players don't mind playing with balls as large as coconuts. But, I also realize that some people are drug dealers and hookers, or belong to a cult that believes in alien love gods from the planet *Bardot*. However, those players who don't mind playing with balls with more hair than a shampoo commercial, also love playing on slow courts.

Tennisological studies, via research grants from the USTA's Department of Superior and Municipal Courts, have shown that players that inhabit slow courts are themselves usually small and fast. In fact, these players give normal people like you and me the unmistakable impression that we are playing rodents in sweatbands.

Of course, slow courts proved useful when I played serve-and-volley type opponents. I would stay behind the baseline and wing winners past them, unless they could actually volley, or until they stayed back, too. The point is I lost regularly, regardless of court type.

Once I played a guy on the slowest slow court I have ever seen. I'm talking "acoustic ceiling." Really. This court looked like a cement acoustic flooring. Remember when all new homes were erected with acoustic ceilings? Those ceilings were so ordinary and prevalent that we referred to them as (unbuttered) "popcorn," partly to assist those fashionable and trendy homeowners who needed to be regarded as "above average." Yes, those ceilings became so common that they eventually became unfashionable in trendy homes. Today, nouveau fashionable and trendy homeowners hire non-trendy workers to take down the "popcorn" ceiling and put up, you got it, "it's-so-old-it's-new" plaster. Of course, they don't actually call it *plaster*. That's far too ordinary. Now it's re-marketed as something new and expensive, like *Sassoon's Wall Reviver and Molding Compound*.

Needless to say, but I will, acoustic ceiling courts are SO slow, they have earned the ultimate *suicidal* rating by the Association of Serve and Volleyers (ASV).

You may not be familiar with the ASV's court ratings, so I will introduce them. I am also providing you with court ratings as devised by the Society of Baseliners (SOB), and how they compare one to the other. If you are not a member of either one of these groups, don't worry. I am even providing the traditional, non-denominational categories at no additional charge, and against my nature.

## COURT RATING TERMS BY ORGANIZATION

| Non-Denominational | ASV | SOB |
| --- | --- | --- |
| Slow | Retarded | Homey |
| Very Slow | Comatose | Resort |
| Extremely Slow | Suicidal | Sex on the Beach |
| Normal | Androgynous | Androgynous |
| Fast | Dart Board | Excedrin |

| *Non-Denominational* | *ASV* | *SOB* |
| --- | --- | --- |
| Very Fast | Shooting Gallery | Migraine |
| Extremely Fast | Stealth Bomber | Laser Lobotomy |

The ASV and SOB are tennis court rivals. They are similar to the Corvette and Porsche car clubs that used to race each other around our nation's parking lots. These two car clubs would regularly get together to speed around tracks designed by one of the clubs and that favored their particular car. Afterwards they would sit back, drink high-octane beverages, and show off their favorite car pin-ups. They got very excited. I think they must have been suffering from some type of sexual dysfunction. Ha, ha. Just kidding! I like cars as much as the next guy–that likes girls! (Note to self: Just in case, cross off "jay-walking" from list of extreme sports to try this year.)

The ASV and SOB have chapters in almost every major city. These chapters lobby the Parks and Recreation Departments for construction and re-surfacing rights of their pet court types. You should see some of these lobbyists. Ooo-la-la. (Definitely no dysfunction here!)

All seriousness aside, slow courts can be hazardous to your health. Take the acoustic ceiling court I described. Tennis players who have fallen down on that Cuisinart surface are disfigured beyond all recognition. They require major reconstructive surgery just to be able to JOIN a support group for the aesthetically impaired.

## *Clay Courts*

To reap the benefits of a slow court while avoiding the cost of cosmetic surgery, it is worthwhile to play on clay courts. Clay courts don't grind your knees into compost. In fact, playing on clay courts is delightfully comfortable, like betting with other people's money. The only thing a clay court does is deposit a fine colored dust all over your shoes. This dust is like fairy dust. It has the magical benefit of making you look as if you have been playing in exotic places such as Paris or Acapulco.

This upscale look makes you appear to have a lifestyle of the rich and famous, or at least plaster ceilings, both of which lead to new and close friends of the opposite sex.

In Southern California, clay courts are extremely rare. They say clay courts require too much up-keep in this parched climate. They say clay courts need to be constantly watered down to keep them from drying up and blowing away. Perhaps. Personally, I'm inclined to believe those who know somebody, who say that we have an exaggerated number of hardcourts in Southern California because the ASV hires those girls who fail as actors or models to lobby for them in Sacramento.

Southern California is home to a diverse group of tennis courts. Many players here even enjoy playing on grass. You can readily identify those grass-court enthusiasts because they blurt out comments like, *Isn't it amazing how the ball just kind of…you know, BOUNCES?* If the shot you hit was an unmistakable winner, they'll hazily announce, *Far out, man,* which means, 'Excellent shot, dude.' However, serious Type A opponents typically pop an aneurysm and explode into their favorite violent, anti-social behavior when they hear it describing their blistering winners. Those Type A's won't even stop for the two-fingered "peace" sign—unless you poke them in the eyes with it.

So, after a painful self-examination of court types and my own game's style, I have come to realize that there is no type of court that favors my style of tennis, that being the old style. This old style has proven to be the tennis equivalent of an evolutionary dead-end, like the Neanderthals. But, I continue to play anyway. And, as far as court types go—any court in a storm. However, I am ready and willing to listen to all arguments. Any ASV lobbyists out there? We'll do lunch.

# 40

## *Racket Tech*

Have you ever asked yourself, a friend, a relative, or even the kid who delivers your newspaper the hypothetical question, *could Edberg have beaten Laver?* I am using Stefan Edberg as a "modern" comparison because he was the number one player in the world not *that* long ago. But mainly I chose him because he is my wife's idea of the perfect guy, and she promised to bake me something every time I mention his name. If you want to indulge in some hypothetical thinking of your own, use the number one ranked player today and Rod Laver, or Billie Jean King.

I chose Rod Laver as my "old" number one because I always admired him, and he has a fabulous name for an athlete (as does Billie Jean). Both Rod Laver and Billie Jean King are deservedly in the Athlete's Name Hall of Fame. They are enshrined along with such names as Babe Ruth, Willie Mays, Joe Montana, World B. Free, and others.

Incidentally, the Classical Music Name Hall of Fame has a totally different standard for entry into its hallowed halls–the names must be foreign or foreign sounding. Hence, Americans George Gershwin and Yo-Yo Ma are in it. Of course, virtually all classical composers and artists are inducted by law. Mozart, Tchaikovsky, Pavarotti, and the Vienna Boy's Choir, are just a few.

An example of the difference between the two Halls of Fame is: if Spike Jones had been an athlete, his name would be up there with Larry Bird, Sammy Sosa, and Dick Butkus. But as a musician? No way. He would have had to change his name to something more like *Werner von Braun.*

253

# Ice Age Tennis

Actually, it doesn't matter which of today's players we compare to Rod Laver because it is all so pointless. Rod Laver and today's best players played in two entirely different eras. Laver's era was tennis' equivalent of The Ice Age. Today's era is, surprise, the *modern* era of tennis.

The Tennis Ice Age is remembered largely for its archaic rackets and primitive animal gut strings. Players from the Ice Age played with rackets made of wood, then aluminum and, eventually, fiberglass. In other words, materials found primarily today in trees, saucepans, and kayaks.

As I remember it, athletes in the Ice Age were actually encouraged to carefully avoid sex before athletic endeavors. Then, if they did not avoid it, the primitive media didn't think we would care anyway. How barbaric! But times have changed in the sports world. These days, for example, many NBA players ritually father an illegitimate child before a game.

# New Age

Today's tennis involves naked, unfettered power. Subsequently, tennis rackets have evolved beyond those old substances into futuristic materials of mass force. New lightweight, yet stiff and strong materials fuel today's power surge. It's the stuff NASA uses. Those of you still playing with Ice Age artifacts against today's space-age players are getting blown off the court like a shotgun versus a spit wad.

The stuff NASA passes down is known as Residual Space Science Knowledge (RSSK). That is, stuff they learn how to make while building space shuttles and satellites. If a new material works for space shuttles (or even if it doesn't), they sell the idea to every prominent tennis racket manufacturer the world over. These manufacturers then quickly manufacture and market rackets made of this latest high-tech, hand-me-down substance.

The modern era also includes worldwide media saturation and megabuck endorsements. Worldwide media saturation is a recent phenomenon. Thanks to today's high-tech satellite communications, the media is better able to let regular people like you and me keep track of the sex lives of celebrities. When things are slow, the media plods along giving us mundane stories such as *Terrorist Bomb Hits Mid-East Fruit Stand*, until something juicy turns up, like *Kournikova Seen Leaving Woody Allen's Apartment*. Players perceive megabuck endorsements, in part, as compensation for reporters taking notes outside their bedroom windows.

## Modern Rackets

Today's rackets are made of several different high-tech materials; among them are: *graphite, ceramics, kevlar, titanium,* and *boron*. Interestingly, these are substances I thought I already knew about. Graphite? The last I heard they were putting it in pencils. Ceramics? I thought it was burned clay. Kevlar? Wasn't that a character on Star Trek? Titanium? Huh? I thought that was what golfers used as clubs. And boron? Isn't that a verb that describes what PBS documentaries do for pledges?

I guess I've grown to take these new materials for granted because now when I think high-tech, I think "stealth." A stealth tennis racket would be a racket that prevents your opponent from determining whether you are hitting a topspin, a slice, or a net cord winner. I'm sure scientists at the major racket manufacturers are racing even now to be the first on the market with a stealth racket. I can imagine those obsessive-compulsive little engineers hunched over Bunsen burners in their concrete-bunkered labs, performing torque and tension tests on materials such as *Teflon, Akron, plutonium* (glowing reviews escaping on this one), *pandemonium, deuteronomy, quartz,* and *super-compressed oat bran*.

## *Buying a Racket*

So, how does a low-tech person like me know which high-tech racket to buy? Well, today's modern consumers base their choice of rackets on a sophisticated, keen eye and a calculator-like mind. First, you pick out two rackets based on brand name preference and the latest color combination. Then that keenly discriminating eye finds the tags that read "$125.95" and "$299.95." Your brain performs the arithmetic operation, and voila, the second racket is $174 more. Remembering the *You Get What You Pay For* parental lecture, first developed by Old World Jewish parents, you safely conclude that the more expensive racket is the better racket.

I remember when I took my daughter out to buy her first high-tech racket. She had been playing with an inexpensive, post-Ice Age/Pre-Modern aluminum racket, to establish whether she enjoyed the game or not. Well, she did—enough to warrant her own racket. So, we went to a tennis shop to inspect the rackets that only a serious player or an aerospace engineer could want.

My daughter had already made up her mind which brand her racket was going to be (mine, bless her). So, we inspected every racket that company made. She dismissed the cheapest model because it was unreliable. That is, she knew a boy who played with one, and he was not very good. The contending rackets all looked exactly alike, except for color fashions, and were priced from $80 to $300. I asked the salesperson what, besides the colors, were the differences in the rackets. He looked at me as if I was completely unable to perform basic arithmetic. Then he proudly waxed into a soliloquy, using broad hand gestures, about the importance of stiffness, its lightness of being, the levels of the players, and the relationships therein. He talked a lot and said little that was useful. The short version is that the rackets were the same; only the proportion of its aerospace composite materials changed, and that difference profoundly mattered.

My daughter, true to her feminine gene that enables women to ferret out the most expensive item in a store without having to check pricc tags, selected the top of the line racket to not be able to live without. The salesman complimented her on her obvious math abilities. However, (excuse my analogous jump here) I did not want to spend money on a Steinway grand piano until she could play more than *Heart and Soul*. She quickly got over the disappointment of not getting her first choice when I promised her some hot pink strings.

It's difficult to imagine Rod Laver playing with hot pink strings, or Stefan Edberg for that matter. (Brownies this time, dear.)

# 41

## *Tennisium Bicourtilate Chlorogreenaphyl*

The color of tennis courts is of little concern to players. Therefore, I am devoting this chapter to it. If you ask players their favorite tennis court colors, they will usually have to think before forming an opinion. My wife prefers a blue court inside the lines, surrounded by tan. I prefer "Tara." I will go into that later.

It seems the unofficial colors of tennis courts (at least the hardcourt variety) are brick red and a shade of green that only art school dropouts are capable of producing. Indeed, several of these dropouts subsequently formed a for-profit laboratory. Passing themselves off as scientists, complete with long white coats and OSHA-approved protective eyewear, they created the particular green found on tennis courts. The rights to this green have subsequently been purchased by the USTA. It is now only authorized for use on tennis courts, mostly in conjunction with its sister color, brick red.

As you may have noticed, it is a breech of scientific etiquette NOT to give a newly-discovered or invented thingamajig a long labyrinth of a name that you cannot pronounce without the aid of a licensed speech therapist. Since the USTA's Department of Non-White Colors seems to have dropped the ball on this one, I will give this color a proper traditional name.

The traditional choices of language for names are Latin, for discoveries, and science-ese, for inventions. Since I have a sense of tradition, and since the shade of green in question was developed, by accident, in the institute's research and development laboratory while seeking a new dye color for the space-age putty that repairs Saturn rocket micro-fractures, a scientific name would apply in this instance.

Therefore, I hereby dub thee the color, *Tennisium Bicourtilate Chlorogreenaphyl*, or "TBC." Of course, "tennis court green" remains the layman's term because it is a term that normal people can safely say in public without fear of drooling or spitting on persons in close proximity.

Every once in a long while you see a tennis court painted inside out. That is, a court painted brick red inside the lines and TBC outside. Personally, I think the people who order that backward combination demonstrate as much good taste as the Dunce County Burp-Off. Inside-out courts should be listed as "not approved" for players with an NTRP rating of 4.0 or above or anyone with a USTA card.

I have seen similar greens used for tennis courts, but the whole court was green with no red used at all. These courts always seemed better to me, probably because I grew up playing on public courts of brick red/TBC green. Those public courts were in a neighborhood where gangs would gather to sharpen their switchblades on the net poles, and where the vending machines were housed in as much armor as an army tank. The only reason we tennis players were relatively safe was because we wielded heavy wooden clubs with the names of mysterious gods written across them, like *Jack Kramer* and *Pancho Gonzalez*. Then, when Wilson came out with the T-2000, rackets took on an even deadlier appearance. With that wire wrapped around the frame like a snake, the T-2000 looked cold and sinister. It gave the racket the look of a lethal 21st century, martial arts weapon.

Just the same, the only places I ran across the mono-color tennis courts were at posh private clubs. Those courts were always clean, too. At least there was the illusion of cleanliness. Maybe that was because, back then, the clubs insisted that members and players be and wear white.

It used to be very important, in a traditional sort of way, that all serious tennis players wore white. If you wore white, it meant you were a player or, at least, a somewhat knowledgeable wannabe. It meant you attended exhibition matches by the pros when they came barnstorming into town. But mainly, wearing white was how we serious players signaled to other serious players the concept: "Yo! I'm serious here!"

This fashion identification technique worked well at the public courts where I played and where hacker recognition was vital. All sorts of weird people would accost us serious players demanding play time. Yes, it was all too common to see people of the Lounge Lizard School of Fitness lumbering toward us in brown wing-tip shoes, Bermuda shorts, and beer-belly hugging T-shirts with The Devil Made Me Do It printed across the front. Their fashion impairment proved to be our best hacker early-warning system.

Other colors I have seen used on tennis courts are (1) my wife's blue and tan, (2) black (and NOT asphalt), and (3) Tara. Tara is a very pale, burnt red. I call it "Tara," after the name of Scarlett O'Hara's plantation in the movie, *Gone With The Wind*. Tara's soil was that southern, earthy red. In a dramatic scene from the movie, Scarlett's father bent down and scooped up a loose handful of Tara's red earth. Showing Scarlett the soil, he proceeded to admonish her for wasting time flirting with men and causing them to go to war when she should have been falling in love with the dirt. It's not as strange as it sounds; he was drunk most of the time.

## Nature Courts

The aforementioned courts were hardcourts made with artificial colors added and have nothing to do with the so-called *nature* courts, like clay and grass. (I have purposely overlooked the Team Tennis courts. Those courts were conjured up with "spectacle" in mind. Those courts are patched together with different colored pieces of carpet, that when assembled, look like a political map of Eastern Europe—as of last Wednesday.)

Virtually all the mainline environmental groups financially back the "nature" courts, from the *Fishermen for the Ethical Treatment of Earthworms* (FETE), to the always-vocal *Tennis Court Green-peace*. Both of these groups issue sums of money (up to $24.95) to the election coffers of those politicians that champion the construction of "nature" courts.

Some of the more radical groups, like *Earth Courts First*, have been known to protest the spreading "pollution" of unnatural hardcourts by using more direct methods. They throw dirt and grass clippings onto public and private country club tennis facilities.

Of the nature courts, clay courts are often the color of Tara, and grass courts are green or khaki. Although, it seems many grasscourt caretakers are from my personal school of gardening because their courts are like my lawn—Death Valley Brown. (It took three winters worth of fertilizer before I learned that Bermuda grass is *supposed* to turn brown in the winter.) You can see this browning phenomenon at Wimbledon on the last day of the tournament. There, after two weeks of world-class tennis, Centre Court's grass is always reduced to a dirty, five o'clock shadow of its former green glory.

The royal groundskeepers could learn a thing or two from the father of an old girlfriend of mine and some avant-garde stadium groundskeepers in this country. They simply spray-paint their brown grass green.

Meanwhile, if you see any strangely colored courts out there let me know.

# 42

# *"Wimpleton" and the Other Slams*

Tennis, along with golf (and probably darts), has its major tournaments. There are four of them. Together they are called the "Grand Slam" events. *Grand,* meaning, 'big and marvelous,' and *slam,* meaning 'throw down with a powerful force.' Together, the phrase means, 'Throw down with a big and marvelous force.' Go figure. I think the same people who write ballot initiatives invented the term.

Anyway, the winners of these major tournaments are revered as heroes and receive notoriety for the remainder of their sex appeal. Of course, this notoriety is chiefly in the form of revealing and humiliating tabloid headlines regarding secret and intimate, backseat rendezvous with extra-terrestrials.

Tennis' four major tournaments are the *Australian Open,* the *French Open, Wimbledon,* and the *US Open.* We tennis aficionados refer to them in mixed company (of players and hackers) as "slam" events. That way, hackers think we are talking about professional wrestling pay-per-view affairs. Ha, ha!

Grand Slam events are the only tennis events televised by the major networks. Only sports channels or one of the artsy channels, like the Snob Channel, televise the lesser tennis tournaments, collectively known as "the lesser tennis tournaments."

You may be wondering what makes these four tournaments so special. I didn't, but I thought you readers might. According to recently released USTA e-mails, it was decided long ago in a covert meeting of

263

the world's foremost tennis fashion designers, that the first four countries with red, white, and blue flags to hold national opens would henceforth (a term we writers use to sound smart, and meaning 'from now on') be designated the major events. This "flagism" is why the venerable Italian Open (country's colors: Red, white, and GREEN) is relegated to the swollen ranks of the lesser tennis tournaments no matter how much free pizza and Chianti they lavish on visiting tennis dignitaries.

Unlike the lesser tennis tournaments in which winners merely win $100K and a sports car, and where first round losers receive a lovely $5,000 parting check, the "slam" tournaments also provide heartwarming human drama. Why? Because they are the only tournaments in which players fall onto their backs or stomachs, kneel with hands clasped, cry, throw rackets, and climb into the stands. You may think, "So what? Players always whine about line calls and crowd noise." In the major events, they do these things after winning championship and even match points. It's weird. It's backward. It's a "slam."

By traditional definition, winning a *Grand Slam* means winning the Australian Open, the French Open, Wimbledon, and the US Open all in the same calendar year. Holding all four titles at once does not count, and only merits a snobbish *humpf*—like when you ask for a decaf coffee in Columbia. Martina Navratilova even tried it once. (So did Tiger Woods.) "Big deal," the purists scoffed. "What's so difficult about that? Next time check your free-with-no-obligation bank calendar, lint-for-brains!" So, only a few players have been able to win a Grand Slam between Januarys: Don Budge, Maureen Connelly, Rod Laver, Margaret Court, Steffi Graf, and Barry Bonds come to mind.

As a matter of public record, most players don't win a *career* Grand Slam, that is, to win each of these tournaments at least once in their careers. Heck, winning any of these tournaments even once in a career is extremely rare. I know I didn't. But, that's only because I didn't have much of a career. For example, I estimate my career winnings to be, let's see, carry the two, and rounding up to the nearest 100: $100.

We were we? A good segue. The names of the places where these major tennis tournaments are held sound predominately, well, English. Children like to make fun of English names. Actually, adults find them pretty humorous too. Who can hold back a giggle when hearing traditional English names like *Percy*, *Wembley*, or *Flatulence*?

The Australian Open used to be played at Flinders Park. *Flinders* sounds English, but it is actually Australian for 'those who flind.' The name created quite an uproar in Melbourne because it alienated those poor, deprived, and vocal citizens who, through no fault of their own, never had the opportunity *to flind*. So, they changed the name to the less provocative "Melbourne Park."

"Wimbledon" has an uncomfortable similarity to "wimpdom," and is routinely defiled by hackers as "Wimpleton."

The US Open, applying standard American capitalism, sells the rights to hold their tournament to the highest bidder. Therefore, the facility name went from Forest Hills (after a mortuary) to Flushing Meadows (a septic tank company).

Only at the French Open, played in culturally rich Paris, can you proudly play at Roland Garros. Here is a name any English-speaking person can nobly pronounce with little practice. Yes, it is in Paris each May that the world learns about French culture from courteous Parisians when foreign journalists ask them subtle questions such as, "Do you really *eat snails?!*"

As if backhands weren't frustration enough, the major tournaments are played on the entire gamut of tennis court surfaces, except asphalt. Asphalt is reserved worldwide for cars and trucks, and by the public school system in California to discourage students from playing outside in the toxic smog. The Australian used to be played on grass, but now is played on a hardcourt surface. 'Hardcourt' means 'those surfaces where falls are accompanied by the scurrying of caring trainers and concerned tournament officials, each carrying legal documents and urging players to sign liability waivers.' Wimbledon is, and has always been, a grass court tournament. The French Open is, and has always has been, a clay court tournament. And the US Open, in keeping with our uniquely American political philosophy of, *It can't get any worse*, was grass, then clay, and now hardcourt.

Court surfaces are more important than they used to be. So, today's players have adapted their playing styles to the surfaces on which they play: hardcourt or clay. Hardcourt and grass are surfaces that do not slow the ball down when it bounces. Clay is a surface that does. Therefore, slower stronger players with benign groundstrokes can become towering champions on the faster surfaces. Conversely, fast little guys with negative volleys can compete very well as baseliners on slow clay, but get bounced from tournaments with faster surfaces in about the same amount of time it takes a fruit fly to reach puberty.

In yesteryear, all players learned to play pretty much the same way—using an *all-court game*. "All-court game" meant you would always try to serve and volley first serves. You hit one-handed backhands, and running around your backhand was considered a sissy act. Those players able to hit a successful backhand about as often as UFO abductions, and yet refusing to run around them, were considered brave. Stupid, but brave.

In my case, "all-court game" only meant I did not have a *weapon*. In tennis lingo, a "weapon" means 'a reliable shot that can put your opponent in a defensive position.' Of course, nowadays in junior tennis, the term "weapon" often confuses young players. Youngsters will hear about other player's having "weapons" and so respond by "packing heat." Happily, these new terms carry the unintentional benefit of enlarging young vocabularies. Yes, today's youthful players are learning that "having a weapon" and "packing" are often two separate things.

These modern facts of tennis now make winning a Grand Slam rarer than anchovies on pizza, except in Italy where anchovies are a delicacy.

Oh my. I think I'm beginning to understand why the Italian Open remains a lesser tournament.

# 43

## *A Short (and Getting Shorter) History of Tennis Fashion*

In the early 1900's, tennis was considered (as were almost all sports) a mere diversion from life's mundane routines of operating heartless and greedy monopolies, inspiring child labor legislation, and committing global war. In other words, it was a leisure activity.

During this time, tennis players bounded gaily around the court while batting balls with rackets that resembled Cro-Magnon colanders. After a match, players would congratulate each other with a hearty pat on the back. Only after this public display of sportsmanship would any hidden competitiveness be discretely revealed. Frequently, a peeved loser would turn to his valet and whisper, "I say, Charles, do be a good fellow and torch the rascal's carriage."

Without an openly competitive crucible, all tennis attire resembled baptism robes, but more modest. Proper tennis attire for men consisted of long-sleeved white shirts with starched collars, and long white trousers. Women wore hats, long-sleeved white blouses with starched collars, and long white skirts that didn't hide the (at the time) sensuous feminine ankle.

So it stayed until Time marched on. (Have you ever wondered why time always marches for historians? For real people, it ambulates in varying degrees. When you are on a hot date, time positively crawls through dinner and a movie, and then it races when you are alone with your date in the back seat of the car engaging in "body talk.")

In the 1920's, people started loosening up and having a roaring good time. This lax behavior greatly concerned government officials who, being made up of devout, cigar-smoking old men, thought choir practice was about as much fun as anyone could morally endure. Therefore, these officials decided the country needed a good old-fashioned moral Spring cleaning. To purify the nation, they amended the Constitution to ban the consumption of liquor throughout the country.

Consequently, this amendment had a profound effect on our democratic party system. Suddenly, party hosts were reduced to providing root beer for their guests and playing Charades. Ultimately, partygoers sat around selling each other worthless multi-layered marketing gimmicks and pyramid schemes. Losing money while sober made the partygoers very depressed, even melancholy. Because of its abysmally dull parties, this era became known as *The Great Depression.*

Thankfully, enough congressmen were blackballed from the Washington Social Register's Charades League and expelled from choirs for smoking during practice that they re-thought their political priorities. So, once again, they passed a Constitutional Amendment to fix the Constitution back to the way it was before they broke it.

Fun and revelry were legal once more, and parties were again entertaining. Daring men started sporting short-sleeved shirts to easier bend their elbows while hoisting a brew. Also, ladies' skirt hems rose to the sensuous female mid-calf and then quickly to the sensuous female knee length. (This last fashion statement was introduced by women who, in spontaneous celebration of fun soirees, lifted up their skirts while dancing the can-can at bus stops.)

## World Crisis

Elsewhere, in an attempt to increase their liquor exports, a few countries got together and started World War II. Events went this way: Germany, believing they brewed the superior beer, began violently exporting it to neighboring Slavic countries. Anxious, France fortified its Maginot Line to protect its haughty wine society from a ghastly beer invasion. Japan, thinking no one was looking, began forcing sake down the throats of its Asian neighbors. The Italians thought that if they entered into a mafia-style venture with Germany, they could begin shipping Chianti into Africa via a network of Ethiopian trade routes. Russia concluded they needed to expand their vodka exports in the worst way. That way turned out to be a pact made with Germany, wherein Germany received the lucrative beer concession in Poland while Russia got exclusive vodka rights to Estonia, Latvia, Lithuania, and Finland. England was quietly getting nervous. Not only was its own gin industry imperiled, but also its Commonwealth buddy, Scotland, was worried that its Scotch markets were drying up. And, Ireland increasingly became concerned should their Irish whiskey be eradicated by Aryan whiskey. Finally, on December 7, 1941, all the pieces came together when America entered the donnybrook in response to a sneaky boycott by Japanese liquor storeowners in Honolulu who refused to sell American bourbon.

Then, in a coincidence of truly mediocre proportions, the world's liquor crisis ended, *and* tennis became a career path. Players started turning professional when they realized they could earn their livings by barnstorming around the country playing each other in front of paying crowds.

This infusion of money led to a deep, yet overt, competitiveness. Soon, men's trousers became shorts when brew-hoisting tennis players decided to improve their court mobility by applying the brew-inspired, short-sleeve technology to their pant legs.

Impressed, the exclusively male designers of ladies' tennis attire made a thorough study of women's legs and came to the startling conclusion that skirt hems were not high enough. To remedy this hem-length problem, designers shortened women's skirt hems to above the sensuous female knee. Women started buying these skirts; some even tried playing tennis. Tennis' popularity was climbing to feverish heights.

While these shorter skirts titillated male tennis players, they absolutely excited the tennis garment manufacturers. "Hey!" they marveled, "Sex sells. Let's raise hems again!" So, an old adage was born and women's skirts rose to the sensuous female mid-thigh. Soon thereafter, male players, in hyper-testosterone rapture, invented mixed doubles.

Playing tennis in these bouncy shorter skirts that concealed nothing might have been embarrassing, except for the generosity of the tennis fashion designers who came out with a line of modestly priced tennis panties. Tennis panties are panties that, even though laced like bridal veils, males tend to view with minimal arousal (a difficult and entirely overrated achievement). Soon, after the appearance of these panties, tennis skirts hit bottom—if you know what I mean.

Eventually, some bored sportswear designer did some investigating and discovered that, due to a typo, men's tennis fashions had not changed in thirty years. Subsequently, in a bold stroke of design innovation, color was implemented. Instead of all tennis shirts being completely white, these intrepid designers made shirts of various pastel colors that made tennis players look like half-dipped Easter Eggs.

These colored shirts became an instant hit with most male players, who realized they could easily identify their league teammates dressed in handsome, yet ready for poaching, colored shirts. On the other hand, young anti-establishment players (those without mortgage payments) ignored designer shirts and, instead, preferred playing in torn and catsup-stained T-shirts to make various important social statements like, *Crud is beautiful, man.*

Meanwhile, women's fashion continued to be an object of experimentation. Remember the bodysuit? The less said about that fiasco the better. And the halter-top—that didn't halt her top? Yes, one redeeming quality about the halter was that it provided considerable breast freedom. Occasionally, a liberty-loving breast would free itself of its bonds and quickly inspire numerous offers of asylum by all freedom-loving males.

Over time, the women players became more competitive as well. In response, tournaments have popped up for them all over the world. Designers, heeding this competitive trend and ignoring their good old adages, devised the industrial strength sports bra. This device is a cheap relative of the straightjacket. The sports bra was specifically designed to oppress the freedom of breast movement. These bras are engineered to be so unattractive that women can, and do, take their shirts off and cruise around in public. And nobody cares! At the same time, we men can't help fantasizing about what women wear OVER them.

The prosperity of the tennis fashion industry has begotten more tennis fashion designers. To create more business for themselves, these designers are now designing warm-up suits, ensembles of matching bags, socks, headbands, towels, grips, and even racket strings.

Personally, I think there is still *a lot* of work left to be done on sports bras.

# 44

## *The Sweatology of Sports Drinks*

For tennis players in the old days, liquid refreshment was either a rare soft drink, or more likely, a drinking fountain. Of course, that drinking fountain was inevitably encrusted with a primitive life form that resembled moss, but gripped the fountain like a barnacle. Unfortunately for us tennis players, the discharge (to use a scientific term meaning 'leakage') from these water fountains was so slight, only the mossy life form could derive sustenance from it. On hot days, desperately parched young players would inevitably form gangs and brandishing their rackets as weapons, hijack rides to a liquor store. Concerned parents soon began to complain to the USTA because this unfortunate behavior took vital practice time away from their young future pros.

Those "old days" occurred around the Kennedy administration. It was a time when the government decided to push physical fitness on an unfit public. In 1961, the federal government undertook a study of random smorgasbord restaurant clientele in major cities and compared them to the voters in the polls. Using the Enron trick of slanting the numbers by carrying an extra "1" into the millions column, the study concluded that the low voter turnout was due, in large part, to the fact that most Americans could not squeeze into the standard voting booth. Figuring that free public service announcements were cheaper than buying larger voting booths, the government began promoting physical fitness as a way to get people to vote.

As an example of how efficiently a typical government-endorsed policy runs, 25 years and five administrations later the country went on a nationwide health kick when sugar was discovered to be the leading cause of communism. (Nationwide, that is, if we ignore the Midwest and South, who to this day, regard "deep fried" as a culinary rite of passage into triple by-pass heart renovation.) Anyway, due to unintended consequences and unforeseen events, (although voters began slipping more easily into the poll booths) more voters than ever are not voting.

Today, voters suffer from TVRDA, or *Television Remote Deprivation Anxiety.* TVRDA is, as you might guess, a communicable disease. It has a debilitating affect on its victims. TVRDA causes its sufferers to sweat and hyperventilate when they range beyond the limit of their television remotes. TVRDA's most common symptom is watching reruns of *I Love Lucy* and *Wheel of Fortune* in the kitchen, until you fall asleep in your pudding cup.

Back on the tennis courts, scientists and entrepreneurs, eager to cash in on this emerging health market, conspired and began concocting sports drinks to replenish various and dangerous chemicals that your body actively sweats out. You see, your body understands that these chemicals are unhealthy poisons created during mild exercise, like breathing.

Modern sweatologists disagree with your body. They say your body doesn't know what the heck it is doing. It is not generally known, but these same sweatologists failed in their advertising ploy to get us to apply their deodorants before playing tennis. Trying a different tack, they devised drinks that would put these chemicals back *in* your body. The only problem is, if you don't start sweating within an hour of consuming a sports drink, your body is overcome by an irresistible urge to power-lift heavy objects. This urge can lead to embarrassing moments, such as in churches where the most accessible heavy weights are dressed in choir robes.

This brings us to the type of liquid refreshment currently preferred by players with Land Rovers and Rolex watches. These days, people aren't looking for just mere health drinks, but *natural* health drinks (like, guess what, water). Except, if you don't buy your water in plastic bottles, then your water is not natural. In fact, only a deranged hermit or former coma victim would commit the faux pas of drinking health-dubious tap water.

Uncovering the unnaturalness of tap water took diligence. Professional health freaks, taking nothing for granted, thoroughly investigated the benefits of water in a healthy diet. And it's a good thing they did, because they discovered that most metropolitan water supplies contain more toxic chemicals than your car's anti-freeze. Career health freaks were very disappointed that good old natural tap water was neither good, nor natural.

As it turns out, some French health-freak named Perrier bottled some water that he swears comes out of the ground (as in bacteria-infested dirt), and not some city purifying system (as in toxic chlorine). He also swears his water has NATURAL carbonic acid. Thank goodness. We wouldn't want to drink just *any* carbonic acid. To me, playing up natural carbonic acid is similar to advertising the benefits of tap water with natural CHLORINE.

There must be 50 water producers today. All of them list 100 percent natural water as their main ingredient. It reminds me that virtually every soft drink has a list of ingredients that includes "natural and artificial flavors." STU-PID. As if someone would read the ingredients and say, "Well looky here, Edna. It says here on this can that this here sody pop has 'natural flavors.' I guess Mom's Down Home Deep-Fried Family Restaurant has started servin' up a hay-ulth drink."

Well, of course every drink has its natural flavors! Then some highly paid tasteologist with human-like taste buds actually sampled those natural flavors and gagged, "Blaaaahh! What is this? Rat bile?! Get some unnatural flavors in here to cover up this natural crap!" So, chemical engineers came up with a chemical gimmick to cover up the otherwise tasteless nature of natural water. Yes, they engineered artificial fruit flavor molecules to make water salable at prices exceeding BEER. Sacrilegious!

Tennis players on the forefront of fashionable fads drink this purified bottled water into which the bottler has added those synthetic taste molecules. Now, we can enjoy natural water with a hint of the artificial essence of fruit, or whatever. However, all drink labels retain "natural flavors" on their list of ingredients so you will think there is some health benefit associated with drinking their product. In short, "artificial and natural flavors" means you get the blah taste of natural water with the cool taste of artificial fruit chemicals.

Of course, the only necessary evolutionary change beer-drinking tennis players have to negotiate is whether to get light or regular beer. Come to think of it, those players seem a lot less stressed! Stress is not good for you. Stress causes heart attacks and a squeaky voice.

Even so, I'm prepared for those antique water fountains at public courts. I carry one of those ubiquitous sports bottles filled with our town's own noxious tap water (with ice artificially added). Call me a deranged hermit, but I'll be damned if I'll buy designer water!

# 45

## *Dave's Laws of Tennis*

Tennis has its place in nature, along with mildew and Lamborghinis, because it, like everything in the world, is subject to the forces of nature, and nature is subject to natural laws, which in turn are subject to interpretation by the Supreme Court. Result: tennis sticks to natural law like an ugly dinner date to your arm.

To civilize and manage tennis, mankind has developed its own rules and codes to administer and control play. These rules are ordinarily strictly enforced at tournaments and are only arbitrary to the extent you can deliver 10,000 paying customers through the gate. Rules are very important. For instance, rules tell us how to keep score, which in turn tells us when to stop playing and get a beer.

Some of nature's more famous laws are: *Gravity, Thermodynamics 1, 2,* and *3, Averages, Supply & Demand,* and *Murphy's.* Murphy is credited with having been the first person to recognize the existence of a set of natural laws that are peculiar to human beings. Historically, these laws have been described as *bad luck,* or in robe-intensive cultures, *karma.* However, Murphy suspected that these laws were more than mere fortune. Ultimately, Murphy discovered a clandestine thread of commonality that exists between these laws and which serve to frustrate us at every turn. Conclusion: the Chicago Cubs are not some random accident!

As Murphy theorized, tennis is also subject to its own peculiar set of unavoidable natural laws that can drive players crazy. With the aid of some of the world's leading tennisologists, I have diligently documented these laws and their affects on your basic backhand-fearing tennis player. I am voluntarily publishing these laws in the crass effort to sell this book.

The following are derived from observation and experience. Witness for yourself:

## Dave's Laws of Tennis (DLT):

**DLT #1:**     On courts under jungle law (under no governing authority), if you are waiting to play on an occupied court and ask the players their score, the reported score will never be further along than 2-1.

**DLT #2:**     Under jungle law, if people are waiting for your court, they will not be able to ask you the score less than once every game.

**DLT #3:**     The angle of your shot never exceeds the speed of your opponent.

**DLT #4:**     The odds of your opponent making a bad call increases with the importance of the point.

**DLT #5:**     The likelihood of losing a match is equal to the amount of bragging your opponent will engage in if he or she wins.

**DLT #6:**     The more effort you expend in getting to break point, the more likely it is you will be aced.

**DLT #7:**     The odds of being struck by the ball while playing doubles vary directly with the number of short lobs supplied by your partner.

**DLT #8:**     After any tournament match that you lose, your opponent and your opponent's friends and family will all congratulate you for playing so valiantly.

| | |
|---|---|
| **DLT #9:** | The greater your desire to win, the more your opponent will cheat. |
| **DLT #10:** | The more crucial the point, the closer to the lines your opponent's shots will land. |
| **DLT #11:** | "Lines" are that unit of measurement that makes your side of the court larger than your opponent's. |
| **DLT #12:** | The person losing will take the longest total time to change sides. |
| **DLT #13:** | The odds of running back for a lob and having the ball bounce off your head vary directly with the number of spectators. |
| **DLT #14:** | The decibel level of insults shouted between mixed doubles partners is equal to the depth of their relationship. |
| **DLT #15:** | In the NTR playing range of 0.0 to 3.5, the total sum of money spent on tennis clothes and equipment is inversely related to that person's playing level. |
| **DLT #16:** | All else being equal, the doubles team will beat the team that plays separately together. |
| **DLT #17:** | The quality of your drop shot never exceeds your opponent's ability to retrieve it. |
| **DLT #18:** | The feebleness of your weakest shot varies directly with your opponent's ability to exploit it. |
| **DLT #19:** | The odds of losing in the first round of a tournament vary directly with the amount of time |

and personal sacrifice involved in arranging to play it.

**DLT #20:**  One hour before your scheduled first round match in a tournament in which your draw is unbelievably great, you or your wife will go into labor.

**DLT #21:**  The distance from the alternate tournament site you must travel to play your first round match varies directly with the distance you traveled to get to the primary tournament site.

**DLT #22:**  The larger the number of your friends and relatives who come to watch your match, the worse you will play.

**DLT #23:**  The odds of playing on a court next to a bunch of inconsiderate hackers are directly related to the significance of your match.

**DLT #24:**  (Hacker's Law): The shortest distance to an open court is through courts with matches in progress.

**DLT #25:**  Under any given set of possible adverse playing conditions, those conditions will throw your game off more than your opponent's.

**DLT #26:**  If 95 percent of all first round matches are byes, you will be in the other 5 percent.

**DLT #27:**  The number of challenge matches you receive is equal to the number of days it took to get over your most recent illness or injury.

**DLT #28:**  Your opponent's volleying skill increases as the depth of your groundstrokes decreases.

**DLT #29:** A person's inability to play tennis is equal to the effort he or she expends in trying to imitate a top professional.

**DLT #30:** Your "let" serves will occur on otherwise obvious aces.

**DLT #31:** All left-handers have wicked serves.

**DLT #32:** The depth of your lobs never exceeds your opponent's ability to hit overheads.

**DLT #33:** All crucial-point, net-cord shots will drop on your side of the net.

**DLT #34:** Against any given opponent, your strengths will play directly into your opponent's strengths, and so will your weaknesses.

**DLT #35:** A tennis ball tends to roll to the nearest inaccessible place.

**DLT #36:** If there is liquid anywhere within a city block, your tennis balls will find a way to roll into it.

**DLT #37:** The odds of showing up for a recreational tennis match and discovering that no one brought the balls increase with the level of trouble involved in arranging your schedule to play it.

**DLT #38:** No matter how many people you know who are better players than you are, you will be asked to play by someone who will utterly destroy your game.

**DLT #39:** No matter how many precautions you take, you will lose one tenth of your "basket" of practice balls every time you use them.

**DLT #40:**   No matter how poorly you play during your tennis lesson, your pro will have nothing but praise for some aspect of your game.

**DLT #41:**   The odds of getting caught playing in the rain vary indirectly with the number of days since you got your racket strung with gut.

**DLT #42:**   The odds of losing your serve increase with the size of the lead you once had.

**DLT #43:**   A woman's skill level is determined by the size of her bra cup.

**DLT #44:**   There is no such thing as a "setup," only opportunities you haven't missed yet.

**DLT #45:**   The fastest way to the poor house is through tennis lessons, and keeping abreast with "new" tennis fashions and racket technologies.

**DLT #46:**   You cannot teach, practice with, or talk about tennis with your spouse without having Armageddon ensue.

**DLT #47:**   The strings of your favorite racket will not break until the third game of an important match.

**DLT #48:**   The odds of a ball rolling onto your court and disturbing play increase with the extent you have forced your opponent to hit a weak return.

**DLT #49:**    (Tarshis' Law[1]): When exhibiting the proper stroke technique to someone, your first demonstration attempt will fail.

**DLT #50:**    The closer your match gets, the more far-sighted your opponent becomes.

**DLT #51:**    The worst players gravitate to the best courts.

**DLT #52:**    At any one time, only three people will be playing a "friendly" game of doubles.

**DLT #53:**    Tournaments will assign the best matches to the worst courts for viewing.

**DLT #54:**    The odds of your next tournament match being played on "fast" courts are directly related to the amount of time you spent practicing on "slow" ones. NOTE: The reverse is also true.

**DLT #55:**    Your best shots will be hit during the match warm-up.

**DLT #56:**    The length of time your opponent keeps his or her warm-up suit on varies directly with how easily you will be beaten.

**DLT #57:**    Your serve never exceeds your opponent's service returns. NOTE: The opposite is also true.

**DLT #58:**    When the going gets tough, the tough run around their backhands.

**DLT #59:**    (Whitehead's Law): Practice makes blisters.

If you readers discover a law not covered in this chapter, you can submit it to our panel of distinguished tennisologists. Just send it, in

---

1.    Acclaimed writer Barry Tarshis was the first to publish this law in Tennis magazine.

care of me, at the address of this book's publisher, or e-mail me at **Fuzzball@bounce.net**. If our eminent panel accepts your rule, it will be awarded its very own number! Or, if you have a better name for a rule, besides its chic number, submit your suggestion. Example: "Whitehead's Law."

# 46

# *Dave's Absolute Tennis Ability Rating System*

I devised Dave's Absolute Tennis Ability Rating System (DATARS) as an aid to (a) rate yourself more accurately, but mainly to (b) red-light any hacking geeks that would publicly humiliate you to the point where only the Federal Witness Protection Program could give you a good name.

I'm serious about protecting hard-working players from unrepentant hacks. With the DATARS system of identification, you will be able to readily discover anyone's tennis knowledge and skill. All that is required are a couple of keen observations along with a shrewd question or two: *Nice day if it don't rain. By the way, what's your DATARS level?*

The following are a list of definitions of all the categories of tennis skill and awareness into which every man, woman, and child fall, now, and until we're overrun by aliens.

## *Dave's Absolute Tennis Ability Rating System (DATARS):*

**0.0:**        Subhuman. These people inhabit remote, desolate areas to escape the "Feds" and misspell the word "tennis." They think tennis balls are fuzzy dog toys, that the nets are for tightrope walking, and that courts were made for roller hockey and vandalizing.

**0.5:** These people can identify a tennis court when they see one. They play once every federal budget surplus and have to borrow a racket and balls. They can hit the ball only if they bounce it first. They pick up balls with their bare hands and hold the racket by its shaft.

**1.0:** These people own a racket bought at a garage sale for $1 and a can of balls given to them on their birthdays five years ago. They play tennis once a year in their hiking boots. They hold the racket like a frying pan. They keep score: one, two, three,…

**1.5:** These people can make contact with the ball about 50 percent of the time and will play with broken strings. They think *doubles* are bar drinks and that the US Open is a foreign trade policy. They refer to Chris Evert as "Chrissy Everett."

**2.0:** These people can make the ball hit their strings more often than not. They can keep 9 out of 10 shots from flying over the fence. They use an old wooden racket press on their Dollar-Mart metal rackets and rally for serve. When they get thirsty, they quit and head for a tavern.

**2.5:** This person knows how to keep score (excluding tiebreakers). She knows at least one other person who plays tennis. She begins serving with her racket across her shoulder. She has no idea that a spin shot is coming and thinks a *singles* tournament is for unmarried players.

**3.0:**    This person realizes his forehand is easier to hit than his backhand. He double faults, on average, around 50 percent of the time and knows which lines are for singles and which are for doubles. He thinks a *default* means your credit is shot.

**3.5:**    This person picks up balls using the foot and racket method. Missing easy setups annoy her. She recognizes that a spin shot will bounce funny, but she will not know in which direction. She understands that playing on grass and playing "stoned" are two different things. She thinks asphalt is a bona fide playing surface.

**4.0:**    These players realize *Goolagong* is not a toy made by Wham-O. They own a pair of $25.00 cotton warm-ups purchased at Clothes-R-Cheap. They can spell "Wimbledon" correctly and can name the number one men's and women's players in the world. These players can roll a ball up onto their strings. They use *tennis elbow* as their stock excuse for losing.

**4.5:**    These players know how to play the 12-point tiebreaker method. They can flip the racket in the air and catch it by its handle. They can tell you who won Wimbledon and the US Open. They carry a tennis bag and pick up balls by bouncing them up with their rackets. They become perturbed when their opponents hit good shots.

**5.0:**    This player can juggle three balls. He can serve in the sun effectively and tell you the names of the current major tournament titleholders. He brings tap water from home to drink. He has read all the tennis biographies, and declares (correctly) *asphalt* to be a medical term for constipation.

**5.5:**    This player owns a $150.00 warm-up suit. She can tell at a glance whether or not the net is too high or too low. She can return left-handed serves. She is familiar with all tiebreaker methods since 1970 and knows the names of the French Open semi-finalists. She brings a bottle of water purchased at Waters-R-Natural.

**6.0:**    This player hits backhand overheads on purpose. He owns more than one $150 warm-up suit. He knows the first round scores of the Singapore Sling Open; he also knows which players are using which brand of tennis shoe and the name of Chris Evert's husband[1].

**6.5:**    This player plays tennis for a living and has a sponsor. She gets her equipment for free, but must qualify for the major pro tournaments. She flies coach and rides buses. She plays primarily for Grand Prix points. She knows the year-to-date earnings of the top 50 players.

**7.0:**    These players fly first class to all tournaments. They are paid large sums of money to use tennis equipment. They date aspiring models and/ or rich people. They have linespeople for every

---

1.    Olympic skier Andy Mill

match and play doubles to supplement their singles earnings.

7.5:    These players travel via chartered jets. They play only major tournaments and exhibition matches. They receive appearance money and have the power to remove linespersons. They do not play doubles. They get media coverage outside of tennis magazines.

8.0:    This player makes TV commercials for non-tennis related products and marries a famous person far better-looking. When they retire from the game, he or she becomes a "name" television analyst for a major network. The paparazzi follow them into middle age.

# 47

## *Excuseology (A Hypochondriac's Reference Guide)*

Everyone who has ever had a sore arm or played a challenge match has heard of *tennis elbow*. Tennis elbow flare-up is the most popular USTA-endorsed excuse of club players. You have probably even invoked this excuse yourself. (Many players even wrap Velcro straps around their forearms as props!) Still, like pregnancy and warts, tennis elbow is also a real medical diagnosis. Since doctors can find "tennis elbow" in their reference books, you can not only suffer from it, but you can pay them upwards of $150 or more to advise you to "rest it" too.

Tennis players are tough. They have to be because they are constantly subjected to a large number of tennis-related injuries unknown to players of other sports. Sure, football may have its ruptured ligaments and compound fractures. And, baseball may have its torn rotator cuffs and ball-induced concussions. All these are very respectable injuries. But, for sheer number and variety of physical ailments, I'll take tennis.

After a highly over-priced consultation with Dr. Bill Padder, the USTA's leading authority on Extenuating Circumstances, I have provided a random list of many of the other physical ailments associated with playing tennis and their primary causes in case you are asked, because you will be. But you know what that means: more excuses!

**Tennis Elbow**—An extremely sensitive and painful elbow condition brought on by stroking the ball every which way but correctly.

**Cheater's Eye**—A black and blue discoloration around the eye, usually in the shape of a fist.

**Netman's Neck**—A stiff neck caused by watching an excessive number of lobs fly over your head and out of reach of your overhead.

**Gofer's Shoulder**—A sore shoulder caused by repeatedly running into fence poles while chasing after your opponent's put-away shots.

**Server's Shin**—A painful black and blue discoloration of the shin caused by smashing it with your racket while serving.

**Poached Belly**—Pink welts on your stomach and chest caused by continually being struck by the opposing netman's poached volleys off your partner's service returns that make noodles look forceful.

**Rip Van Ankle**—A twisted ankle caused by stepping on a tennis ball that you were too lazy to move out of the way.

**Hacker's Knee**—Painfully stiff knee joints caused by a lack of bending.

**Partner's Revenge**—Angry, red welts on your back caused by your partner missing his laser-like serves directly into your backside.

**Whiffer's Head**—An aching head due to swinging wildly at overheads, missing the ball entirely, and having it bounce squarely off the top of your head.

**Faulter's Foot**—Painful fallen arches, brought on by irate opponents stomping on your foot in protest over your constant foot-faulting.

**Bragger's Lip**—A swollen, sometimes bloodied lip, due to bragging above and beyond the call of good manners and good sense about a victory over an irritable opponent.

**Lineman's Ear**—A ringing in your ear or an earache because of loud, acrimonious swearing directed at you and your parentage.

**Pumper's Arm**—A sore arm due to excessively pumping it up and down after winning a point.

**Showman's Crotch**—A deep, excruciating pain in the groin, typically caused by violent contact with the ball while attempting a between-the-legs trick shot.

**Liner's Finger**—A sore finger contracted by constantly pointing "out" at every ball that lands within a ball's width of the line and having angry, amateur, chiropractic opponents give it an on-court adjustment by bending it back until your eyes straighten out.

**Rocket Wrist**—A painful condition of the wrist caused by excessive attempts to launch your racket into space by way of throwing.

**Slapper's Thigh**—A deep, painful bruise on the side of the thigh caused by constantly slapping it for self-encouragement.

**Shaker's Hand**—A painful bruising of the hand resulting from the obligatory post-match handshaking with an ape-like, excessively macho jerk.

**Tired Toe**—A painful toe bruise caused by bouncing up and down on your toes like a yo-yo, the way your pro keeps harping at you to do.

**Splinter Buns**—Large, soft, sore buns typically caused by watching more tennis than you play.

# 48

## *P.S., B.S.*

Finally, I would like to conclude this brilliant tennis classic with a populist chapter—P.S., B.S.. This abbreviation combination is short for *PostScript, Bumper Stickers*. In this extremely short chapter, I document the few noteworthy tennis-related bumper stickers that I have had the pleasure to read over the years, and a couple that I would have liked to read, but didn't because I hadn't thought of them.

To keep vital tennis creativity alive, I am inviting you, the reader, to submit your favorite tennis-related bumper sticker sayings and sayings you would like to see on a bumper sticker. If your "bumper sticker" is viewed as "book-worthy," it will be listed below in subsequent editions. Send your submittals to me at my e-mail address: **Fuzzball@bounce.net.**

**Actual Bumper Stickers:**
"'Tis better to serve than receive"
"It takes three balls to play tennis"
"Tennis players have fuzzy balls"
"I play best on grass"

**Should be Bumper Stickers:**
"Tennis is a bitch, and then you lob"
"Tennis isn't brain surgery…except for the blood"

# Dave's Tennis Glossary

Like all activities in life, from banjo strumming to test tube babies, tennis has produced its own terminology. This distinct and inventive vocabulary provides us real players with yet another way to effectively expose hackers, which then allows us to avoid them.

Example: You and some dipstick in dark socks are watching a tennis match from courtside. You casually mention that one player is "choking." If the dork runs off to dial "911" he is a severe hacker and should immediately be ushered from the courts by brawny guys with fat arms and narrow foreheads.

For the benefit of future real players I have compiled a list of tennis' terms and their meanings, all of which are applicable in the delightful world of tennis. Here is...

## DAVE'S TENNIS GLOSSARY

**Ace**—What your opponents serve, seemingly at will. What you serve before the umpire yells, "Foot fault!"

**Approach Shot**—The kind of shot you use to set up your opponent's passing shots.

**Backhand**—

- *One handed*:—When executed correctly (one-handed), the world's most difficult tennis shot. One of the two main reasons for club tennis pros.

- *Two handed*:—Legalized cheating.

**Baseline**—The area on the court where cheaters operate 90 percent of the time.

**Baseliner**—A player anchored to the baseline by his or her invincible forehands and diabolical, two-handed backhands.

**Charting**—A method of research and development that produces a game plan that will supposedly result in you beating a better player.

**Choke**—The term used to describe what happens to competitors whose elbows fuse at a 90-degree angle during important points.

**Close the Gate**—A term shouted by real players to instruct ignorant hackers on what to do when entering the better tennis courts.

**Club Ladder**—A club's public record of the real players and the clueless hacks.

**Club Pro**—A sadist that receives large sums of money to exhaust students by making them dash back and forth and all over the court while he/she stands there telling them what they're doing wrong. Then he/she makes them pick up the balls.

**Computer Ranking**—The output of a computer program that factors a player's tournament results, level of opposition defeated, and the next lunar eclipse to determine what can best be described as The World Ladder.

**Cross Court**—How hackers get to where they are going.

**Double Fault**—The other main reason for tennis pros.

**Doubles**—

- *Men's:*—Tennis' version of male bonding.

- *Women's:*—Where women meet to compete as usual, only they play tennis.
- *Mixed:*—1. Tennis' version of birth control. 2. Grounds for divorce.

**Down the Line**—The shortest route the ball can take to the net.

**Drop Shot**—A shot that real players use to demonstrate their out and out contempt for dweebic opponents.

**Fast Court**—What you call a court when your shots keep slicing off to the side fence.

**Fault**—What your opponents yell when you serve.

**First One In**—How hackers start a match, before they realize they don't know how to keep score and quit.

**First Volley**—A volley hit by the President of the United States.

**Foot Fault**—1. A favored method of cheating in which you serve from inside the baseline. 2. Athlete's foot.

**Forced Error**—An error that is not YOUR fault!

**Forehand**—The world's easiest tennis shot.

**Gamesmanship**—To invite your opponent to "tank" the match by acting like a jumbo-sized jerk.

**Grand Slam**—An overhead that bounces over the back fence.

**Grips**—

- *Eastern:*—The grip that snobbishly positions your hand toward the Western part of your handle.

- *Western:*—The grip that radically positions your hand toward the Eastern part of your handle.
- *Continental:*—The lazy man's grip type. Located somewhere between East and West, perhaps near Atlantis.

**Hacker**—The only tennis court litter with civil rights.

**Half Volley**—A type of shot you hit when you can't think of any normal stroke to hit.

**Hardcourt**—Not one of the "nature courts" (grass or clay).

**Hobbyist**—A tennis player who doesn't do drills or work out unless the aerobics instructor is "hot."

**Let**—Short for, *let's take it over.* It is issued to the server to indicate that his serve touched the net. Consequently, the returner was unfairly forced to cope.

**Linesperson**—A trained expert in the Science of Bounced Balls.

**Lob**—1. The shot most often used by whiny, gutless players. 2. What Grand Slams are made from.

**Lob Volley**—1. A painfully stupid shot. 2. An improbable winner. 3. A baseliner's volley.

**Mine**—Doubles code word for: *Yippee! It's a setup!*

**Net**—The place that, without thousands of dollars worth of tennis lessons, attracts fuzzy, yellow, round objects.

**Net Ball**—A term for the mechanism that transforms scorching winners into lazy setups.

**Oh and Oh**—A term used by winners to relate their match score of 6-0, 6-0. ("Oh and oh" losers never give the score; in fact, they won't recognize that the match ever occurred.)

**On Serve**—Tennis scoring lingo meaning: 1. Neither player can get a lead of more than one game. 2. WARNING! You are headed for a tiebreaker.

**On the Rise**—A shot hit when you are late for your half volley.

**Out**—What you yell when you need a point.

**Overhead**—1. The easiest way to hit yourself on the head with a tennis ball. 2. What you tell the IRS your house is.

**Play Two**—What you bellow when a ball rolls onto your court, as your opponent is about to slam your short lob away.

**Poach**—1. How to show your contempt for your opponents. 2. How to demonstrate to your partner that his/her game sucks.

**Put-Away**—Same as for lay people, what you do with beer.

**Putz**—1. A soft, looping serve used as a last resort. 2. A hacker's only serve.

**Quick Serve**—The serve you hit while your opponent is tying his/her shoes.

**Rally**—The only way to show off your best shots (because you choke in matches.)

**Real Player**—Not a hacker; a serious tennis devotee who already knows these terms.

**Return of Serve**—What brings on those feelings of dread when you realize you have to serve yet *again*!

**Scoring Terms—**

- *5*          = 1 or 15
- *15*         = 1 or 5
- *30*         = 2
- *40*         = 3
- *Ad Out*     = You are one point from losing the game.
- *Deuce*      = You are two points from losing the game.
- *Ad In*      = You are three points from losing the game.
- *Love*       = Nothing at all, zip, zilch, el squato.

**Seed**—A player you don't mind losing to in a tournament.

**Serve**—The shot responsible for your serve lessons and your falling 401(k) total.

**Singles**—A type of tennis for hyperactive sweat-hounds.

**Slow Court**—What you call a court when you lose because your opponent kept hitting all your shots back.

**Spin**—1. What real players produce on purpose. 2. What hackers cannot figure out how to return.

**Split Sets**—A match in which you only play well for one set.

**Split Step**—A technique used to step in two opposite directions at the same time.

**Switch**—Doubles code word for, *Quick, let's hide my backhand.*

**Tank**—To repeatedly and intentionally attempt the lowest percentage shots imaginable; usually in response to some unfair stimuli, such as having to go to work the next day.

**Tennisologists**—Medical school dropouts that use empirical methods to study the sport of tennis.

**Tennis Publication**—A magazine devoted to making money by convincing you that you can improve your game by reading and looking at pictures.

**These Go**—Tennis code for *commence cheating and choking.*

**Tiebreaker**—1. A tennis scoring innovation to cycle players on and off the court faster. 2. That part of the match where the most chokes occur.

**Tournament**—A place where you pay money to play someone who wouldn't otherwise be caught dead on the same court with you.

**Umpire**—The person who sits high in a chair above your court, and because of her gross partiality, incompetence, or both, causes you to lose your match.

**Unforced Error**—1. When you miss your shots because of diabolically powerful and invisible forces such as: (a) your strings were not spaced evenly; (b) a fuming case of crotch itch; (c) your dog ate your lucky socks. 2. Reading this book.

**Volley**—1. A shot tired players hit so they don't have to run back and forth along the baseline. 2. What players from ex-monarchy countries say instead of "rally."

**Winner**—1. What makes you tell your opponent, "Nice shot." 2. An accomplished cheater.

**Yours**—Doubles code word for, *YIKES!*

**Zoned**—A term referring either to the fact that, 1. You are parked in the red so as to keep your court reservation. 2. For some inexplicable reason, your shots keep landing in the court.

0-595-25828-X

Printed in the United States
R1843000002B/R18430PG39524LVSX00006B/5}